THE COMPLETE BOOK OF LONG-DISTANCE AND COMPETITIVE CYCLING

BY TOM DOUGHTY

1976, 1980 U.S. Olympic Cyclist
1979 Gold Medal Winner, Pan-American Games

and Ed Pavelka
and Barbara George
of Velo-news

SIMON AND SCHUSTER
NEW YORK

A Division of Simon & Schuster, Inc.
Simon & Schuster Building
Rockefeller Center
1230 Avenue of the Americas
New York, New York 10020

SIMON AND SCHUSTER and colophon are registered trademarks
of Simon & Schuster, Inc.
Designed by Irving Perkins Associates
Manufactured in the United States of America
10 9 8 7 6 5 4 3 2 1
Pbk. 10 9 8

Library of Congress Cataloging in Publication Data

Doughty, Tom, date.
  The complete book of long-distance and competitive cycling.

  Bibliography: p.
  Includes index.
  1. Bicycle touring. 2. Bicycle racing. I. Pavelka,
Ed. II. George, Barbara. III. Title.
GV1044.D68 1982   796.6   82-5863
                                     AACR2

ISBN 0-671-42433-5
     0-671-42434-3 Pbk.

All photographs, unless otherwise noted, are copyright © 1982
by Robert F. George

ACKNOWLEDGMENTS

Grateful acknowledgment is made to the following individuals and organizations for their help with the information and photos in this book: *Bicycling* magazine; Bikecentennial; Tim Blumenthal; Sam Braxton; Ed Burke; Claude Gouin; Fred Matheny; June and Greg Siple; Betsy Whittaker.

To my family

CONTENTS

CONTENTS

A FEW WORDS ABOUT BICYCLING

1

They used to call it a fad, a craze, a phenomenon with about as much significance as the Hula Hoop. But now it is being seen as a cultural revolution, a basic change in human ideals that is playing a real role in the shaping of the future. It is personal physical fitness, and its practitioners in America number in the tens of millions. They run, they swim, they play racket sports, they dance, they lift weights—they do whatever gives them enjoyment and, even more important in the minds of many, whatever causes sweat and labored breathing. When it comes down to it, happiness begins with good health and can last only as long as life does. This is the primary reason why so many people are now making exercise a part of each day's activity.

There is something else that used to be called a fad, a craze, but now it too is being viewed as an ever-increasing influence on life in the years ahead. It is the bicycle. As a way to gain physical fitness, cycling has taken a prominent place in the lives of many Americans. But unlike every other means to better health in vogue today, bicycle riding is able to take a person far beyond the well-documented benefits of physical fitness and into a realm in which the activity provides everything from basic transportation to adventurous long-distance travel to the thrill of competition.

Because of these opportunities, there can be no better physical activity to choose to become proficient at than bike riding. On one level it can save you money. If you live within 20 miles of where you work or attend school, commuting by bike is a highly practical alternative to driving a car or even using public transportation. The dol-

11

lar savings will mount up fast, and so will the physical benefits. Instead of having to squeeze in daily exercise during another part of the day, you can get it during a period formerly wasted behind the steering wheel or at a bus stop. We'll look more deeply into this judicious use of time in Chapter 2.

It is the purpose of this book, however, to transport you beyond the day-to-day practicalities of utilitarian cycling. The intention is to take you, the enthusiastic but still developing rider, and help you grow into a cyclist capable of great feats. Cycling is an outstanding way to attain physical fitness, but it is also an exciting and challenging way to rediscover the world around you. It will show you how to ride 100 miles a day and enjoy it. It will tell you how to go about preparing for a self-contained tour that spans a weekend or a continent. It will introduce you to the colorful sport of bicycle racing and give pointers for competing well in time trials, the ideal way in which riders of any inclination can measure their self-improvement. It will tell you new things about how to pedal and control a bike, about how to equip it and how to maintain it. In the end it will make you a much more knowledgeable cyclist and, if you are willing to work for it, a person who is capable of using a bike for virtually any type of riding, no matter what the distance and terrain.

The mention of touring and racing in the same breath may strike some readers as incongruous, but it shouldn't. Though it is true that most cyclists gravitate toward one activity or the other—there are about 10,000 licensed racers in the United States, and few show any interest in riding slowly with a load of camping equipment. This will change as time trialing grows in popularity and brings together riders of various inclinations. At any rate, all serious cyclists have good things to learn from racers, because, as riders, racers are the best there are. My own experiences in training and competition have given me much to share about how to improve riding techniques such as cornering, climbing, descending, braking, position on the bike . . . even how to fall down. Racing is my realm, and I think you will like it too if you try it, but I'll not be twisting your arm to join me at the line. Rather, I want to help you improve your basic riding skills and strength, then progress in whichever aspect of cycling you like best.

Cycling's Unique Advantage

What sets bike riding apart from other methods of recreation and healthful exercise is the machine itself. Not only is the bicycle the most efficient use of human power ever devised, it's fun to ride. Once fitness is reached, that enjoyment can be extended to the limits of imagination. Aerodynamically designed bikes and trikes have been pedaled at speeds in excess of the national speed limit in special competitions at California's Ontario Motor Speedway, and we have watched cyclist Bryan Allen make history by using his legs to propel the *Gossamer Albatross* over the English Channel. These vehicles are based on the simple chain-drive gear system that in one form or another is part of every bicycle. Such performances indicate the wonders our bodies can produce thanks to the mechanical advantage a bicycle provides.

Unlike most other fitness-producing sports, cycling offers the excitement of speed. When riding in a car or even on a motorcycle, 25 mph does not seem very fast. But pedal a bike at that speed and there is a sensation of swiftness that is hard to achieve in any other way. A great part of the pleasure comes in knowing that it is nothing but

Author Tom Doughty. Cycling offers the excitement of speed.

your own power which is making the bike perform. Conversely, nothing but a bicycle can amplify your power so well.

There is also a tangible feeling, a vibration that's part of the sensation of speed. It comes from the road, through the wheels, into the frame, and then into the rider. When the speed changes, so does the pitch of this vibration. Even after becoming accustomed to this, it is still noticed subconsciously and it adds excitement. It awakens the sense of awareness.

Because the bicycle allows so much work to be done for the energy expended, it is possible to travel quite a distance even during a routine daily training ride. As opposed to the runner, a cyclist can have a wider variety of routes and the opportunity to see more places. This increases the feeling of freedom and the other oft-cited enjoyments, such as the constant motion and smooth flow of the world going by.

In another sense, smoothness is the reason why cycling is such an ideal activity for such a wide variety of people. The bike supports its rider's weight, allowing health-producing exercise without the danger of the damaging strain on joints, ligaments, and tendons that is associated with sports involving running. The smoothness of pedaling builds up instead of tearing down, which means that cyclists rarely fall victim to nagging injuries that can necessitate medical attention and a forced layoff. Since a key ingredient for a lifetime of good health is a consistently applied exercise program, there's no better choice than bike riding. It's hard to imagine that man will ever invent a machine that can top the bicycle's potential for personal fitness, as well as transportation, sport, and downright fun.

Not to be overlooked is an emotional relationship with the bike that often develops as the miles go by. A skillful rider on a quality bike will feel a sense of oneness with the machine. Even though I've owned numerous bikes—about fifteen different models in recent years—each one has been like a new friend to me. I've found them all to be enjoyable as pieces of machinery, even as works of art. A quality bike is aesthetically pleasing, being cleanly designed and nice to look at. It functions well, it can go fast safely, and it gives a special feeling whenever ridden. It puts the rider in a comfortable groove.

But it's even more than that. It is as if the bicycle can carry you to a true expression of self. It lets you reach out and achieve your best

You don't need to be some fantastic physical specimen to excel in cycling. Jacques Boyer, for instance, is a fit-looking guy, but you'd hardly expect that he is one of the best road racers the United States has ever produced. In fact, his forte is stage racing, and in 1981 he became the first American in history to ride the Tour de France, cycling's toughest event.

possible performance. It always helps, never hinders. It responds to your every movement, seemingly to your every thought. This can reach the point where the bike is not even there, in a sense, because it becomes an extension of your physical and mental being. It frees you to go beyond normal limits.

The Sport for Everyone

The quality, lightweight bicycle is also a great equalizer, allowing people of all ages, body types, and physical abilities to perform not only at their personal best but also on par with each other. These bicycles, like people, come in different sizes, but they are all capable of going just as fast and just as far. Once the bike has been fitted to you it's simply a matter of your ability to function on it. The bicycle puts everyone at the same starting line, and it's often been proved that small riders can be just as good as big ones, and old ones can perform as well as young ones.

For example, back in 1976 a tiny young Belgian named Lucien Van Impe won the world's longest and toughest bicycle race, the Tour de France. There are no fluke winners of this three-week, 2,200-mile contest that traverses the Pyrenees and the Alps, so Van Impe's victory is a testament to the bicycle, the equalizer. He is one rider who would look more at home on a horse in the Kentucky Derby rather than leading a hundred of cycling's best professionals in the Tour. Then, in 1980, the same race was won by lanky Dutchman Joop Zoetemelk. Capping a career that included five second-place finishes in the Tour, he finally earned victory at age 34. Just as remarkably, the man who finished fifth that year, Joaquim Agostinho of Portugal, was in his early 40s—almost twice the age of many of those he defeated.

There are riders as skinny as a spoke who can move a bicycle at incredible speeds and over great distances. A perfect example from the racing world is Mark Pringle, the former U.S. National Road Team member from Seattle. Mark looks as if he hasn't a muscle in his body, let alone in his legs, but he had a very successful career highlighted by a tenth place in the 1977 World Road Championship for amateurs—the best finish in history by an American male. Mark's ex-

Cyclists come in all sizes. Here is 6-foot-11 basketball star Bill Walton on his custom-made track bike.

ample shows that conditioning, riding technique, and desire have a lot to do with who becomes an accomplished cyclist, and anyone can come up with these ingredients.

In the touring world there are many other examples. Consider Ed Delano of Davis, California. In 1970 he pedaled across the country to attend his class reunion at Worcester (Massachusetts) Polytechnic Institute. Now, a transcontinental trip by bike is a terrific accom-

Eric Heiden, winner of five gold medals in the Winter Olympics, is an example of the more stocky type of rider.

This fellow, casually pumping a tire at the Lehigh County Velodrome in Pennsylvania during his first visit to America, is almost universally recognized as the greatest racing cyclist who ever lived. He's Eddy Merckx of Belgium, and this photo was taken in 1978, just four months after he retired at the age of 33. Looking at those spindly legs, you'd be hard pressed to explain how he had the strength to win five Tours de France. But cycling suits all body types, and it takes much more than muscular legs to make a champion.

plishment for any rider, but that reunion was for the Class of '30—
Delano was 65 years old when he made the 36-day crossing. But
that's not the end of the story. He rode to the 50th reunion in 1980 at
age 75 and went faster than he had ten years earlier. This time he
covered the 3,100 miles in 33½ days.

"When you think of it," Delano told the WPI magazine, "bicycle
riding is one of the best things you can do to keep in good physical
condition. There's no danger of damaging your legs and feet as you
can do in running. Besides, you can go about three times as fast and
see three times as much on a bike. If you ride hard you can give the
old heart a good workout. It's like any muscle in your body—the
more you make it work the stronger it gets."

Delano races, too. In the 1980 national championships he won the
time-trial division for riders aged 70–74, covering the 25 miles in 1
hour, 12 minutes, and 56 seconds. That's a tremendous achievement.
I know because I set the U.S. record that year on the same course by
clocking 52:25. If I lose only 20 minutes in the next 47 years I'll be a
very happy man. But as great as Ed Delano is, he's not unique. In
fact, he wasn't even that close to being the oldest competitor at the
'80 Nationals. That honor went to 84-year-old Fred Knoller of Florida. He rode the 25-mile time trial in 1:31:20 and then set off for

Fred Knoller is 84 and rides regularly near his home in Florida. He also competes
in national and world championships in his age group.

Having fun on a bike helps condition a child's heart and lungs. This is national champion (of her age group) Celeste Andreau.

Austria to race in the Veterans World Cup, a kind of world championship for riders more than 35 years old. On hand were fifty-five riders above age 70, and Knoller was the oldest. He brought home the silver medal in the over-80 category.

Neither is there a lower age limit for cycling. Remember how young you were when what you wanted most in the world was a bicycle? Can you recall your father or mother holding you up on your first two-wheeler as you wavered down the sidewalk ... and that thrill when you suddenly found yourself pedaling on your own? I think learning to ride represents one of the great moments in the life of a child. The bike gives a youngster a taste of freedom, the first chance to independently go places and see new things, even if it is just to the outskirts of the neighborhood. But better than that, a kid on a bike is developing a healthy body. All that fun is helping condition a young heart and lungs and is developing endurance. Children might not know and probably won't care about such things, and I think that's the way their exercise should be. Cycling is such a thrill that kids will do it even if they find out it's good for them.

In fact, kids take to bikes so well that cycling is an ideal activity for the family as a whole. Because the bike is such an equalizer, parents and children can ride together and still maintain a pace that is enjoyable for all, whether it be a Sunday-afternoon picnic trip to a nearby lake or a coast-to-coast odyssey. This is possible in part because of the phenomenon of drafting, which is discussed in Chapter 5. Suffice it to say here that a moving cyclist creates a slipstream and anyone directly behind will not have as much wind resistance. This means that the second rider (child) won't have to pedal as strongly to keep up with the first (parent), and both can cover the same amount of ground comfortably.

If you think this is farfetched, consider the Bradley family of Davenport, Iowa. A few years ago the father, Mel, began cycling with son Jeff and daughter Jacque. They were quite young then, so Mel spent most of the rides leading them around, the kids just sitting on his wheel, as the saying goes. Jeff and Jacque still had to do plenty of fitness-building work to keep up with Dad, but he had the benefit of doing about 30 percent more—such is the difference between breaking the wind and drafting. Mel was able to improve his own physical condition while still enjoying the companionship of his children.

This worked so well for the Bradleys that Jeff and Jacque became national cycling champions in their age groups and have grown up to be stars in the sport. Mel himself has been a successful racer in the Veteran class and remains an active cyclist, though now the roles are reversed on those family rides. Today it's Jeff and Jacque who set the pace and work hard against the wind as Mel reaps the rewards of parenthood in their slipstream.

Let's Get Rolling!

Such examples help illustrate how well cycling is suited to the human body and human enterprise. There seems to be no limit to what a person of any age can do on a bike. When we hear stories of how pre-teens have ridden lengthy tours and how those over 70 compete in major championships, the benefits of the sport are apparent—health, enjoyment, and personal accomplishment. It's proof

When a small town like Somerville, New Jersey, hosts a criterium, it can bring daily business to a standstill.

that cycling is one of those rare physical activities that can be done virtually every day for a lifetime.

If you have the desire to expand your cycling ability to include long-distance riding of any kind or to enter the world of racing, you're about to learn what you need to do it right. You can specialize in one particular use of the bike or combine any number. As long as you keep pedaling you've got plenty of time to enjoy it all—just ask Ed Delano and Fred Knoller.

TIME BUDGETING AND DIET

2

The road that leads a cycling enthusiast into long-distance touring or racing is often strewn with question marks. Realizing that a commitment to high mileage is going to require increased time on the bike and personal effort, a cyclist is bound to wonder:

- How am I ever going to find the extra hours for riding?
- Should I alter my diet somehow to meet the new energy demands?

These questions are so basic to an upward move in cycling that they need to be dealt with even before turning attention to new riding skills and training routines. The reason is that their answers are critical to the success of a serious touring or racing program. Without the time to train effectively and the knowledge to properly care for and fuel the body, there is little chance of success. Let's look into these concerns to lay the foundation for development in whichever aspect of cycling you choose.

TIME BUDGETING

Fitting enough bicycle riding into your daily schedule can take some doing. If you're a student or you work for a living, time is no doubt of great importance. Add family responsibilities and the desire to include other interests besides cycling in your life and each minute becomes even more precious. Still, you want to be as good a rider as you can. Not an Olympic racer perhaps, but at least someone who can be considered a true athlete—someone who has excellent fitness, who can ride all day on tour, and who can perform well in time trials. Given your limited time for the sport, is it possible?

Yes. The key is successful time budgeting, and there's no one who has learned to do it better than Fred Matheny, a man well known to cycling enthusiasts as the author of the *Velo-news* column "Ready to Race." Consider this: Matheny, in his mid-30s, is married and the devoted father of a young son. He teaches senior English at Montrose High School in Colorado and has additional duties as chairman of the department. Further, he is an instructor at Western State College at night and during the summer. As a freelance writer he has authored more than fifty articles and one book, *Beginning Bicycle Racing*. Formerly an all-star offensive lineman at Baldwin-Wallace College, he is now active in cross-country skiing, running, weight lifting, backpacking, and mountaineering. And, despite it all, he has found the time to become a nationally ranked racing cyclist, training virtually year-round and frequently exceeding 250 miles a week. His personal best of 58:27 in the 25-mile time trial puts him in the top rank of riders his age.

How does he do it? Ambition and dedication are certainly important, and so is awareness. Because he wants to ride as much as he can, Matheny has looked for ways to fit cycling into daily time slots that would otherwise not be used nearly as effectively—the trick is to recognize the opportunities and then make use of them. He has written articles discussing several techniques which have worked for him and other limited-time riders, and with a little effort you can successfully apply them to your own situation.

Commute by Bike

The easiest way to ensure some miles every day is to use the bike for commuting to and from work or school, even if you have to take a roundabout route to make the distance worthwhile. A basic 10-mile trip should take about 30 minutes, and this will give you an hour's worth of riding each day, a helpful amount. The homeward leg can be lengthened some days for variety and to build up saddle time.

Commuting by bike does have some drawbacks, although they are

A long shadow is the constant companion of a rider who must fit in training rides before or after the many responsibilities of daily life.

not insurmountable. One problem is how to carry your lunch (and breakfast, if you prefer not eating just before riding) as well as a change of clothes, books and papers, etc. The best way is to use one or more bags from your touring ensemble or a soft teardrop-shaped backpack like those sold at bike and mountaineering shops (get one with a waist strap to prevent it from bouncing). If you ride in cycling shoes, keep a regular pair at your destination so you won't have their weight and grime in the pack. Thanks to modern permanent-press fabrics, clothes can be rolled up and carried without much danger of wrinkling.

Another concern is the perspiration you will work up during the ride. "Everyone has a fear of smelling like a gorilla's armpit at work all day, but such social misgivings are unfounded," notes Fred Matheny, who points out that athletic sweat has little odor and merely needs to be toweled off. For the more fastidious, a quick once-over in the rest room with a wet washcloth or one soaked in rubbing alcohol works almost as well as a shower. It is wise to at least clean the crotch to help prevent the buildup of skin bacteria which can lead to saddle sores.

As for the bike, it's best to take it right into the room where you spend the day. If that's impossible, make friends with the building's custodian and he'll probably be glad to find a secure place for it. Make every attempt to keep the bike out of the weather, and no matter where it's parked, lock it up—just in case.

Some of this may seem inconvenient, but once you begin commuting by bike you'll find you can work out a streamlined system that suits your personal situation very well. Also, you don't need to make it a daily routine. It's good to take one or two days a week off from riding to give the body a chance to recuperate and grow stronger, so you can schedule weekdays for this. For instance, take off Monday to recover from your long weekend rides and then take off Friday so you'll be rested for your Saturday and Sunday efforts. With a system like this you can use Monday to transport street clothes so you won't have to pack them in your Tuesday, Wednesday, and Thursday commutes. Then drive the clothes back home on Friday, or stuff them into your backpack if you choose to ride six days a week instead of five.

Early-Bird Special

If for some reason you can't commute by bike or don't wish to, there are two other alternatives for getting in your weekday rides: cycling before going off to work or school, or cycling afterward. (I really don't think it's practical for a rider to squeeze an exercise session into the lunch hour, as some runners do. With the time it takes for dressing, warming up, cooling down, undressing, and cleaning up, there just aren't enough minutes left for beneficial riding.)

Psychologists tell us and physiologists confirm that some people just can't get it going in the morning. That might be your self-image, but is it based on athletic experience or on a life-style that has conditioned you to a schedule of late to bed and late to rise? It's really hard to be certain until you give morning exercise an honest try, and that's what I suggest you do. Everything considered, early morning is better than late afternoon or evening for training.

There are several advantages to arising at the crack of dawn for a bike ride. Environmental conditions are usually at their best—the wind is rarely bothersome and the air is often cooler and cleaner than it will be at any other time of the day. Traffic is usually very light, allowing you the freedom of an open road. With sunlight in the sky well before 6:00 A.M. in the summer months, there is enough time for a beneficial ride even if you must punch the clock at 8:00.

Matheny, who much prefers morning rides, has found that "perhaps the biggest advantage for the limited-time cyclist is that early workouts are seldom interrupted. That time is your own. Afternoons, however, have a way of getting filled up with the unexpected. If I get my workout early I can then handle whatever the day throws at me. If I put it off until later I have a fixed anxiety that it will get bumped by other responsibilities." He cites another important benefit by saying, "The feeling of accomplishment that I get from my riding is a positive way to start the day. That success carries over into other activities."

The primary disadvantage of sunrise cycling centers around the difficulty of forsaking a warm bed for the harsh realities of physical exertion. The best tactic is to get out from under the covers immediately when the alarm goes off, before you have time to think. After the first few weeks it will be routine. At any rate, it's almost always the case that once you are up and out on the road it is more enjoyable than a sleepy imagination suggests it will be.

Another problem is the danger of sleep loss. If you don't go to bed earlier to compensate for getting up earlier, you run the risk of deep fatigue that will negate the beneficial aspects of exercise. Since time budgeting for cycling is basically a matter of borrowing from one activity and transferring to another, the sleep stolen by early workouts must be repaid.

P.M. Pedaling

Scheduling rides for late afternoon before the dinner hour or evening engagements makes it hard to keep cycling from infringing upon other interests and responsibilities. It also puts your bike time in constant danger of being cut short or canceled due to unexpected obstacles or bad weather that develops during the course of the day. There is also rush-hour traffic and its pollution to contend with. Therefore, the 4:00–6:00 P.M. time slot can be a rough one for regular workouts, unless they are simply an extension of your commute by bike. Of course, I'm looking at this through the eyes of someone who lives in a city or a thickly settled suburb. If you are in a small town or rural area and only minutes from quiet country roads, late-afternoon riding is more practical.

There is one other alternative, although I'll admit it sounds quite outlandish. It is riding at night in the period from about 10:00 P.M. to midnight. As crazy as this sounds, it does offer some real benefits and it's been known to work for a number of riders, especially racers whose daily routines leave them no other suitable time to train.

Nighttime produces some pleasant conditions for cycling. In summer the day's heat will have subsided, while in winter the evening temperature won't be as cold as in the early morning. Relatively few cars are on the road to produce pollution and interference. A late ride can give a person something to look forward to during the course of a hectic day, and, as noted above, some people simply start functioning better as the evening hours approach.

The big disadvantage of the "midnight special" is obvious, and you've already guessed it: darkness. In general I advise against riding at night, because too many bad things can happen, most of them the fault of inadequate lighting on the bike. However, if you invest in a serious system such as a Soubitez generator set, a Belt Beacon rear flasher, and a reflectorized vest to augment the bike's reflectors (an amber set for the rear of the pedals is a must), you will be both visible to motorists and able to see in dark patches between streetlights.

I do not recommend riding on completely dark roads, because bike lights aren't enough to let you push along at a beneficial pace and still be sure of seeing and avoiding all hazards. Also, the dazzling headlights of cars coming out of the blackness can make it very hard to see the road and hold a straight line, a very dangerous situation if a car is approaching from the rear at the same time. All too often an oncoming driver will neglect to dim the headlights, making it so difficult to see anything that you become disoriented.

The lack of scenery and the confinement to routes which have streetlights—parks and suburban neighborhoods are best—can combine to make night riding boring. Some racers prefer it this way, because they concentrate better without visual distractions. For others, though, there is the danger of making cycling seem like a chore instead of the enjoyable activity it should be. Fatigue is another drawback if the night cyclist lets his or her time on the bike take away from time in bed. This problem is compounded for a person who gets charged up by workouts and then has trouble falling asleep afterward.

Weekends

Ah, Saturday and Sunday. Whether you are up each weekday to ride at dawn, out each night pedaling into the witching hour, or determinedly commuting by bike, the weekend is when you reap the dividends. As your Monday-through-Friday cycling program heightens your fitness and riding ability, you'll be looking forward to weekends as never before, anxious to explore new roadways and physical capacities.

Subsequent chapters contain specific training information for touring and racing. Both endeavors require plenty of long miles, and even the rider who lives by the appointment book should be able to find time during the weekend to pile them up. Still, you do have certain obligations, interests, and a family and friends you don't want to neglect. How can you expand your cycling horizons and not be reported by your roommate as a missing person or perceived by your wife as someone who cares more about that damn bike than the kids?

If you are married, one solution is to make cycling a family affair, pedaling at least part of the way with your spouse and/or the children. If they are also involved in bike riding they won't feel shortchanged by losing you to the sport for an extra hour or two after you've had a family outing. Make a loop together, drop them off at the house, and then continue on for a while longer. Thanks to the equalizing effect that drafting provides, even pre-teenage kids can manage several miles at a good pace when they are sitting in behind an adult.

As for your friends, it's my guess that as you become more deeply committed to cycling many of the people you enjoy most will be riders. You'll meet them down at the local shop, at bike club meetings, and out on the road. The weekend offers a great opportunity to ride together, something that may be impossible on weekdays because of divergent schedules. In fact, the chance to ride in the company of others provides the solitary cyclist with more than a break from routine; it is an extra incentive for sticking with the less-than-thrilling daily training.

The combination of good exercise and good friendship is hard to beat, and it can definitely make you a better rider. When cycling with others, you can extend your strength by sitting in now and then, thus riding longer and at a stronger pace than you could handle alone. The socializing adds interest to the ride and helps the miles go by briskly.

A good time to take the big ride of the weekend is early Saturday morning. True, there will be less traffic on Sunday, but the day might dawn rainy or windy and thus put a crimp in your plans. Should the weather wipe out a Saturday ride at least you have Sunday to fall back on.

If you are riding alone or with friends instead of family, an early departure will have you back home by midmorning, just about the time everyone else is up and about. How long you should try to ride is based on your daily average. If you are accustomed to riding for about an hour at least four times a week, you should be able to pedal at least twice that long before beginning to feel drained of energy and strength. A good carbohydrate breakfast such as pancakes, French toast, or cooked cereal grains will provide plenty of fuel, and it can be eaten within a half hour of the ride. For an extra-early getaway, you can stuff your jersey pockets with fruit and eat during the first few miles as you pedal easily to warm up.

If Saturday's long ride goes as scheduled, the remainder of the weekend is then clear for other activities. Of course you'll want to ride on Sunday as well, but this session needn't be nearly as long—you won't want it to be the day after a lengthy bout in the saddle. Loosen up by taking a cruise with members of the family, or slip in an hour's ride while they are into their own pastimes.

With a little forethought it is possible to make the long weekend ride part of a family outing. Plan a day at the lake, beach, state park, etc. and schedule your departure by bike and the family's by car so that all of you arrive at the same time. Or if the distance is too far for you to ride, work it out so that the car overtakes you at a prescribed time—say, three hours down the road. In this way you can get in all the riding you want and still be part of the family's main activity. Put the bike on the car rack and enjoy your relaxation the rest of the day. You've earned it, and you're welcome to indulge in that prideful feeling that results from knowing how far you've come as a cyclist.

DIET

"The area where faddism, misconception, and ignorance is the most obvious in cycling is nutrition," states Ed Burke. His preeminent position in U.S. cycling physiology has put him in close contact with hundreds of riders of all ages, interests, and abilities, and he has found that cyclists, like athletes everywhere, run the gamut of dietary dogma. Some riders adhere to strict vegetarian regimens while others are junk-food addicts. Some take vitamin and mineral pills by the handful, others never touch them. Some load up on pancakes before a long ride or race, others eat eggs. Some carry a banana in their jersey pocket, others a ham sandwich.

Few indeed are the serious cyclists who haven't wondered if their diet is helping or hurting their riding performance. Some put much more importance on the nutritional question than others do, of course, and this is why the subject always leads to controversy. But what is the reality? What has Burke, in his work as chairman of the USCF's Medical Committee, discovered in his discussions and practical experience with many of the country's finest competitive cyclists?

Sorry, there are no great revelations. Burke has found that the best diet for the serious cyclist is basically the same one we've had drummed into us since grade school, the one that includes portions from all the major food groups—milk products, meats, grains, vegetables, and fruits. A well-rounded diet with a good balance of carbohydrate, protein, and fat, as well as the essential vitamins and minerals, will provide both excellent fuel for cycling and the nutrients necessary for good health. The problem with this for many people is that it's just too simple to be true.

Well, there is something to that sentiment. Certainly some basic information needs to be digested in order to make sure that the daily diet has the best proportion of food types and nutrients for long-distance riders. There is also the important consideration of caloric intake and how it affects body fat and overall weight. Some of you may be interested in losing a few pounds through cycling, and every competitive rider will want to make sure he or she is as light as possible without sacrificing strength. Let's now look into these and other dietary concerns, with emphasis on Burke's findings as he has detailed them in his writing for *Velo-news,* the journal of bicycle racing.

Meat or Meatless

"Nothing is more amusing than to sit at a dinner table and listen to cyclists argue over whether a vegetarian or meat-and-potato diet is better for performance," says Burke. "However, no one can win this argument. There have been many successful athletes using each diet, just as there have been athletes who have suffered from malnutrition due to too much rigidity in their eating."

In order to explain the nutritional advantages and problems of these two dietary regimens, Burke uses an example which deals with the caloric, protein, and fat content of meals. Each of his two hypothetical cyclists must consume 5,000 calories a day to equal the number they burn in their daily cycling and general activity (5,000 is quite high except for road racers and long-distance tourists). The cyclists weigh 75 kilograms (165 pounds), and this means they each have a minimum daily protein requirement of 60 grams (0.8 grams for each kilogram of body weight). If these riders eat one-third of their daily calories and protein at each meal, this requires an intake of 1,667 calories and 20 grams of protein per sitting. The table gives an example of a meal the typical meat-and-potato cyclist might eat.

"Examining this rider's intake of 2,128 calories in this single meal, there will be a probable excess of 1,380 calories per day," Burke notes. "At this rate the cyclist would put on one pound of fat, which is equal to 3,500 calories, in three days unless he rides more miles. In fact, it is relatively easy to consume excess calories when large amounts of animal fat are eaten. Further, over half the fat intake is saturated fat, which recent research says may lead to atherosclerosis. Fat is a necessary nutrient, but more should be taken in the unsaturated form.

"Also, the protein requirement for the whole day has been exceeded in this meal alone. While protein is an essential nutrient and meat protein contains most of the essential amino acids, any excess will be broken down and used for energy or stored as fat. Considering today's meat prices, this is an expensive source of food energy."

Protein molecules can include about twenty-five amino acids, but some do not contain all of those which are termed essential—the ones that are not synthesized by the body and must be obtained through the diet. High-quality or complete proteins contain all the essential amino acids, and it turns out that the foods which supply these best come from animal sources such as beef, pork, chicken, eggs, and dairy products. Plant protein lacks some of the essential amino acids and is therefore termed incomplete or poor-quality. This means that the vegetarian must be careful to eat foods which com-

Meat-and-potato Diet

Food	Calories	Grams = Fat	Grams = Protein
10 oz. pot roast	818	113	56
1 med. baked potato	180		6
2 Tbsp. margarine	200	24	—
2 pieces bread	140	2	4
1 lettuce salad	20	—	—
2 Tbsp. French dressing	130.	12	—
1 slice cherry pie	350	15	4
2 cups 2% milk	290	10	20
TOTAL	2128	176	90

From *Inside the Cyclist* (Brattleboro, Vt.: *Velo-news*)

Vegetarian Diet

Food	Calories	Grams = Fat	Grams = Protein
1 med. baked potato	180	—	6
1 cup cooked carrots	45	—	1
½ cup cooked beans	30	—	2
1 lettuce salad	20	—	—
1 tsp. olive oil	125	14	—
1 Tbsp. margarine	100	12	—
1 banana	100	—	1
1 apple	160	—	—
¼ cup cashews	195	16	6
TOTAL	1026	42	16

From *Inside the Cyclist* (Brattleboro, Vt.: *Velo-news*)

bine to create the high-quality protein so important to each body cell and life itself.

While overboard in calories and protein, the meat-and-potato cyclist's meal is very low in fiber, the only significant amount being in the lettuce salad. This can be a problem, because low-fiber diets may mean that food isn't mixed well in the intestine. Mixing is necessary to help nutrients come into contact with the walls where they can be absorbed. Thus, though this meal may appear balanced at first, it is actually high in saturated fats and low in nutrients, especially if all the nutrients that are eaten aren't assimilated.

Looking now at the vegetarian's meal, we see that the amount of food eaten is quite large but its calorie total is about 650 fewer than this cyclist requires. At the end of the day he will have eaten almost 2,000 calories fewer than he has expended, which means he will have lost more than half a pound of body weight.

"This problem of maintaining weight is common for many cyclists who eat a meatless diet," Burke says. "As a result of the low caloric content of their food, they have to eat almost constantly during periods of hard training, racing, and long-distance touring."

And there is another concern. Being high in fiber, a vegetarian diet increases intestinal action to the point where food can move through so quickly that nutrients may not be fully utilized. This is why in a stage race where energy requirements can reach 8,000 calories a day, I only have to look in two places to find a fellow rider who is a vegetarian—in the kitchen or in the restroom.

To assure that all the essential amino acids are obtained, a vegetarian should include a variety of whole grains, dried peas and beans, nuts, and various fruits and vegetables. When these foods are eaten together they can supply an adequate amount of high-quality protein. The vegetarian meal is short of the 20 grams of protein needed at each sitting, putting this cyclist in danger of having a deficiency in both the quantity and quality of the protein he is eating. However, he is in good shape in terms of saturated fat and cholesterol, consuming enough for the body's needs but without the excess that can lead to various medical problems.

Probably the wisest dietary change that a cyclist who prefers not to eat meat can make is to become a lacto-ovo-vegetarian. In contrast to plant-only strict vegetarianism, this includes the eating of dairy products and eggs, thus making it easier to gain complete protein and calories as well as important nutrients like calcium, iron, and riboflavin which may otherwise be in short supply. Importantly for the athlete, this also provides sources for vitamin B-12. Lack of B-12 causes pernicious anemia, which affects the blood and nervous system, and B-12 is not found in plants.

"The ideal diet for a serious cyclist lies between the extremes shown in the two tables," Burke states. "The meat-and-potato rider should cut down on his intake of saturated fats and include more veg-

If you love to eat, especially those naughty foods rich in carbohydrates, you've found the perfect sport in long-distance cycling. Thanks to the high caloric demands of riding hours at a time on weekends and training each day, it is actually necessary to eat well and often. But make sure meals are composed of portions from all the major food groups to ensure the intake of necessary nutrients.

etable fats, fish, and poultry. The vegetarian would do well to add one egg and two cups of 2 percent milkfat milk to a meal such as this."

Burke's conclusion is that "the available evidence does not seem to favor one diet over the other in improving performance in athletes. The choice of a vegetarian or meat-and-potato diet is an individual one, but the mixing of both appears to be the most nutritionally sound."

Vitamin and Mineral Supplements

It's rare to open a sports magazine and not see an ad promising you the "winning edge" if you take this vitamin, that mineral, or some supplement that combines fifty of them. While the International Olympic Committee lists dozens of unpronounceable substances which are forbidden to athletes because they can increase performance in an "artificial and unfair manner," there are no restrictions on taking vitamins and minerals. Given this open door, a number of top cyclists gulp pills by the handful in the expectation that their riding will be improved. There is probably some psychological value to this practice, but it's doubtful that vitamin and mineral supplements can make a physical difference in a rider who has a well-rounded diet.

Vitamins have no caloric value, but function as catalysts in nearly all metabolic processes. There are two basic groups: vitamins which are soluble in fat and those soluble in water. Vitamins A, D, E, and K are in the first group, while C and the B-complex vitamins are in the second. This is important for knowing which vitamins can be stored in the body (fat-soluble) and which are passed off in urine and thus must be supplied daily. It also determines if there is danger of a toxic buildup should large doses be taken.

According to Burke, a cyclist needs to be mainly concerned with getting enough vitamin C and the B-complex vitamins. The former is found in fruits, vegetables, and their juices, especially citrus, while good sources for the B-complex include brewer's yeast, liver, and whole-grain cereals.

"If a rider does not have enough B and C vitamins, a decline in performance will be seen in a few weeks," Burke says. "They are needed for the production of energy and, being water-soluble, are not stored in the body to any significant degree. On the other hand, if stores of the fat-soluble vitamins have been accumulated over a period of time, a rider may get along on inadequate amounts for several weeks."

A vitamin deficiency can be caused by a poorly balanced diet, of course, but there are other factors to consider. For instance, a racer or tourist who is away from home a lot may frequently sit down to restaurant meals which have a low vitamin and mineral content because of food storage, processing, and cooking. In fact, cooking can result in a 50 percent loss of water-soluble vitamins. Additionally, hard riding increases the metabolism of foods to produce energy and this in turn increases the use of vitamins and minerals; taking certain medicines such as antibiotics decreases the body's ability to absorb vitamins; and there is evidence that vitamins can be lost through sweat, which is of concern in hot weather and during periods of hard training.

The need for minerals is often neglected amid all the publicity that vitamins receive, but they are also regulators of the physiological processes involved with exercise. The most important minerals are calcium, phosphorus, magnesium, sodium, potassium, and chloride, all of which are needed in levels greater than 100 milligrams per day. Additionally, there are a number of trace minerals which are present in the body in much smaller amounts.

Burke points out that there are studies which say vitamin and mineral supplements are unnecessary, but he says it may yet be proved that large doses of either or both can have a beneficial effect on performance. While the jury is out, a daily vitamin C and B-complex supplement seems in order, and cyclists who just aren't sure if they are covering all bases with their daily diet might do well to take an all-in-one vitamin and mineral tablet.

Reducing Body Weight

The more I'm around bike riders the more I'm amazed at how many guys who are easily 10 pounds overweight will constantly search for ways to lighten their bikes. They'll spend hundreds of dollars on drilled-out components, titanium frames, superlight wheels, and so on, hoping to save an ounce here or there and thus be able to ride faster and farther with less effort. Better they should save the money and lighten their bikes by doing something about the weight of the object which covers the saddle.

As a physiologist, Burke has taken particular note of this phenomenon. "Ten pounds may not seem like a lot of excess weight," he says, "but think about how often in cycling it must be lifted and accelerated. We have to climb hills, get back up to speed after a stoplight, spring away from dogs, get moving at the start and turnaround in time trials. And extra pounds isn't the only factor—fat is composed of cells which need a blood supply. This blood could do more good in working muscles and in dissipating heat."

If you have 10 pounds to spare—or 20 or 30 or more—you can certainly become a more efficient engine for your bike by shedding the excess weight. I'm sure this doesn't come as a surprise, but how to lose weight properly through cycling may not be so obvious. Let's see how you can use your bike as a means of slimming down.

First, you must find out how much of your total weight is actually fat so you'll know how many pounds can be safely lost. The bathroom scale can't tell you this, but your doctor's skinfold calipers can. Burke's studies on top competitive cyclists have produced recommended levels of 10–12 percent body fat for male riders aged 16 to 18, 6–9 percent for men 18 to 34, and 12–15 percent for women 18 to 34. In contrast, the average U.S. male has approximately 18–21 percent body fat and the average female 21–23 percent. Everyone at such levels has plenty they can safely lose, though once 5 percent is reached, that's the limit; some fat is needed by the body for fuel, vitamin storage, and insulation.

Despite everything you read and see advertised, there are really just three ways you can lose weight: (1) increase energy expenditure while keeping calorie intake constant; (2) decrease calorie intake while keeping energy expenditure constant; (3) a combination of 1 and 2. The first way is the best for the obvious reason that your method of energy expenditure—i.e., cycling—will help you build cardiovascular fitness and muscular strength as you shed the pounds.

Since the way to lose a pound of fat is to burn 3,500 calories without replacing them, it is possible to maintain your present diet and reduce weight by simply riding your bike. The graph shows how

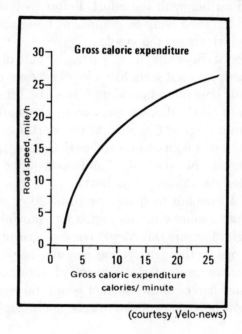

(courtesy Velo-news)

many calories per minute you will burn when riding at various speeds by yourself on a flat road. It is based on a rider weighing 170 pounds. If you are heavier than this or are a relatively new rider and not yet an efficient pedaler, the curve moves upward. If you weigh less than 170 the curve moves down somewhat.

The best approach, according to Burke, is to knock off from 500 to 1,000 calories a day through a combination of decreased food intake and increased exercise. In one week's time this will produce a weight loss of between 1 and 2 pounds. Admittedly, this plan won't excite a person who wants to reduce rapidly, but, as Burke notes, body weight lost gradually and systematically is more likely to stay off. You must also consider that the energy requirements of cycling can leave you feeling lifeless the rest of the day (not to mention during rides) if you drastically cut calorie intake in order to accelerate weight loss.

The Value of Carbohydrates

Cyclists not concerned with reducing their weight can rejoice in knowing that carbohydrates are the best source of fuel for working muscles. Foods rich in carbohydrates are those which many people enjoy eating, most of which have long been looked upon as being fattening—sugars and starches in the form of breads, cereal products like spaghetti, fruits, sweet deserts, and other delights. Yes, they will plump up the sedentary person, but not the cyclist burning several thousand calories a day. Instead they provide both enjoyable eating and the glycogen and blood glucose needed for muscle energy and the proper functioning of the central nervous system.

The benefits of carbohydrates have led to a dietary technique which can increase the body's store of glycogen well beyond normal levels, the idea being to help a cyclist pedal stronger longer. It is called carbohydrate loading, a term already well known among distance runners. In its strictest application the procedure calls for a long, hard ride to deplete muscles of glycogen, followed by six days of moderate exercise. After the depletion ride and throughout the next three days, meals are virtually devoid of carbohydrates and heavy on protein and fat. The diet then switches to high-carbohydrate foods during the three days before the event, thus saturating muscles and blood with high levels of sugars. By the time of the event, muscles may contain almost three times their normal amount of glycogen and the rider will experience a big boost in endurance.

It sure sounds good, but there is growing evidence that carbo loading can be dangerous to the body, especially if practiced frequently. High levels of glycogen in muscle tissues have been reported to produce blood in the urine, tightness in muscles due to accumulation of water in the cells, abnormal EKGs, and increased concentrations of fat in the blood. Further, the long-term effects of carbohydrate loading are unknown and need more investigation. Some riders have found that a significant benefit can still be gained by eliminating the depletion stage—quite an unpleasant experience, anyway—and simply increasing carbohydrate intake over normal levels during the days preceding the event. As long as you use this loading technique and save it for a few widely spaced races or century rides, there probably isn't any health risk. One caution, though: Loading doesn't mean stuffing yourself silly, it simply means increasing carbohydrate intake at the expense of other types of food. Overeating is never good for you.

Fat is another important source of energy, especially for the road racer and long-distance tourist. After several hours of riding, the glycogen supplied by carbohydrates diminishes, forcing the muscles to turn more and more to fat as their energy source. This isn't to suggest that you should eat a high-fat diet; rather, you must train your body to use the fat stores it already has. This is easy to do in one sense because it begins to happen after about three hours every time you take a long, continuous ride. However, the experience of crossing the boundary from sugar fuel to fat fuel can be rather unpleasant until enough rides have conditioned your system to it. You are likely to feel weak, empty in the stomach, and even slightly sick, but you must realize that the experience is necessary for becoming a strong and proficient distance rider.

Especially during long road races and all-day rides, cyclists can be hit by the "bonk." This might sound funny but it won't bring any smiles out on the road—it's an extreme case of the symptoms just described, occurring to such a degree that it is all but impossible to carry on. There are a number of reasons why the bonk occurs, including lack of blood glucose to fuel the brain and nervous system, depletion of the glycogen needed for muscle energy, and loss of fluids, minerals, and electrolytes because of prolonged sweating. To fend off the bonk many cyclists snack frequently on high-sugar foods like raisins, dates, and other fruits, and this usually works during long training rides and tours. But there is evidence that putting food in the stomach during races is counterproductive, as Burke notes: "The stomach requires a greater blood supply during digestion of food and this causes a diversion of blood away from the working muscles in the legs." As a better way to replenish carbohydrates, he suggests drinking frequently from water bottles filled with a glucose solution of not greater than 2 percent (one tablespoon of sugar per bottle). "If higher concentrations are ingested, the rate at which water leaves the stomach is reduced and it may even cause water to be drawn into the stomach," Burke cautions. "The majority of commercial replacement drinks contain too much sugar to be effective."

Fluid Replacement

Burke strongly advocates drinking plenty of fluids before, during, and after cycling, whether it be a 2 percent sugar solution, diluted fruit juice, weak iced tea, or just plain water. In fact, he has drawn criticism for his suggestion—seen as excessive in some circles—that during warm weather a cyclist who is racing or training hard should (1) drink 13 to 20 ounces of fluid 15 minutes before riding; (2) drink about 4 ounces every 10 to 15 minutes during the ride; (3) drink plentifully between meals and during the evening even if not feeling thirsty; (4) keep a chart of morning weight to spot a weight-loss trend that may be due to dehydration.

The reason for all this caution is that by tradition many cyclists will embark on a strenuous hot-weather ride of up to 75 miles with only two bottles of water, one in the cage and the other in a jersey pocket. But as Burke notes, "In such a ride a person can lose between 7 and 10 pounds of water weight. Even if he drinks both bottles (approximately 40 ounces) this will replace only 2½ pounds of lost fluid. Such losses put severe demands on the circulatory system, which is about 70 percent water.

"When water is lost," he continues, "plasma has a limited capacity to carry nutrients such as glucose, fats, and oxygen to the working muscles and also remove the by-products of metabolism. Although it may be impossible to offset all water lost in sweating, even partial replacement can limit the problems of overheating and minimize the threat of circulatory collapse."

It stands to reason that if you ride for the physical benefits of the sport, it's foolish to risk ill health by neglecting something so simple as drinking enough water. Some old hands have scoffed at the quantities Burke recommends, but one thing is for sure: Too much water is easier to deal with than too little.

FITNESS FOR DISTANCE

3

In their highly readable and informative *The Bicycle Touring Book*, authors Tim and Glenda Wilhelm make this statement: "We don't consider ourselves athletes by any stretch of the imagination." Can you imagine those words from a pair of cyclists whose extensive touring has taken them thousands of miles, including across the United States in 1976? I respectfully suggest that this is about as perfect an example of unpretentiousness as has ever been written. Anyone who can pedal a loaded bike between 50 and 100 miles a day through all kinds of terrain and weather is an athlete by my account, no less so than the racer who goes out and covers the same ground in half the time. The difference in objectives may be great, but it's the same thing that makes those wheels roll down the road—physical strength and fitness.

There is a division between tourists and racers that holds up quite firmly: Tourists don't race and racers don't tour. Sure, some tour-oriented riders will enter low-key club competition, such as time trials, and some competitors will take a weekend bike trip or two after the racing season ends. But the two disciplines are so different that it is the rare cyclist who doesn't find one much more attractive than the other. The equipment needed, the level of commitment, the basic reason for riding—these factors and others virtually necessitate a choice. Not the least consideration is the type of training required to properly prepare.

As we see in Chapter 10, fitness for racing comes from a lengthy program that first lays a solid foundation of long miles and then moves on to specialized techniques to hone endurance (LSD) and build speed (intervals). This requires sticking to a rather precise daily training schedule leading to weekly progressions of the workload and mileage totals. For touring, on the other hand, much less rigidity in training is needed. The best way to develop the ability to handle the demands of a century ride, a weekend tour, or even an extended journey is simply to spend an ample amount of time on the bike. In fact, a rider who has done so usually has all the base mileage needed for making a successful transition to training for racing, should the urge to compete be felt.

First things first, though, and that means a look into how you can improve your cycling strength to the point where a distance of 50–100 miles is manageable in a day's time. Accomplishing this is not hard but requires the time and dedication to take on a steady diet of riding. There must also be a firm understanding of how training helps develop muscular strength and cardiovascular fitness—the fundamental elements of cycling performance.

The Training Effect

A primary goal of any cycling program, whether for touring or racing, is to produce the training effect. Exactly what this means has probably never been explained better than by Kenneth H. Cooper, a U.S. Air Force medical officer who used the data from tests on more than 5,000 people to create a landmark book in America's awakening to the benefits of endurance exercise. When his *Aerobics* was published in 1968 it not only introduced a new word to our vocabulary, it gave tens of thousands of previously sedentary souls the motivation they needed to get off their soft backsides and into a regular program of running, swimming, or cycling, the "big three" in Cooper's list of best exercises. He promises that if we exercise correctly we will be rewarded with a number of highly desirable changes to our bodies— the training effect—which he lists as including:

- Increased efficiency of the lungs. They will be able to process more air with less effort and thus make more oxygen available for the energy-producing process.
- Increased efficiency of the heart. It will grow larger and stronger and beat at a slower rate because it can pump more blood with each stroke. Further, it will be able to handle the body's demands during

maximum exertion without having to beat at dangerously high levels.

- Increased number and size of blood vessels, allowing oxygenated blood to be carried to body tissue.
- Increased total blood volume, which also allows more energy-producing oxygen to reach body tissue.
- Reduced blood pressure, thanks in part to improved tone of muscles and blood vessels.
- Increased maximal oxygen consumption, due to the improved efficiency of oxygen supply and delivery. The general enhancement of the function of the lungs, heart, blood vessels, and body tissue helps strengthen the body against many forms of illness and disease.
- A firm body due to fat weight being changed to lean weight.

To these remarkable physiological benefits, Cooper lists several important psychological rewards of endurance exercise programs: "The training effect may change your whole outlook on life. You'll learn to relax, develop a better self-image, be able to tolerate the stress of daily living better. And, what is very important, you'll sleep better and get more work done with less fatigue, including desk work."

This is all good news, but when it comes to the specifics of using cycling for physical conditioning, Cooper's advice leaves a lot to be desired. As a runner himself, and because his Air Force research primarily used running in its study of the training effect, Cooper obviously doesn't have the personal or professional experience to understand how a bike should be ridden to build fitness. He shows his unfamiliarity when he says that "the obvious disadvantage [of cycling in comparison to running and swimming] is that you need a bicycle." Indeed! No one who ever had a good bike and learned to ride it right would ever call owning it a "disadvantage." He cites other problems with cycling as not being able to use the bike indoors when the weather is bad (not correct, thanks to rollers and new devices like the Racer-Mate and Turbo-Trainer), and he says riding won't benefit the upper body muscles as much as running and swimming. Well, maybe not swimming, but if the good doctor ever rode a time trial or a century or tackled a long climb he'd have no doubt that cycling does much more than running for the upper body.

In fact, Dr. Fred A. Brandt, writing in the anthology *The Best of Bicycling,* states that cycling is one of the most complete forms of exercise, not only for the legs but for the arms, shoulders, back, and abdominal and diaphragmatic muscles. He notes that cycling utilizes the largest muscle "pump" that the body possesses—the alternating contractions and relaxations of the large muscle masses in the legs— which aids in returning venous blood to the heart and thus enhances circulation.

But the misconceptions about bicycle riding in *Aerobics* pale to insignificance when Cooper states that he bases his exercise program for cycling on the use of an American single-speed bike. Further, he says that if you are riding a 3-speed "racing cycle" you should use the highest gear as much as possible. Nonsense! Although Cooper does supply some of the best information available for the person interested in physical fitness, I think his treatment of cycling actually does more harm than good. In fact, many people seem to have a basic misunderstanding of how a bike should be ridden in order to produce muscular strength and cardiovascular benefits. The plain truth is that a person can't get fit through cycling unless and until (1) the proper riding position is attained, as outlined in Chapter 4, and (2) the bike is pedaled correctly against the proper resistance for sufficient periods of time. Neither can be the case on a single-speed bike nor on most three-speeds, and the fact that so many people do think it's right to use the highest gear as much as possible is why suffering leg muscles end their riding long before the training effect can occur.

Let's now look into the proper way to cycle for physical fitness and then how to develop a training program for becoming a proficient long-distance rider.

Riding for Fitness

Rather than pedaling around in large gears that require plenty of short-term work for virtually no long-term benefit, you must do just the opposite. That is, ride so that leg-muscle fatigue doesn't happen before the lungs and heart have undergone a sufficient period of elevated activity, i.e., before the training effect has taken place. To accomplish this you must (1) select a gear that is low enough to turn quite easily; (2) spin your legs fast enough to bring the heart rate to the training-effect level (see below); (3) maintain this heart rate for at least half an hour. This formula is as simple as it sounds, and it can easily be tailored to your personal needs. First, the practical definitions of some terminology used in cycle training.

Training Effect: In sum, all of the beneficial physiological and psychological changes which occur due to a sustained high level of aerobic riding.

Resting Heart Rate: Find this by taking your pulse after you have been relaxed and sitting quietly for a number of minutes or, even better, before you get out of bed in the morning. Learn to take your pulse by pressing fingertips against the carotid artery, which is located in the neck just to the side of the Adam's apple. Count the beats for a full minute.

Maximum Heart Rate: While this can be determined through medical testing, you can get a good approximation by subtracting your age from 220. For example, for a person 30 years old the maximum attainable heart rate will be about 190 beats per minute. Of course, among all 30-year-olds some will be above or below this figure.

Training Heart Rate: Find your ideal by subtracting your resting heart rate from your maximum heart rate and taking 75 percent of the result (in other words, multiply by 0.75). Add this number to the resting rate and you then have the number of beats per minute which should be maintained to elicit the optimal training effect. Going back to our example, the 30-year-old with a maximum heart rate of 190 finds that his resting rate is 70 beats per minute. Taking 70 from 190 gives 120, and 75 percent of that equals 90. Adding that back to the resting rate of 70 gives him a training heart rate of 160. This means that if he can sustain 160 heartbeats per minute during his cycling he will be gaining near maximum fitness for his time on the bike. However, for many people in the early weeks of a cycling program a 75 percent rate may be too stressful to maintain for the necessary length of time. Should you fall into this category it is fine to strive instead for a training heart rate based on 60 percent and then progress to 75 percent as your ability to handle the workload improves. In the example, using 60 percent gives the 30-year-old a figure of 142 beats per minute, which can be called the minimum rate that will arouse the training effect for him. Therefore, he should pedal at a rate that keeps his pulse above 142 beats per minute, and the closer to 160 the better. (To take your pulse during a ride you will need a digital watch or one with a sweep second hand. You can either stop the bike or make the check while moving. Use the carotid artery where the pulse is strong and easy to locate, and count the beats for six seconds, adding a zero to find the one-minute rate. Make the count without delay, because the heart rate begins to fall off quickly when exercise intensity is reduced.)

Cadence: The number of crank revolutions per minute. Determine this by counting how many times your right foot comes around during 30 seconds and then double the number. Make the check when you are on flat terrain and pedaling along at your usual training pace.

Two things should accompany every riding session, a warm-up before and a cool-down afterward. Each plays a part in preventing muscle injury and soreness.

A warm-up is performed to prepare the body for physical exertion. It should gradually increase both the heart and breathing rates, as well as muscle temperature. This can be accomplished with light calisthenics, and a few push-ups and bent-leg sit-ups will help strengthen upper-body muscles used in riding. Stretching exercises should be included to keep muscles and tendons loose and to remedy specific sorenesses. In this regard I recommend the well-illustrated book entitled *Stretching* by Bob Anderson. Besides listing routines for virtually every sport, he includes diagrams showing which stretches can be used to treat muscle problems in any part of the body.

It varies among individuals, but 15 minutes is usually adequate for proper warm-up. Thanks to the gentle nature of pedaling, the last phase of the warm-up—bringing up a light sweat—can be done right on the bike, spinning easily in a low gear.

The cool-down is just what you suspect, a period of steadily decreasing exertion following the workout. This helps ensure the return of blood from working muscles to the heart, as well as the elimination of waste products from muscle tissue. Each is important for the prevention of tightness and soreness. Cool-down is accomplished best by ending the workout a couple of miles from where you will stop riding. Just putter on in using a low gear so that breathing and heart rates will be down to near normal levels by the time you climb off.

Long-Distance Training

How many miles a week have you been riding? Whether or not you keep a diary of your cycling activity (I strongly recommend that you begin now if you haven't been), try to come up with a weekly average for the last month or so. This is an important figure, because it is your starting point for the progression into longer distances. The goal will be to increase your mileage by about 8–10 percent each week until you have reached the point where your training is sufficient to see you through the longest one-day ride you want to take. This slow but steady buildup will work very well if you let it; the temptation to make bigger weekly increases will almost certainly arise, so beware and try to resist.

Although you won't be putting yourself through the exhausting training routines that racers use, you must be just as concerned with adaptation to stress. It does no good to do everything right on the bike day after day but fail to allow the rest that permits recovery and consolidation of strength. This is the reason for gradual increases in mileage and why it is good to take a day off once a week. Also important is adjusting your sleep schedule should your expanded training program cut into your usual bedtime hours (see the section on time-budgeting techniques in Chapter 2 and review the danger signals of overtraining).

For illustrative purposes I am going to assume that you have a primary goal that is common to many nonracers—becoming strong enough to ride a century. One hundred miles is sort of a magic figure in cycling, being the distance of many formal rides sponsored by clubs affiliated with the League of American Wheelmen. Additionally, it is the day's work many riders like to accomplish when touring. Generally speaking, when you can go out and pedal 100 miles in eight hours or less you have arrived as a long-distance cyclist.

Begin working toward a century by trying to ride six days out of every seven. Assuming you hold down a full-time job or are a student, weekday rides can be hard to manage, but do what you can to pedal at least an hour a day. This is where commuting by bike can really help. By using the gears and cadence necessary to maintain a 60–75 percent training-effect level during these rides, you will improve your cardiovascular fitness. Perhaps just as important, your upper body and your posterior will be subjected to the stresses of increased riding. While the addition of simple exercises such as bent-knee sit-ups, push-ups, and standard weight-training movements will help accelerate the strengthening of upper-body muscles, only riding can condition your sit-down area to long hours in the saddle.

If you can fit in one or two longer rides (say two hours) during the week, so much the better. But don't do more than that, for two reasons. First, the stress of job and school is real and takes both a physical and mental toll. Add to this the rigors of an expanded riding schedule and you have the breeding ground for fatigue and stalled progress. Second, the hard/easy principle applies to cycling just as it does to training for other sports. This means that a long ride should be followed by a short one. Since you will be putting in extra miles on the weekends, one or two relatively lengthy rides during the week are all that can be undertaken without the risk of overdoing it.

Select different routes for the weekday rides if possible. Doing so will alleviate both mental and physical monotony. Even the most enthusiastic rider will soon begin to flag when facing the same routine every day. Also, if you use routes with contrasting terrain there can be quite a difference in the stress applied to the body, an important consideration if you are limited to the same amount of time for training each day. Without the opportunity to make one day's ride longer than another's, you can alternate hilly terrain with flat. As the mood strikes, extra work can be done by attacking the climbs or using the descents to roll out a high gear for short periods.

Proper use of the weekends is the key to preparing for a century. Given the restrictions on weekday training, Saturday and Sunday are for adding the miles that produce each week's 8–10 percent increase.

Further, two long rides back to back will furnish the stress that builds the strength demanded by a 100-miler. (Be sure to make Monday a short and easy day or take it off completely so that recovery and adaptation can take place.)

There are various ways to approach weekend workouts. The objective, however, is always the same: saddle time. Even if you go at a pace closer to your 60 percent training-effect level instead of the 70–75 percent you can manage during short weekday workouts, cardiovascular benefits will accrue. More important, you will be developing muscular endurance as you extend the length of your rides toward the time it will take to complete 100 miles in one day. Duration is actually more significant than the number of miles ridden, the reason being that frequently in the final stages of a century it is comfort, not strength, that plays the biggest role in enjoyment and success. If you pedal at a comfortable cadence in moderate gears, drink frequently, eat energy-yielding foods along the way, and even dismount occasionally to stretch and relax, a century shouldn't be a titanic struggle. But it will be if your shoulders, neck, back, and buns start to mutiny after the 60-mile mark.

The distance/time to strive for during Saturday and Sunday rides is, of course, dependent on where you are in your buildup program. In the early stages you might go for 40 miles on Saturday and come back with 25 Sunday. By the time the century is near, you should probably be handling 75 Saturday and 50 Sunday. The longer day is done first for two reasons. First, you will be riding easily on Fridays to pool energy for the weekend; it makes sense to use those reserves for the week's biggest effort. Second, should Saturday's ride be cut short or canceled for any reason, you can then lengthen the Sunday session. But if you schedule Sunday for the long day and disaster strikes, all those important miles will be lost.

The reason Sunday's mileage (riding time) should be about two-thirds of Saturday's is to help prevent the kind of stress overload that can cause leg injuries and general fatigue. As you pedal past your former limits on Saturdays you will probably be elated to find that it is easier than expected, thanks to the fitness built by your progressive training and the fact that you are relatively rested. But the enthusiasm bred by Saturday's accomplishment has a way of disappearing on Sunday morning when a stiff body faces another long bout in the saddle. Knowing that the ride will be shorter helps greatly. When you start finding that you have the liveliness and strength to duplicate Saturday's distance on Sunday it is a sign that you are truly reaching the kind of fitness required for extended touring. But in terms of century preparation, the best tactic is to then increase Saturday's distance and keep Sunday's proportionally shorter. This is the way to safeguard against both physical and mental staleness.

Once you are beyond 50 miles for your long ride of the week, begin to treat that ride as if it were the century itself. Carry food and drink (use these rides to find which refreshments suit you best) and stop for short breaks if you intend to during the 100-miler. Use your handlebar or saddlebag if you can't fit your provisions, rain jacket, emergency tool kit, etc. in your jersey pockets. Wear the same shoes, clothing, and helmet you expect to use for the century. The idea is to get thoroughly acquainted with everything that will play a part in the real ride.

There is no need to ride 100 miles in training in order to accomplish it on the day of the formal century. Once you have built up your Saturday rides to about 75 miles and have managed this distance with relative ease three or four times, you are ready.

Riding a Century

The best way to ride a century is to participate in an event sponsored by a bicycle club affiliated with the League of American Wheelmen. The advantanges are many and all result from good organization. Scores of centuries are held each year and publicized in the LAW magazine, *American Wheelmen,* providing riders in almost every part of the country with a nearby event. A modest entry fee is usually required (it's often lower for LAW members), and it is well worth it since the organizers provide important things like a map of the course, markers along the way, a meal after the ride, and a sag wagon to make sure no one is left stranded on the road.

Pick a LAW century far enough in advance so that your weekly training buildup will bring you to readiness within a month of the ride. Send for information and mail in your entry early. If the ride originates in a town quite a distance away, go ahead and reserve a motel room. Sure, you could get up extra early and drive over before the start, but why lose sleep and then have anxiety that an unexpected delay could cause you to miss the ride? You've worked long and hard to prepare for the event, so arrive the evening before, treat yourself to a nice room and dinner, and take peace of mind in the fact that when you wake up the next morning you will be where you need to be.

In the week leading up to the century, taper off your training. After the previous weekend's normal schedule of back-to-back long rides, take Monday off and come back with relatively short sessions on Tuesday, Wednesday, and Thursday. If the century is on Saturday, take Friday off and either travel to the ride site or use the time to make sure your equipment and clothing is in good order. If it is a Sunday event, you can ride Friday and use Saturday for getting ready. The objective is to allow time to attend to final details and get plenty of rest.

As discussed in Chapter 2, build meals around high-carbohydrate foods during the three days before the ride. This will help give you energy stores that maximize muscle endurance. On the morning of the ride, eat a moderate breakfast a couple of hours before the start, choosing foods that experience has proved agree with you. Also prepare the liquids and snacks you will carry in your jersey pockets.

Plan to be at the staging area at least 45 minutes before start time. This will give you the chance to get answers to any questions, make a final trip to the restroom, and talk with a few of your fellow cyclists. You may even meet an experienced rider who has the same time objective as you do and who offers to help set the pace; it's comforting to strike up an alliance when you are about to enter the unknown, especially if it is happening in a sea of strangers.

Finally, you're off. Although a LAW century ride isn't a race, you might not be so sure when a number of riders blast off at a crisp tempo. You may be tempted to go with them, but don't. Remember Aesop's tortoise and hare. Put faith in the training you've done and settle into your Saturday pace as soon as possible. You may wind up riding the first several miles faster than normal—it's hard not to owing to your high energy level, the adrenaline that flows from the excitement of the event, the fact that you are in the midst of many good riders now instead of out on the road alone, and the windbreak of having them around you. But the key to making it to the 100th mile with some strength, comfort, and good humor still in reserve is to ride at *your* pace, nobody else's. If it develops that your pace happens to match that of another rider or two, so much the better—companionship and socializing always help the miles go by quicker. Just don't allow it to disrupt your regular pattern of drinking and nibbling, or your breaks from riding if you are accustomed to taking them during long spells on the bike.

If you've prepared and ridden correctly, your journey through the final miles will hold no surprises. You will feel a general fatigue and you will have long since run out of comfortable positions—there won't be a square millimeter of saddle you haven't used—but the effort it takes to reach the finish won't be overburdening. The last minutes may find you questioning your sanity for having put yourself through such a test, but such thoughts will be flushed away by the pride of accomplishment within moments after finally climbing off the bike. In the camaraderie that follows a LAW century, it is the rare cyclist who isn't already thinking about riding another one.

4

POSITION, PEDALING, GEARING, AND BRAKING

Of all the matters you need to attend to when becoming involved in serious cycling, perhaps the most important is establishing a proper riding position. The best equipment and the finest physique aren't worth much if they can't be used to full advantage. Doing so depends on having a frame size appropriate for your body size, and then making the critical adjustments to the saddle and handlebars that will custom-fit the bike to your unique physical dimensions.

It sounds pretty straightforward, but it's not. Since I began riding I've owned about fifteen bikes and have experimented with an untold number of positions in my quest for the magic formula. Along the way, I suffered a lot of physical discomfort—the reward for many of my attempts was an aching back and sore arms. I once thought that sitting straight up was the answer, and so I raised the saddle and bars as high as I could. When I found that this made wind resistance a problem second only to the pain in my rear end, I tried having the seat quite low. That didn't work either, because my knees were too bent for strong and efficient pedaling.

I tried all the traditional formulas that are supposed to result in a perfect riding position, and still I couldn't get it right. But I kept working at it, kept making slight alterations, and I gave each new set-up an honest appraisal by sticking with it for hundreds of miles on the road. It took me five years to achieve the position I now have, a position that lets me use my body and its strength to utmost advantage whenever I ride. Furthermore, I can now take any bike that falls within my size range and adjust it for my optimum position. Using the following guidelines, you will be able to do this, too. The result will make you and your bike appear to be designed for each other.

Determining Frame Size

Finding the right position is difficult because there are a number of variables. First you have to have a frame size that falls within the narrow range of what fits your body. Ten-speed bikes which use standard "adult" wheel sizes (27×1¼ clinchers or 700c tubulars) normally have frames that range from 19 to 25 inches. The exact figure is found by measuring from the center of the crank axle to the top of the seat tube. Because many bikes are built on metric measurements, the figure you get may come out to a fraction of an inch.

I've found that the best indicator of correct frame size is leg length. Make this measurement from the top of the femur bone in the center of your hip to the floor (with shoes off and leg straight).

To determine the frame size that is correct for you, measure your leg from the top of the thighbone to the floor and subtract 13¾ inches. The result should equal the seat tube length (give or take half an inch) of frames that fit you best.

Subtract 13¾ inches from the figure you get (or 35 centimeters if you are in the metric mode) and the resulting number will be equal to the seat-tube measurement—give or take half an inch—of bikes which fit you and should allow you to obtain your best riding position.

Generally, a person whose main interest is touring and who outfits the bike with packs and panniers will find a slight advantage in riding a larger rather than smaller frame, as long as the size remains within the above limits. This is because there will be a bit more room for the equipment on the larger frame. On the other hand, racers and long-distance riders who don't pack much gear should try for the middle ground or even the small end of their size range. Relatively speaking, a small frame is lighter and stiffer, which means there will be a more efficient transfer of the rider's energy. While this is also important in touring, other considerations, such as being able to pack the bike so that nothing interferes with riding position and pedaling, take precedence.

Saddle Position

The traditional formulas claim that saddle height should be determined by a rider's leg length—they say it's just a matter of simple arithmetic. But I have found that the best way is to actually get on the bike and adjust the saddle according to the body as a whole. The method I recommend is the one taught by the U.S. Cycling Federation's national coaching director, Eddie Borysewicz, and it works well for almost every rider who uses it. You will need your bike, your cleated cycling shoes or whatever you most often ride in, a metric tape measure, a plumb line, tools for working with your seat post/saddle and handlebar stem, and a marker. Invite a friend to pedal over so you'll have a helper, and each of you will end the afternoon with bikes custom-fitted to make you stronger riders.

The most critical element in correct position is the location of the saddle. The goal is to sit so that each leg is able to exert maximum force on its pedal when the crank arm is in the forward horizontal position. Since the knee is the leverage point through which leg power is transmitted, it must be directly over the center of the pedal

A little error in riding position can make a difference, so be as precise as possible when setting your saddle height. Here Eddie Borysewicz, the U.S. Cycling Federation's national coaching director, finds that a rider's saddle is set too high. The heel should reach the pedal when the pedal is at its lowest position and the knee is straight.

or just slightly behind it when the crank arm passes through the horizontal.

Put on your riding shoes and get on the bike. Let one of the pedals go to the bottom of its circle and place your *heel* on it (if toe clips are installed just let the pedal hang upside down). When sitting squarely in the middle of the saddle you want your knee almost straight, but not so extended that you can't make it lock and unlock. Raise or lower the seat post accordingly, and then try it with the other heel. Pedal backward using both feet to make sure you don't have to rock side to side to keep your heels in contact. Now you have arrived at a saddle height that is approximately correct.

The second step refines the position. While still in the saddle, have your friend hold a pedal right side up and parallel to the floor at the bottom of the circle. Without moving your pelvis off the center saddle, straighten your leg and slide your foot under the pedal. Have your friend position your foot so that the slot in the cleat lines up directly under the rear of the pedal cage. (If you do not use cleats, line up the ball of your foot under the center of pedal.) Now your friend should hold your foot (still under the pedal) at the angle it makes when you are pedaling normally—usually about 20 degrees to the horizontal with the toe down. If this makes your knee straight and you are still in the center of the saddle, the height is correct. More than likely, though, your leg will not be straight or you will have had to shift your butt to keep your foot at the proper angle. Raise or lower the saddle accordingly. Based on my experience, you'll probably need to raise it a centimeter or so from the position determined in the first step.

Next you have to adjust the relationship between the center of the knee and the center of the pedal when the crank arm is in the forward horizontal position. To do this, first feel the large bones on the inside of your knees (the bones that touch each other when you stand with your feet together). Make a mark in the center of these bones and then climb back on your bike. Put your feet in the pedals and assume a normal riding posture. Bring one pedal to a forward horizontal position and have your friend put the plumb line on your mark. Tilt your knee inward a little so the line can drop between the crank arm and the frame. Now you can see where the center of your

a

To arrive at a position that allows strong and efficient riding, first set the saddle height so your leg will be almost fully straight when you put your heel on the pedal (*a*). Then slip your foot under the pedal so that the shoe cleat lines up with the rear of the pedal cage (*b*), lowering the saddle, if necessary, so the knee will straighten without your having to move from saddle center. The saddle height is now correct. To adjust for best fore/aft position, first mark the center of the large bones that touch at your knees when you stand with your feet together. Then sit squarely on the saddle with the crank arms horizontal and use a plumb line to see how your mark lines up with the pedal axle (*c*).

b

It should be directly over the axle or slightly behind, never in front. Move the saddle accordingly and make sure it is level with the top tube of the bike (some riders prefer a slight nose-up angle) before tightening the seat post clamp. Finally, climb back on the bike in a low riding position to check handlebar location (*d*). When looking down at the front hub, the handlebars should obstruct your line of vision. Raise or lower the bars until this is the case, which should leave the top of the handlebar stem between three and six centimeters below the top of the saddle.

d

knee is in relation to the center of the pedal. Slide the saddle forward or backward until the string falls about a centimeter behind pedal center. This is the best position for most road riders, especially tourists who must pedal against the resistance of a heavily loaded bike and hilly terrain. Riders not facing such conditions and who generally don't use big gears may prefer to be directly over pedal center; in no case should the knee be in front of pedal center.

Before firmly tightening the saddle to the seat post, make sure it is parallel to the top tube of the frame. Usually it helps to lay a yardstick or broom handle on the saddle from front to back so you can see any angle it is making. Many cyclists prefer a slight nose-up slant, but be cautious, because too much can cause discomfort and numbness in the crotch area because of excess pressure when riding in a low position. A saddle should never be angled nose-down, as this will cause you to continually slide forward, resulting in fatigue to arms and shoulders as they cope with the added weight.

Handlebar Adjustment

Only after the saddle has been correctly positioned should you adjust the handlebars. This is because the location of the bars works hand in hand with saddle height to produce the proper weight distribution of 40 percent/60 percent, front wheel to back wheel. To get into the ballpark, move the handlebar stem up or down until it is about 4 centimeters below the saddle (measured from the top center of the saddle to the top tube, compared to the top of the stem to the top tube).

To refine this setting, hop back on the bike and get into a streamlined riding position with your hands on the drops and your elbows slightly bent. Sit very comfortably, as if you could ride in this position for a long time. Now look at the front hub. You can't see it because the handlebars are in the way? Great, that means your handlebar position is correct. The hub needn't be blocked out completely—the center can be a bit in front of or behind the bars—but if it's not close, then raise or lower the stem accordingly. Make the final adjustment based on your own preference for being stretched out a bit more or less, but the stem should end up within 3 to 6 centimeters of the top of the saddle.

If you find that you can't block out the hub and stay inside this range, you probably have the wrong stem extension. To find out the size you need, get in your low riding position and have your friend hold a metric ruler (stems come in metric sizes) along your present stem. As you look down at the wheel you can estimate how much longer or shorter the extension needs to be. When visiting a shop to buy the correct size, make sure to ask if they'll take your old stem in trade, because there won't be much else you can do with it.

It's a more serious problem if you run short of stem before the handlebars are as high as you need. Since a stem is made of lightweight alloy, a good portion of it must remain in the head tube to prevent it from shearing off because of forces associated with stopping and riding rough roads. Some manufacturers indicate minimum stem depth with an engraved line, and in no case should you install one so that you can still see its vertical expansion slot. If you can't raise the bars high enough, it's a good indication that your bike is too small. You can't simply go out and buy a longer stem (as you can a longer stem extension) because they are all made fairly short as a safety factor.

The final step is to set the angle of the handlebars. Simply loosen the bolt at the front of the stem and rotate the bars until the drops make a slight upward angle to the top tube. For most riders this creates the proper alignment for the wrists when riding the drops, and it puts the tops in the right position for the various hand placements. However, personal tastes and riding habits can produce quite a variety of workable angles. Some tourists, for example, prefer to position the tops as flat as possible because that's where they ride much of the time, and they pay little heed to how this affects the drops. Experiment to discover what works best in the type of riding you do most.

Riding Posture

Your riding posture is important to every bike-handling skill and for producing the proper weight distribution between saddle and handlebars. Since overcoming air resistance is a primary concern, a sleek, low position that creates a minimal frontal area is the ideal. But this isn't very comfortable for an extended period and it is not natural or easy to achieve. So compromises are in order, and by using the following tips you should be able to develop a relatively stream- lined posture that also works well for long-distance riding.

Rather than bending forward from the middle of your back, keep your whole top half straight and lower yourself from the waist, as far down your spine as possible. A flat back is what you are striving for.

Keep your shoulders flat and wide. A lot of riders tend to sit in a round-shouldered position. This might feel low and streamlined, but what it's mainly doing is reducing lung capacity. Especially when you must increase muscular effort, such as when going uphill or into the wind, more oxygen is needed. And yet the tendency of most riders in stressful situations is to make things harder for themselves by hunching forward. At times like these you should concentrate on

Australian Danny Clark is one of the world's fastest bike riders. He holds many velodrome speed records in Europe and does just as well in short-course road races and criteriums. His position on the bike is a reason why—he is low and streamlined and yet relaxed, as the fingers of his right hand disclose. Keeping tension out of upper-body and arm muscles is also a key to comfort and delaying fatigue during long periods on the bike.

keeping the torso relaxed and letting the arms and legs do the work. If it seems to take a lot of effort to breathe and if the muscles in your chest and diaphragm feel fatigued after a ride, you probably have this very problem.

Don't lock your elbows. Loose and flexible arms are important for keeping the upper body relaxed and for absorbing road shock. It takes some awareness, though, to avoid tightening up. To illustrate the risks of stiff arms, John Allis, the national road champion in 1974, has been known to ride up to someone from behind and grab him by the elbow. This often causes a swerve, but it shouldn't if the arms are bent and as lightly tensed as they are supposed to be. If you find you can't ride without keeping your arms locked straight, the handlebars may be too low or the stem may have too much extension. By correcting the problem you'll improve your bike-handling ability and your comfort—hitting bumps when your arms are rigid can jar your teeth out. On the other hand, elbows must not be tucked into the torso so that chest expansion and breathing is hindered. The usual cause of this problem is a stem that doesn't have enough extension.

Of course, no matter what type of riding you do—racing included—you won't be on the drops for extended periods. That position is used mainly when making an intense effort and for presenting the least amount of body surface to a headwind. Breathing may even be better down there because the forward extension of the arms helps open the chest. But for better comfort and visibility and for fending off fatigue in neck and back muscles, do plenty of riding on the tops. Best results come with the habit of changing hand position every couple of minutes.

Gaining Strength

Even a good position takes some time to get used to. If at first you feel uncomfortable while riding, don't automatically blame every ache and pain on your position. Usually it's a matter of not having sufficient tone in your cycling muscles. You must develop the strength to sit comfortably on the bike for long periods of time, and all this takes is regular riding.

As the miles go by you'll also develop your feel for the two keys to bike handling—hip movement and weight placement on the pedals—which escape most casual riders. Inherent in every bike is what I call a zone of control, something similar to the sweet spot in a baseball bat or tennis racket. Once you have set up your bike properly, you will be in this zone. Then it's just a matter of becoming accustomed to how the bike behaves under you, and of how soon your body adapts to the stresses of your riding program.

Everything I have said about position is a guideline, a place to start. After a while you can make your own small adjustments as you see fit, but make them one at a time and give each several rides to settle in so you can make a correct appraisal. You can drive yourself crazy by constantly fiddling with saddle and handlebar positions. The human body is very adaptable and can certainly perform equally well within a centimeter of any of the measurements I've described. It's best to settle down as soon as you're reasonably sure you have a set-up that meets your requirements. When that happens, copy down all the measurements and keep them in a safe place, and you'll have a big head start when setting up each of your future bikes.

Pedaling Technique

Good pedal action is easier to recognize than it is to describe. As in activities with fluid movements like figure skating and ballet dancing, you can usually tell when it's being done well because it looks easy.

Pedaling is as individual as walking or running. There's really no wrong way as long as the result is both feet moving in a smooth circle with fairly even pressure on the pedals—this is why toe straps and shoes with cleats are so necessary. The importance of circular pedaling is reflected in the way a rider will describe a difficult period on the bike: "I was pedaling in squares."

Though maximum leg power comes at the point where the pedals pass through the forward horizontal position, you can also push through the top and bottom of the stroke somewhat. Most important, as one foot presses down, the other can pull up. It takes concentration to develop this ability because when you are spinning along a flat road it's easy to forget about pulling up, but this is precisely the time to be working on circular pedaling. The goal is to make it a habit, and the way to do this is to practice every time you ride.

There is no strict rule about the angle of the feet, but in general they should be held at about 20 degrees, toes down. If after you have found your best saddle height your feet tend to make a greater or lesser angle than this, don't worry about it. Just keep your ankles loose, cultivate a fluid transition between pulling and pushing, and you'll be fine. However, if you find that your heels constantly drop lower than the balls of your feet, something is amiss. Recheck your position, make sure you're not using gears that are too large, and concentrate on keeping your feet at least horizontal. Sinking heels seem to be a natural tendency when climbing or pedaling a big gear, but try to avoid it or you will be reducing the arc in which power can be applied to the pedals.

As for the knees, make sure they move up and down fluidly and quietly—there should be no movements to the side, no exaggerated motion. Your hips should be stationary, not rolling from side to side. Pedaling is done with the legs only. If you find you have a problem keeping your hips quiet, recheck the saddle height. Too low will

Good position can vary from one cyclist to the next, depending on body build and the type of riding being done. But note the one constant between these two racers—knees are well bent at the bottom of the pedal stroke, which is necessary for development of power and prevention of knee problems and other internal leg injuries.

cause you to bounce; too high will make you rock to reach the pedals, resulting in a lot of discomfort in a short time. Your rear end should show very little movement if your riding position and leg action are correct.

In order to ride long distances well it is essential to establish and then maintain a constant, rhythmic pedal cadence using a moderate workload. This ability must be developed in training rides. Once it becomes ingrained, the legs will virtually send up the message when a gear change is needed to keep them turning at an efficient rate. Exactly what this rate is depends on the length of ride, terrain and weather, load on the bike, level of fitness, and personal preference. For touring, a good cadence (the number of revolutions made by one foot in a minute) is 70–80 rpm, and some riders favor 80–90. On a long one-day outing without a load, 90–95 is not unreasonable for a fit rider. Of course, these are figures for flat terrain; cadence naturally falls on climbs.

Frequent coasting will break your rhythm, and muscle stiffness and cramping may be the result if you don't keep the legs turning on the descent after a hard climb. However, brief coasting to stand and relieve saddle pressure and stretch the legs can markedly improve comfort. If you will be riding for several hours and don't plan to stop, go ahead and do a few seconds of stretching on the bike every 30 minutes or so. Let one heel and then the other drop as low as you can to stretch your calf muscles. Arch your back and roll your shoulders. When you sit back down you'll feel quite refreshed.

Gears

You can ride at your strongest and longest if you are putting out approximately the same amount of moderate effort all the time. The key to accomplishing this is using the gear system properly. This means changing the gear anytime that anything causes you to lose your personal pedal rhythm.

There is no such thing as a right or a wrong gear. That is, you could ride the same route every day for a week straight and use different gears each time, depending on how you feel, how hard you want to work, and the wind conditions. The gear system is there to do your bidding; you pick the gear, it's not the gear that picks you. If you want to go fast, use a big one. If you want to take it easy, pick a small one. If you are riding for fitness, pick gears that provide enough resistance to ensure a constant, moderate workload. When touring, use those that will let you parcel out your strength for the hours you will be riding each day.

Anticipation is the key to smooth operation of the gear system. Since shifting is best when done under a moderate chain load, you should plan to make gear changes before you find yourself spinning without resistance or bogging down. For example, when approaching a steep hill you should shift into low gear before the incline makes you start pressing heavily on the pedals. If you try to shift after you've begun to put a load on the chain, the derailleur may not be able to respond. The only way out of this situation is to ease the pressure for a few pedal strokes to let the derailleur operate, but this will cause you to lose a great deal of momentum. If the hill is a more gradual one, you should have no problem making a gear change in the middle of it. Simply let up on the pedal pressure slightly just as you make the shift, then press on.

For purpose of comparison, the easiest way to talk about gears is to refer to the number of teeth on the chainrings and cogs. For example, if you have the chain on a 42-tooth chainring and a rear cog with 17 teeth, you would say, "I'm riding a forty-two seventeen." But how does this 42×17 compare with the 45×19 your friend is riding in? Which is the higher gear?

There are several ways to find out. One is to figure the distance each bike will travel with one revolution of the cranks. This is called gear development. On a bike with standard 27-inch wheels, one crank revolution in 42×17 will move it forward by 17 feet and 2 inches. In a 45×19, one revolution will produce 16 feet and 5 inches. So, to answer the question just posed, 42×17 is a higher gear than 45×19.

Development seems like a good way to compare gears but unfortunately it is rarely used. The more common system is a leftover from the olden days of cycling when people rode highwheelers and there was no chain drive. The pedals were connected directly to the hub of the front wheel, the size of which determined the "gear." When multispeed bikes were introduced, people continued to refer to gears in relation to wheel diameter, and so this is the system we seem to be stuck with today. To determine a gear ratio using this method, divide the number of teeth on the chainring by the number of teeth on the freewheel cog, then multiply that result by the diameter of the wheel in inches.

So if you are in a 42×17 and have 27-inch wheels, you are said to be riding in a 66-inch gear (42 divided by 17, times 27). A 45×19 would be a 63-inch gear. Again, this illustrates that 42×17 is the higher of the two. By counting the teeth on your chainrings and

GEAR RATIO CHART
Number of teeth on rear sprocket

		13	14	15	16	17	18	19	20	21	22	23	24	25
	40	83.1	77.1	72.0	67.5	63.5	60.0	56.8	54.0	51.4	49.1	47.0	45.0	43.2
	41	85.2	79.1	73.8	69.2	65.1	61.5	58.3	55.3	52.7	50.3	48.1	46.1	44.3
	42	87.2	81.0	75.6	70.9	66.7	63.0	59.7	56.7	54.0	51.5	49.3	47.3	45.4
Number of teeth on front chainring	43	89.3	82.9	77.4	72.6	68.3	64.5	61.1	58.0	55.3	52.8	50.5	48.4	46.4
	44	91.4	84.9	79.2	74.3	69.9	66.0	62.5	59.4	56.6	54.0	51.7	49.5	47.5
	45	93.5	86.8	81.0	75.9	71.5	67.5	63.9	60.8	57.9	55.2	52.8	50.6	48.6
	46	95.5	88.7	82.8	77.6	73.1	69.0	65.4	62.1	59.1	56.5	54.0	51.8	49.7
	47	97.6	90.6	84.6	79.3	74.6	70.5	66.8	63.4	60.4	57.7	55.2	52.9	50.8
	48	99.7	92.6	86.4	81.0	76.2	72.0	68.2	64.8	61.7	58.9	56.3	54.0	51.8
	49	101.8	94.5	88.2	82.7	77.8	73.5	69.6	66.1	63.0	60.1	57.5	55.1	52.9
	50	103.8	96.4	90.0	84.4	79.4	75.0	71.1	67.5	64.3	61.4	58.7	56.3	54.0
	51	105.9	98.4	91.8	86.1	81.0	76.5	72.5	68.8	65.6	62.6	59.9	57.4	55.1
	52	108.0	100.3	93.6	87.8	82.6	78.0	73.9	70.2	66.9	63.8	61.0	58.5	56.2
	53	110.1	102.2	95.4	89.4	84.2	79.5	75.3	71.5	68.1	65.0	62.2	59.6	57.2
	54	112.2	104.1	97.2	91.1	85.8	81.0	76.7	72.9	69.4	66.3	63.4	60.8	58.3

The formula is:

$$\text{Gear ratio} = \frac{\text{no. of teeth on chainring}}{\text{no. of teeth on freewheel cog}} \times \text{wheel diameter in inches}$$

freewheel cogs and looking up the ratios in the adjoining chart, you will be able to see whether or not you have a good variety of gears or several that are almost identical, thus making your bike something less than a 10-speed. Serious riders have been known to spend hours poring over a gear chart, figuring which combinations provide the best ratios for their specific needs. This can be very important in touring when the terrain and load demand a wide range of evenly spaced ratios. Once you have decided on your optimum chainring and freewheel sizes, a good bike shop should be able to supply them no matter how out of the ordinary they may seem.

One final point: Although there are ten possible gear combinations on a 10-speed bike, you will do best to operate it as an 8-speed. The two combinations to be avoided are the extreme crosses—the small chainring with the smallest freewheel cog, and the big chainring with the biggest freewheel cog. It's not that these combinations don't work—they do—but they don't work well. The problem with both is that the chain must make a maximum angle from freewheel to chainring, and this results in rough running that you can often feel through the pedals. Additionally, the angles will cause wear on the chain and the teeth it touches that is much more severe than with straighter alignments. So for these practical reasons you should avoid the big-to-big and small-to-small combinations. They also don't make sense from a theoretical standpoint. The small chainring is used to establish the low range of gears, so why combine it with the highest gear on the freewheel? Conversely, when you go to the large chainring you are in effect saying you want high gears, so why couple it with the lowest freewheel gear? You should be able to locate another chainring/freewheel combination that gives you the gear ratio you are looking for, but one that runs more smoothly and doesn't produce excess wear.

Braking

For reasons discussed in the chapter on equipment, I think sidepull brakes are superior to centerpulls. But whichever type you have, braking technique is the same and begins with hand position. If your fingers are long and strong enough, you can apply the brakes from on top of the lever hoods. Most cyclists ride on the hoods more often than any other position, so it's essential to be able to brake from there. Let your first two fingers of each hand move down onto the lever handles and activate them—you won't be able to apply a lot of force, but you won't have to when making small adjustments to speed or when coming to unhurried stops.

Of course, your best leverage and most precise feel will come when your hands are down in the hooks of the handlebars. This is the best braking position when touring with a loaded bike, since the momentum of the gear being carried will significantly reduce any caliper brake's stopping ability. The best technique is to get a good hold on each lever, slide your weight back on the saddle, and hold yourself in position by pushing against the pedals. If you will be stopping from a high speed, such as during a descent, alternately apply one brake and then the other. This will help prevent a blowout caused by overheated rims, and in the case of tubulars it'll keep the glue from melting and letting the tires come free.

The keys to proper braking are anticipation and smoothness. If

This photo sequence shows the various hand positions that can be used for special purposes and for altering upper-body position to delay fatigue on long rides. The first shows hands on top, a position used when climbing in the saddle. This is also the best place to locate hands before one is taken from the bars to reach for food, the water bottle, etc., because a grip near the stem helps prevent accidentally jerking the bars and losing control.

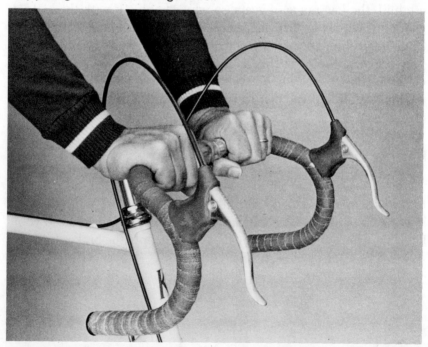

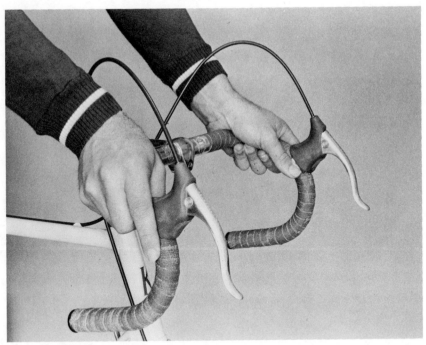

This grip allows an upright riding position but puts a larger proportion of weight on the front of the bike.

This is the favorite hand position of most riders, particularly when climbing out of the saddle. It provides excellent support for the hands and upper body and exposes less frontal area to the wind. Also, hands don't have to be moved in order to apply the brakes; the first two fingers of each hand can be extended to the levers easily.

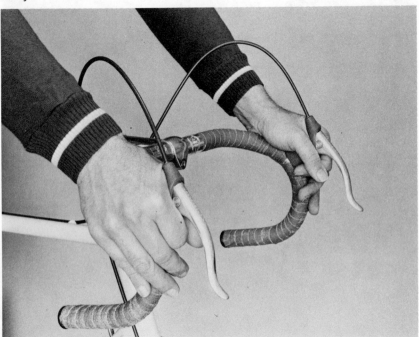

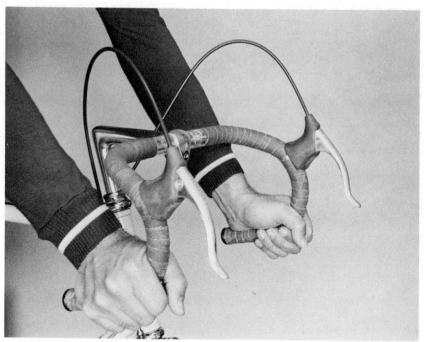

This is a restful position used on long descents. It is also good for minimizing frontal area when riding against a headwind.

This is a grip often used by competitors during hard efforts. It allows the arms to be well bent, thus giving the most streamlined position. It also gives easy access to the brake levers and thus is the best position to assume on curvy downhills.

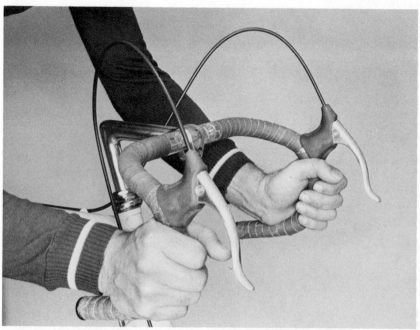

you anticipate so as to stay mentally one step ahead of yourself, it is possible to complete entire rides without using the brakes at all. When you must brake, you will be able to get the pads on the rims in time to decrease speed before finding yourself in a panic situation. If you have to grab the levers and yank them hard you can easily skid a wheel and ruin a tire.

When you brake any bike, loaded or not, weight transfers forward. This means the front brake will do a better job of bringing you to a stop than the rear. You may even prefer to do almost all your braking at the front wheel—entirely possible if your anticipation lets you avoid situations that require emergency stops. When sudden deceler-

When braking on a descent, it helps to sit up high so that your body catches more air and helps reduce speed. U.S. pro Jacques Boyer's technique is to apply steady pressure with the rear brake and "feather" the front to make precise adjustments to speed. When actually coming to a stop, the front brake will be applied more firmly since it is more effective than the rear as weight transfers forward.

ation is needed you should use both brakes, remembering that it will still be the front that gives you the most stopping power. Moderate the forward forces by keeping yourself well back on the saddle and by bracing against the pedals, but hold your head up to let your body catch air and help reduce speed.

It takes longer to stop in wet conditions than dry, simply because initial brake pad contact with the rim is doing little but wiping off water. The wetness of the road also decreases tire adhesion. In rainy weather, then, you should anticipate that it may take as much as three times the normal distance to come to a stop. Also of concern is the slickness of the road because of factors beyond the water itself. For example, in Puerto Rico when the U.S. team was in final training for the 1979 Pan-American Games it rained every afternoon, making it difficult to even ride in a straight line because of the oil and grease that the water floated up. Roads will often be slickest right after the rain starts, improving considerably following a few minutes of rinsing.

On slippery roads or those with loose surfaces, not only do you have to increase the time and distance for braking but you have to be more gentle. Any sudden squeezing of the levers can easily cause a skid and loss of control. One way to prevent this is to "feather" the brakes—apply a light, almost delicate on-and-off pressure. This will help you keep tabs on your speed without the danger of locking a wheel.

BIKE HANDLING

5

Good bike handling depends on riding position, pedaling technique, experience, and confidence. When all of these factors are right, a bicycle can really be made to perform. That's a great thrill in itself, but even more important is the safety it adds to every ride you take.

Riding a Straight Line

It may sound overly elementary to say it, but the first thing every cyclist must master is how to ride in a straight line. Most beginning or infrequent riders can't perform this seemingly simple feat because they don't have the two main ingredients—proper position and pedal action. You'll see them weaving down the road, posing a threat to any riders they are with and making motorists react in irritated ways. But watch experienced cyclists cruise along and it will look like they are on some kind of invisible rail. Their steadiness comes from being relaxed and comfortable, they pedal in even circles, and they look well ahead so any changes in course can be made smoothly, not suddenly.

The reason why keeping a straight line is so important becomes immediately apparent when riding in auto traffic or with a group of cyclists. But even when all alone you should make it a habit to maintain a steady course. It's certainly more efficient, and once the ability to stay straight is mastered it becomes ingrained and allows concentration to shift to other aspects of bike handling and safe riding.

When the pavement is in good repair and there's no dangerous dropoff along the edge, ride about 6 inches inside the painted line that defines the road from the shoulder. This will keep you out of the

The ability to ride a steady, straight line is important in every type of cycling but is nowhere more apparent than in the team time trial. Here Tom Doughty takes his turn at the front on the way to an American gold medal at the 1979 Pam-Am Games in Puerto Rico. Precise bike control is a must when your teammates are just inches from your wheel for 100 kilometers (62 miles) of all-out effort.

traffic flow and yet reduce the chance of a puncture from the debris usually found just off the main road surface. One way to develop the ability to ride straight is to concentrate on keeping a constant distance from the edge line as you pedal along. You'll soon learn to keep your upper body relaxed and make minor course adjustments not with the handlebars but with slight hip movements—this is the key to steering. While six inches from the edge doesn't seem like much room for error when on a road with a bad shoulder, it will be more than enough after you have gained confidence in your control. When traffic conditions allow, you can practice precision handling by picking out small marks on the road ahead and running over them. After you've mastered that, try rolling through the space between road debris such as gravel, twigs, leaves—nothing that could cause a problem if you miss. This is a good way to practice for possible emergency maneuvers and become familiar with the responsiveness of your bike.

One thing you must do if you will be touring with racks and panniers is use them on several of your training rides. Their weight and location will alter the bike's center of gravity, stability, and responsiveness and how it is affected by the wind. It is wise to set up the bike exactly as you will be using it on tour, even to the extent of packing the identical items you plan to carry. The handling characteristics will probably be so altered that it will take several rides to accustom yourself to what in effect is a different bike. These trial runs are also good for making sure the panniers are properly packed and stable and don't allow weight to shift. Once the tour does begin there won't be any unpleasant surprises, and you won't have to spend several unsteady hours learning how the bike is going to behave when cornering, climbing, braking, or simply riding down a straight road.

On long one-day rides this is of no concern, because you should be able to carry all your needs in your jersey and perhaps one small handlebar bag or saddlebag. While pockets full of extra water bottles, fruit, and a sandwich or two may be noticeable on rough roads or when you are out of the saddle on a climb, the actual behavior of the bike won't be affected.

Cornering

Cornering is one of the most satisfying moves you can make on a bike. It's fun, it's exciting, and it also happens to be one of the hardest things to learn. Even an experienced rider can always improve this facet of bike handling, and that's what cornering is—the essence of bike handling, the ability to sweep through a turn with full control no matter what the conditions. This might mean racing at 50 mph on a curvy descent, but just as critical is the ability to negotiate a sharp turn at 15 mph while touring with loaded panniers. In both cases there are some general techniques that apply.

When going very slow you can steer through a corner using the handlebars. But as speed increases, any sudden turning of the front wheel will likely result in loss of control due to oversteering. It's almost a braking effect as the front wheel tries to go one direction and the rear wheel continues straight—a rider can literally be catapulted off the bike. To avoid this, a bike must be turned by leaning it, by steering with the hips instead of the handlebars. On sharp turns of more than about 70 degrees even this is not enough; you must also lower your center of gravity toward the pedals as much as possible to help keep the bike from slipping out from under you.

When you are cornering correctly you will feel very solid. It's a good feeling, like a ride on a roller coaster—exciting but not really dangerous. You will come out of the turn where you want to, not courting disaster up against the curb. But when road width does make it necessary to corner from curb to curb, you should be able to do it when there are inches to spare just as confidently as if there were no curb at all.

Let's start at the beginning. The first thing to do when approaching a turn is adjust your speed to the conditions and the line you intend to take. The line is the path you will follow into, through, and out of the turn. A wide arc is best because it will enable you to safely retain much of your speed—you won't waste energy by having to slow way down and then pedal back up to the speed you want. (For example, when approaching a right-hand turn, move to the left of the road as far as conditions permit, cut directly through the corner, and emerge as wide as your speed naturally carries you. The idea is to make every turn as shallow as possible.) Have your speed under control by the time you give the slight hip movement that begins the turning process, because you won't be able to change it effectively from that point on.

The safest way to get through a sharp turn is to coast. Experience is the best guide to how far you can keep pedaling into a turn without striking your inside pedal on the pavement and suffering either a

Criterium racing demands excellent cornering ability. U.S. National Road Team members David Ware, front, and Mark Pringle show just how far a bike can be leaned safely through a turn. Each has his weight fully on the left pedal, with the right knee used for pointing into the turn. Note that their hands are off the brakes—all braking must be done before entering the corner or else there could be a loss of control.

loss of control and crash or at least a good scare. Once you quit pedaling, drop your outside pedal to the bottom of the stroke and shift your weight to that foot; the faster you are trying to corner the harder you must press. This will allow you to safely lean the bike to a degree that a bystander would call frightening.

In fact, both legs play a part in cornering. When you put your weight on the outside pedal, don't lock that knee; leave it bent slightly and let it rotate with your hips in the direction of the turn. It'll help steer you through, as will your inside knee if you let it point into the turn. This will stabilize you, it catches a bit of wind to help you control your speed, and you can feel the turning force that it creates. You should try these techniques with each leg independently until you get the feel of how they affect bike control. Soon you will learn just what is needed to safely negotiate turns at various speeds with the bike both loaded and free of panniers. Remember that fast cornering is not dangerous if done properly and it will help you be a more efficient rider.

A great place to practice cornering is in a surburban neighborhood during hours when traffic is light. The only way to learn to turn is to do it—it's not something you can read about and immediately be good at, though it is important to understand the principles and recommended techniques. In the end it takes confidence to handle a bike through corners, and that's something that can only come with experience. It's a good bet, though, that almost everyone with a desire to corner well will take a fall sometime. Don't be discouraged and don't let it make you afraid—it's just part of the learning process. Common reasons for falling include leaning over too far because of an incorrect line, trying to change the line in the middle of the turn, or pedaling too far in and having the inside pedal strike the ground.

Perhaps the surest way to spill is to brake in the middle of a turn. Because braking slows the wheels it disrupts the forces acting on them and tends to make the bike go back toward the vertical. This will straighten out the bike's path and send you places you'd rather not go. Resist the temptation to brake if you feel you are going too fast to make the turn. Instead, rotate your outside hip down, stand hard on the outside pedal, and aim your outside knee towards the inside of the turn. The rear wheel may slip slightly and chatter along the road, but your chances of making it through will be better than if you hit the brakes. Even if you go down, a sliding crash is going to be less damaging than riding headlong into the far curb or other obstruction.

A bike in a turn has a lot of stability when it is handled right. It can be leaned 30 degrees or more and still have enough tire on the road for sufficient traction. The essential thing is putting in lots of practice time (especially with the bike outfitted as you ride it during your day trips and tours) and making sure that everything is correct—equip-

With his weight firmly planted on the outside pedal, Tom Doughty leans his bike through a corner in a criterium. He has just released the brake levers, having made sure to adjust speed before the turn so he won't have to touch the brakes while in it.

ment as well as technique. No matter how good your ability, wheels and tires must be strong and in good condition if you are to corner safely. For those who ride on tubulars, this means tires must be securely glued on and inflated to proper pressure. If they aren't you'll find yourself cornering on your rims . . . but not for long.

Climbing

At 6,288 feet, New Hampshire's Mount Washington is the highest peak in New England. An 8-mile-long partially paved road leads to the summit, and for a number of years this has been the course of one of the country's most demanding running races. Bobby Hodge of Boston owns the hillclimb record with a time of 62:08 and, through the 1981 event, is the only runner who has ever averaged better than 8 minutes a mile. While that sounds like a pedestrian pace by most standards, it's testimony to the steepness of the grade and to the frightful weather conditions that have made the mountain renowned in meteorological circles. Shirt-sleeve temperatures at the base frequently give way to howling wind and frozen rain or snow at the summit, where the brave men who operate the weather station have recorded the highest wind gust ever measured on the earth's surface, 231 mph.

Well, cyclists aren't any less crazy than runners when it comes to meeting such challenges. Since 1973 there has been a hillclimb as part of the annual Mount Washington Valley Grand Prix bicycle races, and a curious situation developed. Whereas many riders can, for example, cover the marathon distance (26.2 miles) twice as fast as the world's best runners, it wasn't until 1980 that someone pedaled up the mountain faster than Hodge. It took a rider who is recognized as one of the country's best climbers to do it, Dale Stetina of Indianapolis. The two-time national road champion reached the summit in 57:41 to set a human powered record that no runner is ever likely to seriously challenge.

On a shallow grade there's no doubt that a person can go faster on a bike than on foot, but on a steep grade it becomes more difficult. The reason is that both body weight and the bike's weight must be lifted against gravity. This means that a 150-pound rider will in effect be carrying about 175 pounds—considerably more if touring with camping equipment. Even so, it should take a terribly steep grade to force a good rider to get off and walk, and it never need happen if the bike is geared properly for the terrain and the rider uses correct climbing technique.

In Chapter 4 I discussed techniques for shifting gears and the importance of planning ahead for climbs, of making sure you are in the low gear you need before your forward motion starts bogging down. How low a gear you go to depends on your fitness, your climbing style, the weight you are carrying, and the steepness and length of the hill. Or, on a short hill, you can elect not to shift at all—just press the pedals hard and grunt on over, either in the saddle or out.

When you remain seated on a climb you should change your pedaling technique slightly. Obviously you won't be able to maintain your flatland cadence and you will have to put more effort into turning the cranks. To make the effort a bit easier, slide back on the saddle—this happens almost involuntarily—so that the angle at which you push the pedals will be altered for the better. It will enable you to apply force a little sooner coming over the top of the pedal circle, producing a slightly longer power stroke.

It can also help to do something that should be avoided at all other times—namely, let your upper body sway or bob to a moderate extent. Normally such excess movement will work against bike control and efficiency, but when climbing in the saddle it can help you establish a beneficial rhythm. As your arms pull on the bars and your top half rocks to and fro, your legs will pick up the beat and it should carry you over the top a little more quickly and less strenuously than if you resisted this natural rocking motion. You can experiment with hand positions to determine which help your in-the-saddle climbing technique, but most riders find that a wide grip on the tops works best because it produces an upright upper body, which aids breathing. Since it's the grade of the road and not air resistance that is inhibiting forward progress, a low, streamlined position is not needed.

Rhythm is important to any kind of climbing and can be established mentally as well as physically. Some riders like to sing to themselves, some do a chant, some count out each pedal stroke. When I'm climbing I simply try to tune in to what feels right. This

When climbing in the saddle, the best hand position is on the top of the handlebars. This lets the arms pull in unison with the legs, and the overall effect is a slight upper-body rocking motion. It sets up a rhythm that helps a rider keep a strong, steady pace up and over the top. In the lead is John Howard, the country's top roadman in the early 1970s. He was a rider of all-round ability who won five national championships.

means that my rhythm on a certain climb can vary from ride to ride depending on a host of variables, but I always try to maintain each day's pace from bottom to top. If I'm riding with others I still try to find a rhythm, though it is often dictated by the lightweight guys who seem to be able to go uphill even faster than on the flats. Adjustments in rhythm are made through gear selection—you can climb in the saddle using a fairly low gear with a relatively high cadence, or select a larger gear and stand on it. The latter may work best when you are getting tired because it lets you use your weight and momentum to compensate for fatiguing muscles. If you let your body be the guide, you should be able to find a helpful rhythm for each hill.

I used to do all my climbing sitting down before I first rode in Europe, where many ascents are so steep that the best way to handle them is out of the saddle. I found that some riders prefer always to climb standing up because they can use a bigger gear and the rhythm of it feels comfortable to them. It also gives them a chance to relax certain muscles and stretch out of the sitting position. It's really a matter of individual preference, the gears available, and the load being carried, but when you choose to stand there is a special technique which helps ensure a smooth transfer of strength and weight from one pedal to the other. One way to describe it is to say that it will make you look as if you are running on the pedals.

As when climbing in the saddle, you will be using more upper body than you do on the flats. The pedaling sequence starts with your top half preparing for a downward lunge. You lean the bike away from the power-stroke side so that your leg has a straight downward shot at the pedal. As you step hard on that side you pull up the opposite pedal—here is where it is really important to have your toe straps snug and to pedal with both feet at the same time. As the stroke is completed the bike is brought smoothly back through the vertical to lean to the other side. Your weight is now transferred to the opposite pedal, which is passing through the top of its power stroke, and the movement is repeated. This technique lets you apply a great percentage of your body weight and leg strength to forward motion.

The easiest way to learn to climb like this is to practice on a long hill that has a consistent grade. Use a larger gear than you would if

Most riders who climb out of the saddle do so with hands gripping the brake levers. This provides wide and stable control of the bike, while keeping the chest area open wide to promote breathing. Also note how David Mayer-Oakes is pulling up hard with the right foot as his weight comes down on the left.

you were sitting, and a slow pedal cadence so you can feel the full range of motion. In the beginning it may not seem as smooth as climbing in the saddle, but it is efficient because you will be able to use your strength and the momentum of your weight to pedal. With practice you will be able to climb like this without any wasted motion—your upper body should move side to side less than the bike does. Grip the bars using the hoods of the brake levers, which gives good upper-body support and keeps the arms spread away from the chest to facilitate breathing.

This climbing technique can take quite a while to perfect, so don't feel frustrated if it doesn't seem natural right away. You can tell

During their winning breakaway in the 1979 National Road Championship, Steve Wood and Tom Doughty displayed two entirely different ways of handling the same hill. Wood used the out-of-saddle technique of throwing his bike side to side to let his body weight come down on each stroke. Doughty, using a lower gear but higher cadence, managed the same speed in a less dramatic style.

when you've finally got it because you won't feel as if you're fighting with the bike anymore. You will be able to go out of the saddle, complete the climb, and settle back into your normal sitting position with no interruption of the fluid rotation of the pedals. However, if the bike is outfitted with panniers the extra weight will make it harder to handle when you are flip-flopping from side to side, so be sure to practice this technique with your touring load. If it is uncomfortably unsteady, you should certainly gear the bike low enough so that all climbing can be done sitting down. You will still want to stand occasionally to stretch legs and relieve saddle pressure, but extended time out of the saddle may sap a lot of your energy if you must put undue effort into controlling the bike.

Once you have reached the top of a climb, don't be in too big a hurry to shift into a higher gear. Your leg muscles have been working hard to get you to the top, so give them a breather by spinning your low gear for a few seconds. Then begin a steady progression to the gear the new terrain calls for. If there is a descent right after the climb, it's best to avoid coasting and keep the legs turning even if against no resistance. Doing so will promote the blood circulation that carries away metabolic waste products caused by the effort of climbing. This helps prevent muscle tightness and cramping.

Group Riding

A long ride with others is often more enjoyable than going it alone. It's nice to have company, and as a member of a group you should be able to cover more distance with less effort than if you rode by yourself, thanks to the phenomenon of drafting.

We saw a good example of drafting in *Breaking Away*, the award-winning movie. In one scene the main character was out for a training ride and was able to get behind an 18-wheeler. Thanks to the slipstream (draft) he kept right up even as the truck reached 60 mph and the driver was pulled over for exceeding the speed limit. Of course, our hero's several excursions out from behind the trailer to see the driver's hand signals indicating their speed was not an authentic portrayal. If that happened anywhere but in Hollywood the rider would practically be blown off his bike. But it did give a good representation of how fast a rider can go when air resistance is eliminated.

A bicycle rolls so efficiently that air is the primary impediment to speed. The faster you want to go, the more air resistance you must overcome. By the time you reach 20 mph you are using more than half your energy just to push through the air. The resistance progresses logarithmically, with the result that to increase speed another 10 mph, about 90 percent of the additional effort must go into breaking the invisible wall and only 10 percent into pedaling the bike faster. So imagine the benefit if there is another cyclist directly ahead putting a hole in the air. By riding close behind his rear wheel you can travel the same speed while doing approximately 30 percent less work. When the two of you take turns drafting one another, the result should be more miles covered at a faster pace than either of you could accomplish when cycling alone. The advantage is greater yet when four to six riders—the optimum size for a group—are sharing the work at the front.

To benefit from the drafting effect you need to keep your front wheel about a foot from the rear wheel ahead of you. Within 6 inches is even better, but riding that close requires so much more care and concentration that it really isn't worth it when on tour. You'll want to be able to see the scenery and what the road ahead is offering, and you can't do it if your attention is riveted on a threatening wheel inches away. By maintaining a 1-foot gap you can look past the front rider, letting your peripheral vision keep you advised of where you are in relation to his bike. Once you gain experience you will be able to ride your own line almost as if there was no one ahead, and yet remain close enough to have the full benefit of the draft.

However, you must always be cautious when following a wheel. It can be an unsettling feeling to know that the guy in front of you holds your safety and health in his hands, and yet that's exactly the situation. If he does anything to cause your wheel and his to contact, all he'll feel is a slight bump as you go crashing to the ground. Not that you'll always fall, but the braking effect of touching wheels can cause your front end to twitch right out from under you. To prevent the possibility you have to anticipate the other rider's movements and, in effect, ride a bit defensively.

Of course, experienced riders will understand your predicament because they know what it's like to draft. They'll often point or call back to warn of things like broken pavement or a dog that might cause them to make a movement you won't be anticipating. This helps a lot, but the drafting rider must also be aware of normal riding actions which can cause the person in front to pose a threat to safety.

A time this is likely to happen is when the front rider stands up to pedal, because the effect is to send the bike backward several inches. The suddenness with which this happens can cause wheels to contact, so you must try to anticipate such actions and then put your front wheel a little to the left or right, or a little farther behind. This is another reason to be looking past the front rider instead of at the rear wheel. If you're not, you might never notice his rise out of the saddle until it's too late. As a safety margin, some riders always keep their line just to the side of the person they are following, instead of directly behind. This also helps them see down the road better. However, wheels should never be allowed to overlap—a crash will almost surely result if the front rider veers suddenly.

When three or more riders are together, a pace line is the best way to make use of the drafting effect. If there is no crosswind, all the riders should be in single file about 12 inches apart. But if a wind is blowing from either side, those behind should angle off to the downwind side of the leader. The resulting formation is called an echelon.

Because the rider on the front must pedal harder against the wind than those in the slipstream, it is important to share the work. After you take your turn in the lead, pull over to whichever side has been agreed upon or, if it is a windy day, to the side the wind is coming from. Let's say the wind is blowing at you from the left. Everyone will be echeloned off to your right, so all you have to do is move over to the left a bit farther and decrease your speed slightly. As you begin to drop back toward the end position, the rider who was immediately behind you will assume the lead.

The reason you decrease your speed after pulling off the front is so the rest of the group can come through at its steady pace. If the others had to accelerate to get past you it would waste energy and cause gaps to open between riders. You should drop straight back along the pace line, staying close enough to the others to enhance the draft. In the case of an echelon, sort of stairstep your way back so that you ride momentarily behind each rear wheel. As you get to the next-to-last rider, start to pick up your speed. Don't wait until the last person comes by or you'll have to jump hard to catch on, which defeats the energy-saving purpose of the pace line. Move over smoothly to the caboose position and begin another steady progression toward the lead.

The length of your pull at the front depends on your strength, on the strength of your companions, and on the type of riding you are doing. During a distance ride at moderate speeds each person might stay on the front for as long as 10 minutes. But it's more advantageous to change pace frequently, say every couple of minutes, because everyone will stay fresh longer. If you start overdoing your turn in the lead, you won't be able to recover before reaching the front again and soon you may not be able to contribute to the group effort at all.

Everyone doesn't have to do the same amount of work, though, and that's another benefit of using a pace line: It allows cyclists of different strengths and abilities to pedal together. For example, four people can go for a beneficial and enjoyable ride even though one is a racer, one is a tourist, one is in his 50s, and the other is his daughter. The reason it works is that each rider can stay at the front for as long as he or she wants, or not at all. One person can take a 10-minute pull while the next immediately moves over after reaching the lead position. This helps developing cyclists improve their riding ability and confidence, while experienced riders are able to do all the work they are capable of. Thus the pace line can serve as an equalizer for a touring group composed of riders with a relatively wide range of strengths, as long as a speed is set that everyone in the draft can handle. Of course, even when riders of equal ability tour together some may feel stronger than others on a given day. Using a pace line, spunky riders can sit on the front and let out their energy for the benefit of those in the slipstream. There is a big enough difference between the two positions that the group will be able to stay together.

Gear selection in a pace line is determined by how fast the group wants to travel. Since the idea is to maintain a steady speed, everyone will be in about the same chainwheel/freewheel combination. Riders in the slipstream may want to select a gear slightly lower than the leader so they can continue to pedal briskly in the reduced wind resistance but not overrun him. Upon reaching the front, each rider will have to shift into virtually the same gear the leader was using if the pace is to be kept steady. Make the change slightly before he begins to pull off, approximately 10 pedal revolutions and take the front position without any sudden acceleration that will break the rhythm of the riders behind.

Braking is another important consideration, and the best advice is to resist doing it. Especially when learning to ride in a pace line you will tend to go for the brakes often as you try to maintain proper distance behind the wheel you are following. However, by using the brakes you will tend to slow too much, a gap will open, and you will accelerate to catch up, but to keep from overrunning the wheel you will hit the brakes . . . and on and on. You can imagine the chain-reaction problems this causes for those behind you. (If you can't, they'll tell you about it soon enough.) Instead, use the brakes only when absolutely necessary and make minor speed adjustments with your pedaling. If you are getting too close to the wheel ahead, keep turning the cranks but not so that power is going to your wheel—this is known as "soft pedaling"—and in a second or two your bike will lose enough speed to drop back slightly. Then smoothly increase your pedal cadence until you again match the speed of the rider in front and the distance stays constant. Almost all speed adjustments you will need to make in a pace line can be done with pedal pressure.

It might not seem that pace lines or echelon formations would be safe in traffic, but in some ways they are. A number of riders will be able to fit into half a lane, and because they are bunched up they are easier for motorists to deal with than if they were strung out. Cars will often be able to get by the entire group at once, but cyclists should show some common courtesy if conditions make passing a problem. You may need to stop riding in echelon and go into single file along the road edge until the traffic gets past. This is especially true if the group numbers ten or more.

WEEKEND TOURING

Long rides are done to build fitness and also, as in a century, to meet the challenge of covering a specific distance. Each is a worthy goal in its own right, but each demands a certain regimented attitude toward the use of the bike. This isn't necessarily bad, though if carried too far it can tend to make cycling more a chore than a recreation. A great way to make sure this doesn't happen is to get into weekend bike tripping.

In bike tripping, getting there is 99 percent of the fun, especially when "there" is simply right back to where you started. The goal is

(Photograph courtesy of Schwinn)

to ride all of one day or two, not to simply reach the end. That's where cycling differs entirely from most other means of travel and in particular sets the rider apart from the motorist. While the time spent behind the steering wheel is viewed as a necessary evil by most drivers, the hours behind the handlebars are the most attractive part of taking a trip by bike. There is no better way to experience the sights, sounds, and smells of the countryside as you pass through.

Best of all, there are no wrong ways to do it. When it comes to one- or two-day bike trips the possibilities are limited only by one's imagination. You can design a trip around any objective or no objective at all. For example, you might ride to a distant town to have lunch at a restaurant you've heard good things about, and then return home by a different route. Or you can carry your victuals and set off on roads you've never cycled before, stopping at any point of interest that intrigues you. The key to bike tripping is to plan the ride just enough to get yourself headed in one direction or another, but never so much that you can't make spontaneous changes along the way.

ONE-DAY RIDES

One-day bike trips are great because you can travel so lightly. If you can't carry everything you'll need in your jersey pockets, a handlebar bag or saddlebag should certainly be sufficient. This will leave the bike unencumbered by the kind of add-on weight that extended touring requires, weight which disrupts handling and makes hills more of a strain. In addition to sufficient food and water for a day in the saddle, items to carry include a small assortment of tools and spokes for emergency repairs, a rain jacket if there is a chance of afternoon showers, walking shoes if you ride with cleats, and a frame-mount pump and spare tube or tire, which can be strapped under the saddle. You may also wish to have a camera, a watch, and an odometer. The latter two items can be helpful for judging when to begin the journey back home, especially if the outward leg has included time-outs for snacks, sightseeing, a dip in a stream, etc.

Another handy item is a road map (see discussion of maps in Chapter 8). You may be familiar with the route you expect to take as you wheel out of the driveway at dawn, but a map gives you the option of later altering course should you feel the urge to go exploring. Take along some money, too—have change for a pay phone and stash a $20 bill and maybe even a credit card, just in case. Also carry some identification that lists who to contact in case of an emergency and your special medical requirements, if any. It's always smart to tell someone back home where you are headed (even if you are only sure of the general direction) and what time you expect to return.

Riding Pace

The main difference between a one-day bike trip and either LSD training or a century ride is pace. The long, steady distance trainer pedals at a consistently high cadence, striving to keep his heart rate at a 60–75 percent training-effect level for between two and four hours. He ignores the temptation to reduce the workload, let alone get off the bike for a rest or snack. The rider in an organized century is intent on cycling 100 miles, not so much within a certain time but at a pace he can hold to the finish—the satisfaction comes in completing the distance, and most riders choose to go at the task with minimal time out. For the bike tripper, however, the objective is to spend an enjoyable day traveling by pedal power. That could mean 50 miles or 150, depending on factors ranging from riding strength to personal whimsy.

In general, the riding segments of a seven- or eight-hour bike trip will not be strenuous. A rider should have no sense of urgency; instead, he should feel free to ride easily and stop frequently. Someone who finds himself looking more at the road than the scenery around him is missing the point. Most fit riders will find that a cadence of 75–80 in a gear of 42×17 or 18 can be managed for hours in rolling terrain when there is no bothersome wind, especially if they treat themselves to occasional breaks. This sort of riding isn't designed so much to build fitness as it is to enjoyably use the fitness developed by other types of cycling.

Solo or Not?

Many cyclists find a special pleasure in riding alone. Solo bike trips provide a great way to get off by yourself, make your own decisions, and be as venturesome as you please. And because there are so few distractions while riding on quiet back roads, you can get a lot of creative thinking done. Personally, I find that the routine rhythmic exercise of pedaling can put me into a trancelike state in which time seems to fly by and my imagination and senses are heightened.

However, riding with a friend or two on day-long outings also has its pleasures. It can be enjoyable to share a cycling adventure with someone else, and there is safety in numbers. That is, if a physical or mechanical breakdown occurs, help is right at hand. Also, if the day becomes windy there will be someone to share the task of putting a hole in the invisible wall—racers aren't the only riders who can benefit from drafting techniques. Taking turns at the front can be just as helpful in the final few miles if exhaustion begins closing in.

The big drawback to riding with another person—and this goes for just about every type of cycling—is if the two of you are incompatible in some respect. You must get along smoothly on a personal level, be well matched physically, and share the same objectives. If not, friction is bound to occur as the day wears on, making the trip far less enjoyable than if you'd gone it alone. For example, if you are a relative newcomer to extended rides, be wary of partnering with an old hand. You may wind up riding at a pace that's too brisk, which will cause your energy and comfort levels to come crashing down well before they otherwise would. It's just as frustrating for an experienced rider to have to pedal slower than his most enjoyable pace in order to keep a companion from falling behind. So find someone you like who is close to your own ability and who has the same goals and desire.

One of the most common disagreements between riding partners is how often to stop and for how long. Some people like to take a regular rest break—say, 5 minutes at the end of every hour. Others stop sporadically to enjoy the scenery or have a snack. Then there are those (usually competitors accustomed to LSD training) who never want to stop at all except when a trip into the bushes becomes neces-

A weekend is the perfect opportunity to enjoy the pleasures of traveling by bike. Make your one-day or overnight trips unhurried and get a taste of what it would be like to undertake an extended tour. Be sure to allow time for any diversion that strikes your fancy, whether it be photographing the rising sun or taking a short snooze in its warmth after it is high in the sky. (*Photograph courtesy of Greg Siple*)

sary. They prefer to eat right on the bike and use downhills for stretching and loosening up. I belong to this group, because I'm always looking for physical improvement from my riding and I don't like to give my heart rate too many opportunities to decrease. But for most riders on a weekend bike trip, it certainly makes sense to stop occasionally to relax and fuel up so that the entire ride is as comfortable and enjoyable as it can be. Save the "training" for other occasions.

TWO-DAY RIDES

A weekend overnighter is the best way to get a true taste of bicycle touring. Despite all the romanticized, enthusiastic accounts of lengthy tours you can read in cycling publications, you might find that this use of the bicycle simply isn't for you. On the other hand, you may be so turned on by touring that you can't wait for each vacation so you can begin another journey by bike. It's hard to know if tours of two days or longer will appeal to you until you've at least sampled an overnight trip.

There are a couple of ways to go about it. The simplest, of course, is to treat the overnighter as a pair of long one-day rides connected by a stay in a motel or the home of a relative or friend. If you use accommodations like these and have home-cooked or restaurant meals, you will have to carry very little gear. Besides those items mentioned above, probably the only other things needed will be a clean pair of riding shorts for day two, toilet articles, and some civvies to wear in the evening. You will still be able to get by with but one or two touring bags and thus enjoy nearly normal bike handling.

Although some dedicated tourists prefer to motel-hop even on extended trips, I strongly suggest that you use a weekend overnighter to try camping out. Doing so may prove without a doubt that it is worth the money for a hot shower and cozy bed at Murray's Motor Court, but you also might find that a night under the stars adds greatly to the adventure and pleasure of bicycle touring. In fact, the chance to be almost completely self-contained is what attracts many people to long-distance travel by bike.

However, until you are absolutely certain that extended touring and camping is for you, try to borrow or rent the major items you'll need—tent, sleeping bag, cookstove and utensils, bike bags and racks, etc. Otherwise you may make a large investment only to find that some of the equipment is inappropriate or unneeded for the type of touring you settle into. Wait until you've made a couple of bike camping trips, talked to experienced tourists, and researched the many brands and models of equipment on the market before finally deciding.

A big advantage of one-night camping trips is that they keep you relatively close to home. Surroundings will be somewhat familiar, and this helps reduce fear of the unknown. Even though you may be 50 or 75 miles away from where you live and feeling some apprehension as you attempt your first overnighter, there's comfort in knowing that help is just an hour or two away should a major problem arise. Once you gain confidence that you can successfully cope with the demands of a short trip you will have much less doubt about your ability to handle the unexpected on an extended tour.

Preparation

If you haven't camped before and are worried about how to do it right, it makes sense to undertake a trial run right in your own backyard. Practice pitching the tent and spend one night in it using your sleeping bag. Try out the cookstove if you will be carrying one, although it is certainly not a necessity even on long tours, especially in the warm-weather months. In general, the more familiar you are with your equipment the more confident you will feel on the actual trip.

Another consideration is how the bike will handle once it is encumbered with the racks, bags, and equipment needed for a camping trip. Naturally, the more weight and bulk being carried the greater the effect on the various aspects of bike control. If you are used to riding with no more than a handlebar bag or saddlebag, you must make an effort to accustom yourself to the added weight, altered center of gravity, and increased width of the bike.

To begin this process, install the racks and put on the touring bags, filling them out with crumpled newspaper. This is important mainly when using rear panniers because of the width they add. Until you get the hang of riding with them you may find yourself brushing against objects as you corner or ride in congested areas. It's better to make a mistake with bags full of soft newspaper than items which won't give. After a couple of rides to get used to the bike's new dimensions, add the bulky items (sleeping bag and pad, tent) that will go on top of the rear rack and experience the difference they make in how the bike behaves.

Finally, pack the bike with everything you will carry on the trip and take at least one test ride which includes varied terrain. Strive to make the weight the same on each side of the bike and put only a light load in the handlebar bag. We'll look more deeply into proper weight distribution in the next chapter when extended touring is discussed, but suffice it to say that the heaviest items should be packed at the bottom. During the ride make sure that items don't move around when you are stopping and cornering, and that there is no danger that anything will contact the wheels.

If this is the first time you have ever ridden a loaded bicycle, be cautious until you get the hang of it. That quick, nimble machine you're used to is a different bike now. Acceleration will be slower and deceleration will take longer. Road bumps and riding out of the saddle may cause bouncy, whippy sensations, and the bike may tend to twitch and shimmy on a high-speed descent. Depending on front/rear weight distribution, front-wheel response could be either quicker or more sluggish than normal. Crosswinds are more likely to blow the bike off line because of the increased side area the bags produce. Riding experience combined with a cautious respect for the possible dangers will help make all of these conditions entirely manageable.

Camping Out

Good destinations for an overnight tour include state parks and public or private campgrounds. Such facilities often have drinking water, toilets, and a good choice of sites for pitching a tent. Sometimes they are near a stream or lake, which can be used for a refreshing, cleansing dip (make sure any soap you use is biodegradable). A fee is usually required for camping privileges, but the conveniences are worth it. You may also appreciate that there are other campers in the area and that the grounds are likely to be supervised by the owner or a person from the regulating agency.

It's possible to camp on public or private land, of course. On an unstructured bike trip you may wish to ride until the sun starts sinking, then stake a claim to the next inviting spot you come across. In the wide-open West there may be no other choice, since formal campgrounds are few and far between. Obtain the permission of the landowner if that's possible; otherwise, help yourself but be sure to leave the area just as clean as you found it. It's best to select a site out of view of people passing by on the road. It will be quieter and you will feel more secure.

Arrive at the camping area at least two hours before dark, or earlier if you will be cooking dinner rather than eating raw foods or something already prepared. Choose a site which is off the beaten path to the toilet or water supply and, if it is mosquito season, away from wet areas. Unload the bike and pitch the tent on a level spot, laying down a plastic groundcloth first (if there is no level place, position the tent so that you can sleep with your head uphill). Roll out the sleeping pad in the tent and open the sleeping bag so it will air out. Once these chores are done, get yourself cleaned up and then have dinner. As dusk settles, stow all your gear in the tent. Turn in as the stars come out, and try not to be spooked when you hear the voices and rustlings of the animals in the wild. You're in their domain now, and many are creatures of the night. There is little to fear unless you're in bear country, and if you are, don't keep any food in the tent; suspend it from a tree a good distance away and you should have no problems.

When dawn wakes you, roll out and leave the sleeping bag and tent open so both can air. Get dressed, stretch, have breakfast, clean up any utensils you've used, and go off for your morning constitutional. Upon return, roll up the sleeping bag and pad, empty the tent, and pack the bike bags. Then sweep out the tent, take it down, and roll it up, hanging the groundcloth over a tree limb or bush so the underside can dry. Before putting the bags and other gear back on the bike, check the trueness of both wheels and tire pressure, and look for anything embedded in the tread. Make sure all rack attachments are secure and that gear and brake cables are tight. Now begin loading the bike, making sure, as always, that the weight is evenly balanced and items won't shift during riding. Fill your water bottles, check the campsite for any item you might be about to leave behind, and then walk the bike out to the pavement. Set off at an easy pace to let the kinks work out, then plug into the rhythm that will get you back home by the end of the day—with time out for occasional stops along the way and a leisurely lunch, of course.

Assessing the Experience

One or two overnight trips should be enough to indicate whether you have what it takes to be a successful tourist. But don't be put off if the second day's ride isn't as enjoyable as the first; it's normal to be less comfortable because of muscle stiffness and tenderness from the saddle, and you may not sleep as well as usual if it is one of your few times in a tent. These problems have a way of disappearing as experience is gained. In fact, during longer tours most riders report a phenomenon akin to the second wind—the body adapts to the daily rigors so well that morning soreness suddenly ceases a few days into the ride. Even saddle comfort, often so hard to come by early in a tour, generally improves as the riding routine is established.

The tip-off to your potential as a touring cyclist boils down to your answer to this two-part question: Do you enjoy riding to your destination as much as finally arriving, and, once there, does camping out add to the cycling adventure rather than detract from it?

Those who come up with a no to both parts are probably riders of a competitive nature or who view cycling primarily as a means of improving physical fitness. I am certainly among them. No matter when I get on the bike I like to keep it moving. My idea of a long weekend ride, even in the off-season, is to put in a steady four hours or so at a pace that lets me look around and enjoy the countryside but includes just one brief stop, if any, and that only for eliminative purposes. I really do take pleasure in a ride like this, and part of the reason is that I feel I've accomplished something beneficial when I'm done. For me that's more important than things like stopping along the way to sit for a few minutes by a waterfall.

If you answer yes to the first part of the question but no to the second, you probably have the makings of a happy touring cyclist if you can spend nights in motels or hotels or with friends and relatives along the way. Or you may simply need more camping experience to gain a tolerance for and appreciation of the challenge of living outdoors. As I'll note in the next chapter, one way to tour is to camp out most nights but hole up in a motel at least once a week. Just knowing that a hot shower and cozy bed is in the near future can help a rider get through some uncomfortable times in the wild.

Anyone who can give a hearty yes to the whole question has the attitude it takes to be a successful, self-contained touring cyclist. With adequate equipment and the time to use it there should be little to prevent such a person from pedaling virtually anywhere with confidence and enjoyment. Two other important ingredients are desire and an understanding of how to plan an extended trip. If you can supply the first item, the next two chapters will help you with the other.

7

EXTENDED TOURING

"Our modern technology of transportation has made the world smaller and smaller until there's nothing left to see. What a bicycle does is make the world big again."

These are the words of Greg Siple, a man who knows better than almost anyone just how big the world really is. He and his wife, June, and some friends cycled the length of two continents—from Alaska to Argentina—on an 18,272-mile trip dubbed Hemistour, which was detailed in the May 1973 issue of *National Geographic*. As Greg has found out firsthand, there is nothing like a bike to bring back what 55-mph-plus travel has taken away: "The bicycle puts back all those spaces that disappeared between places."

Siple is now the staff cartographer for Bikecentennial, a national nonprofit service organization for touring cyclists. It was founded to create a bicycle route—the TransAmerica Trail—across the United States as a part of the celebration of the nation's bicentennial. In 1976 more than 4,000 cyclists rode all or part of the 4,450 miles, a distance that makes the trail by far the longest recreational "bike path" in the world. Since that inaugural summer, thousands of others have pedaled across the United States and also used shorter, regional routes developed by Bikecentennial. Siple says that in 1980 the organization received more than 20,000 inquiries about bicycle touring.

When it comes to long-distance trips, the people at Bikecentennial are the experts. That's why I'll be borrowing extensively from their literature in this chapter and the next as we look into how to undertake an extended journey by bike. If this is where your cycling interest lies, you will naturally want to contact Bikecentennial directly at Box 8308, Missoula, MT 59807. Much helpful information can also be

(*Photograph courtesy of Nina MacLean*)

found in the pages of the magazines *Bicycling* (33 E. Minor St., Emmaus, PA 18049) and *American Wheelmen* (Box 988, Baltimore, MD 21203). In the following chapter I will include other sources of information to draw from when it comes to planning your specific tour. Right now, let's look into all the physical and mechanical details necessary to help make the venture a success.

PHYSICAL PREPARATION

There are numerous tales of people whose riding background was virtually vacant before they hopped on a bike and pedaled across the country. They began by keeping daily distances relatively short (less than 50 miles) more out of necessity than design. But it wasn't too long before they adapted to the stress and were able to accomplish as much as 100 miles on days when conditions were favorable. Given this, is it really necessary to undertake a training program before embarking on a tour?

I believe it is, and the reason lies in all the stories you don't hear, the ones of the people who gave up and took a bus back home because they were physically or mentally crippled by the demands of all-day riding. Touring simply isn't as easy as many people imagine. Total body fitness is required not only to pedal a loaded bike but to control it. A day in the saddle places big demands on the muscles in the back, arms, and neck, and lack of conditioning here can result in great discomfort. There is also the critical matter of being able to tolerate the saddle mile after mile and day after day, fortitude which is developed best by a gradual buildup in riding time.

So it behooves the prospective tourist to give serious attention to physical preparation. Why suffer through the first week or more when you can begin the trip with the confidence that solid fitness provides? Being in good shape is the best way to ensure an enjoyable experience from the outset.

If you have been riding regularly, say to the tune of 100 miles a week for a couple of months, you've got the necessary base from which to move into training for a tour. By training I don't mean a rigid, structured schedule such as racers must undertake, but a low-key program that will yield the ability to ride about 100 miles in a day's time. In other words, a program similar to that outlined for the century rider in Chapter 3. By way of review, this calls for weekday rides of whatever length you can fit into your schedule, progressively longer back-to-back rides on the weekends, and one day off the bike each week for recovery and pooling of strength.

As your tour approaches, undertake one or two weekend over-nighters as described in the last chapter. These will provide valuable miles, and a chance to ride with a loaded bike and also get acquainted with camping techniques and your gear. In addition, the experience will help you make rational decisions when it comes to planning the daily mileage goals and itinerary for the big trip.

Besides riding, a valuable aid to conditioning is stretching exercises and calisthenics. The former will help keep muscles and joints loose while the latter enhances upper-body fitness. The simple addition of bent-leg sit-ups and push-ups can pay off in greater stamina and comfort on the bike, as can a weight-training program which includes basic movements such as behind-the-neck presses, bent-over rows, bench presses, curls, etc. Do one set of each exercise every other day, using light weights and high repetitions to build strength and endurance without adding bulk.

MECHANICAL PREPARATION

Mechanical preparation is no less important than physical. In fact, it might be more important. While a person may be able to ride into shape during the course of a tour, mechanical failure can stop even the strongest cyclist cold. To help guard against breakdowns, the bike should be given a thorough inspection and all needed maintenance should be completed at least a week before the tour is to begin. This will allow time to ride the bike a few times before departure to make sure it is in tip-top operating condition.

Several components may require special attention, depending on your bike's stock equipment and the road surfaces and terrain you will be encountering. Assuming that you will be a self-contained traveler carrying about 35 pounds and that your route will include some hill country and secondary roads, the wheels, gear system, and bag support racks are going to be critical to efficiency, reliability, and safety.

Wheels

Chapter 14 contains information on rims, tires, and spokes, but I want to emphasize here that long-distance tourists have no business on anything but alloy 27×1¼ rims, high-pressure 27×1¼ or 27×1⅛ tires with a mixed tread, and quality 14-gauge spokes. Given these components, it makes relatively little difference whether the hubs are high- or low-flange, as long as the diameter of the spokes matches that of the hub flange holes so there will be no movement that contributes to spoke breakage.

If your bike has tubular wheels or the new 27×1 clinchers, I don't advise using them, because there is too much chance of failure. Either have them rebuilt or buy a second pair of wheels to use for touring. Besides strength, another advantage of standard 27×1¼ clincher wheels is the widespread availability of replacement rims, tires, tubes, and spokes. In a pinch you may be able to find what you need at a hardware or department store, but not every bike shop carries the components of lightweight clincher and tubular wheels.

Gear System

Unless your bike is a model made expressly for racing, you may have to alter its gearing. Riding experience will indicate whether the present low gear is sufficient; if you must get off the saddle to pedal your unloaded bike up some climbs, you will have no chance on tour. Even when riding with a load during your weekend overnighters no hill should force you off the saddle. Based on these considerations, and with a realistic look at the type of climbing you will face on the tour, a lower range of gears may well be in order.

Using the gear chart on page 72, write down the ratios for each of your ten (or twelve or whatever) front-to-rear chain combinations. Once you are familiar with the strength it takes to climb a steep grade in your lowest gear when the bike is loaded, you should be able to estimate how many more inches, if any, you need to go down in size—i.e., how many more teeth the largest freewheel cog needs to have. (Of course, if the inside chainwheel has more than the standard minimum of 42 teeth, you have the option of lowering the gear range by replacing the chainwheel with one that size or even smaller, if your crankset can accept it.) The best advice I can give is to be honest with yourself in assessing your strength—a day of climbing in the Rockies or Appalachians has no mercy for the macho rider. It's better to gear a little too low than not low enough, especially since a loaded bike has a tendency to sway, wobble, and suck up your energy when it is being pedaled out of the saddle.

Whether you need a lower low gear or not, check all ratios to see that there are no duplications which will reduce even further your usable gears (remember that you should avoid combining the large chainwheel with the largest freewheel cog and the small chainwheel with the smallest cog—see Chapter 4). If you have gears falling within a couple of inches of each other, you should replace freewheel cogs (or buy an entire new cluster) with sizes that produce wider gaps. It's interesting to spend some time with the gear chart and come up with cog and chainwheel sizes that yield ideal ratios for your needs. Touring experts advise a low gear of about 30 inches

(38×34) or slightly less for really mountainous regions, but for more standard terrain a 42×34 (33-inch gear) should be both sufficient and easy to obtain for any bike. The one snag may be that your stock rear derailleur cannot handle more than 28 teeth or so; in this case, you will have to install a long-cage touring model such as the SunTour VX-GT, an excellent derailleur that sells for less than $20.

Since climbing is the most difficult aspect of touring with a load, it's best to have less than 10-inch gaps between each of your three lowest gears. This should ensure that you have a gear appropriate for any grade. The jumps can be bigger between middle gears and larger still between the higher ratios. Some riders prefer to gear more toward the middle ratios by going down to a 50-tooth large chainwheel; combined with a small freewheel cog of 13 teeth this will give a high gear of about 104 inches and more than enough speed when descending with weight.

Once you have customized the gear system to your needs, you must learn to use it fully. Tape the usable ratios to your handlebars until you have them memorized. To ride efficiently you have to know where to shift to get the next higher or lower gear. This is especially important when riding hours a day with a loaded bike, because it has a direct bearing on energy output, maintaining a steady pedal cadence, and prevention of muscle and knee strain.

Racks

Metal bag supports must be able to stand up to a real beating on a long tour. According to one expert, Sam Braxton, writing in the Bikecentennial publication *BikeReport*, "Strength and rigidity are the two key factors in the racks you choose for your front and rear panniers. Racks that are less rigid will 'whip,' or move from side to side as you pedal (often the rack will be moving one way while the cyclist is moving in the opposite direction). Racks that whip will constantly loosen the loads attached to them, which leaves you with panniers in your spokes and sleeping bags lying on the roadside five miles back. Eventually, the constant side-to-side movement will weaken the rack and it will snap at the stress point."

Braxton, a bike shop owner in Missoula, MT, the headquarters of Bikecentennial, has had years of experience with touring equipment. In his opinion, the best rack by far is one that is actually brazed onto the frame. He realizes, though, that this isn't practical for many riders because of the expense or difficulty of finding someone who can do the job. Therefore, he advises, "Your best bet is to get the most rigid rack you can find that provides a level mounting surface when attached to your frame. Three-point attachment racks are going to sway more than those racks that attach at four points. Also, the further apart the two mounting points on the seat stays, the more rigid the rack will be.

"Construction material is another important consideration," he continues. "I think that aluminum is an awful poor material from which to build a bicycle rack. Aluminum will develop hairline cracks at stress points and then completely fracture. Steel will bend and bend before it finally breaks at a stress point. . . . Unfortunately, several of the better mass-produced racks use aluminum. You'll probably be okay using one of them as long as you're aware of the possible problems. Don't overload them, and watch the rack carefully if you suspect that there is any whipping action that could result in cracking and fracturing."

Braxton's recommendation for handlebar bags is to select only a model which has a metal support extending all the way underneath. This will prevent the bag from sagging down toward the wheel, though a hard bump could bounce it backward over the handlebars. To prevent this, some manufacturers add shock cords which stretch from the bag to the dropout eyelets of the fork. Braxton advises using a model like this *plus* a support underneath for maximum safety and stability.

For tips on what to look for in the selection of panniers and other bags, tents, and sleeping bags, see Chapter 14.

TOURING GEAR

The amount and kind of clothing and equipment to take on an extended tour usually is the result of a compromise—you don't want to overburden yourself and yet you want to have everything you might need. As Greg Siple notes, "If you carry very little weight you can do an extra 20 miles every day. You fly over the passes and you feel light and airy—it's great. But then you can't cook any meals because you don't have a stove, you're always worrying about rain because you don't have a tent, you don't have a freewheel remover when you need it. . . ." He sums up the dilemma by saying, "When you're on the bike it's nice to have no weight at all and when you're off the bike you want to have as much weight as possible."

The Siples camped out about 60 percent of the time during Hemistour and carried from 35 to 50 pounds of gear apiece. If that's all they needed on a trip of 18,272 miles, nobody should ever need more. According to Bikecentennial literature, here are the items the properly outfitted camping cyclist should have:

Bike Equipment: Tire pump, racks and panniers, handlebar bag, bottle cage and water bottles, bike locking device, safety flag or slow-moving-vehicle triangle, light and reflectors, tool assortment including spare tube, patch kit, spokes, cables, and anything out of the ordinary your components might require.

Camping: Tent with rain fly, ground cloth, sleeping bag and pad, moistureproof matches, compass.

Eating: Can opener, stove (if desired) and its fuel, utensils, water purification tablets, emergency food supply.

Personal: Hardshell helmet, clip-on rearview mirror, cycling gloves, 2 pairs cycling shorts with chamois lining (or terry cloth for quicker drying), 1 pair tights or leg warmers, 2 jerseys, breathable windbreaker, rain jacket or cape, wool sweater, 3 pairs socks, cycling shoes, walking shoes, 1 pair long pants, 2 short-sleeved shirts, 1 long-sleeved shirt, 3 sets underwear, towel, toilet articles, and, if desired, pajamas and a swimming suit.

Miscellaneous: Hat, sunglasses, sun screen, lip balm, first-aid kit, insect repellent, sewing kit with scissors, candle, roll of nylon cord, toilet paper, pocket knife, camera and film, maps.

Home sweet home. The best thing about touring with a tent is that you have the freedom to spend the night almost anywhere. This can add greatly to the adventure of a tour and a sense of accomplishment once it has been completed. However, nights in the wild are not for everyone, and riders who utilize motels, bike inns, and hostels need not feel their tour is less of an achievement. (*Photograph courtesy of Greg Siple*)

Your weekend overnighters and some serious thought about the specifics of your big tour will no doubt have you adding or subtracting a few items on this list. If you need to buy anything, go for the best balance possible between light weight and durability. Bright colors in cycling clothes add to safety, and, as pointed out in Chapter 16, wool is the best fabric. Color-coordinate your off-bike clothes and you will have the largest possible wardrobe.

How to Pack

Loading the touring bike, like selecting gear ratios, is a subject that fosters many opinions, not all of them in agreement. And just as with gearing, so many variables come into play that it is possible to talk only in basic principles, not specifics. It's up to you to apply the information to your own bag system and equipment.

In general, once the load being carried exceeds 35 pounds or so, at least a third of it should be put on the front of the bike. The traditional way to do this has been to use a handlebar bag, but as the weight in it begins to exceed about 6 pounds there will be an increasingly adverse effect on handling. Sam Braxton recommends a weight distribution of 45 percent/55 percent (front to rear) to help prevent the front wheel from feeling too squirrely and the rear tire from wearing out quickly. To obtain this proportion he advises the use of front panniers in addition to a handlebar bag. Front panniers allow more flexibility in packing, and he traces a reduction in rear-wheel problems to their growing popularity.

However, Braxton cautions, "You shouldn't view front panniers as an open invitation to load your bicycle to the hilt. I think that a good average load for a cyclist using only rear panniers is 35 pounds, and that includes the pump, loaded water and fuel bottles—everything. Front panniers would allow you to go up to 40 or 45 pounds."

The drawback to using front panniers is that they produce more air resistance (particularly noticeable in a crosswind) and they can make handling difficult at low speeds. They also necessitate a fairly precise weight balance; if the bags are loaded unequally there will be steering problems and the danger of high-speed shimmy on downhills, a condition in which the whole bike begins to shake violently. (If you ever experience this, try not to panic. Apply the brakes with moderate force and squeeze the top tube between your knees until you have things under control, then do something about the distribution of the load. High-speed shimmy isn't always caused by improper balance—it can happen even on an unloaded bike due to faulty frame or fork alignment, or problems with the headset, hub or, wheel—but a packing error is the first thing to suspect if it strikes during a tour.)

Once you have selected your panniers and bags (see shopping tips in Chapter 14) and have installed the racks on your bike and laid out all the gear you will be carrying, there are two main rules for how to pack. First, keep the center of gravity as low as possible by putting heavy items in the bottom of the bags. Second, position as much of

A long tour requires plenty of physical and mechanical preparation to help ensure an enjoyable ride from the outset. Special attention must be given to the selection of equipment and packing and loading the bike. Once under way, all the time spent getting ready will be rewarded by an intimacy with the countryside available in no other manner. (*Photograph courtesy of Bikecentennial*)

the weight as you can directly over the wheel axles. As Braxton points out, panniers designed in a tapered or teardrop shape instead of rectangular offer an advantage because they practically force you to position the weight low and in line with the axle. Another benefit comes if you have long feet or use longer-than-standard crank arms—tapered rear bags offer plentiful heel clearance when pedaling, whereas panniers with square corners might have to be moved rearward, which goes against ideal weight placement.

It will take some thought, experimentation, and actual weighings of the various loaded bags in order to pack the bike correctly, and then at least one good test ride to make sure everything is balanced and stable. All the time this takes will be well worth it once you set off on the actual tour. A good idea is to keep specific items (tool kit, eating utensils, first-aid kit, toilet articles, etc.) in the various pockets your bags provide so they are easy to locate. Use the detachable handlebar bag for your valuables, camera, and the items you need most when riding or taking a break. By rolling up your clothing, putting each individual item into a clear Ziploc bag, and packing it all vertically in the large pannier chambers, you will protect your things from the elements and won't have to dig through layers of clothes and other items to find what you want.

To secure your sleeping bag and tent to the top of the rear rack you can use bungee cords (sandows) or nylon straps with buckles. Most experienced tourists recommend the latter. Such straps can be cinched as snugly as needed and they will stay tight, but the elasticity of bungees can allow the load to bounce and shift on bumpy roads. There is also the danger of an errant metal hook catching in the wheel, and there could be a serious injury if one slips and snaps back while you are bent over the bike trying to load or unload gear.

Finally, double-check the necessity of every item you intend to carry. That flashlight won't be needed if you have a detachable bike light; forget that cup and give your water bottle double duty; leave the can opener if your pocket knife has one. Every ounce you can save will be worth a pound on a climb at the end of a long day in the saddle. Keep this in mind throughout your planning and it will pay off in the ability to pedal more miles with less effort.

PLANNING A TOUR

8

Now that we've looked into the physical, mechanical, and equipment preparations needed for an extended tour, we come to the all-important matter of actually formulating the trip itinerary. But before getting out the calendar, maps, and other resource material, it's essential to make a final honest self-evaluation so that the type of tour you decide upon will have the greatest chance of success and satisfaction.

According to the experts at Bikecentennial, even advanced tourists tend to overlook the importance of self-knowledge and mental preparation. You certainly realize that there could be some tough times ahead—headwinds, rain, dust, hills, heat, traffic, bad pavement, mechanical breakdowns, even injury—but are you sure you have what it takes to cope with such difficulties day after day? Bikecentennial has found: "As much as the right equipment, training, and route planning, bicycle touring demands the ability to cope. Knowing yourself and being comfortable with your limitations, motivations, and objectives will do more to ensure a rewarding tour than anything else."

What it boils down to is that you'd better be able to flow along with daily circumstances and not become upset by forced changes in your schedule. As Bikecentennial puts it, "A sense of humor is as useful a tool as the spoke wrench on a long-distance bicycle tour." And because a tour that goes exactly as planned is much more the exception than the rule, the itinerary you finally decide upon should leave plenty of leeway for the unanticipated. It may be wise to add an extra "slush" day or two just so you won't wind up a basket case from trying to overcome the delays that threaten to destroy a precise timetable. A long bicycle tour can be (and should be) a highlight of your life, so put enjoyment first and foremost on the list of priorities as you make plans.

There is certainly such a thing as overplanning a tour, and it can

(Photograph courtesy of Nina MacLean)

be as disastrous as being underprepared. Bikecentennial cautions, "Knowing every bend in the road before you leave can quickly kill the spontaneity of a trip. Be familiar enough with the area through which you'll be cycling so that you can find food, water, and shelter without difficulty. Research your route choices in terms of difficulty of terrain and road conditions. Then put down your books and maps, load (but don't overload) your bicycle, take a deep breath, and hit the road."

Keep this in mind as you read through this chapter. I'll be listing sources for all kinds of information that can be used to plan a tour, but this doesn't mean you should use every one. Decide as early as you can the specific things you want to know for planning the trip, then set out to gather that data. Once it is in hand, let it help you reduce the unknown but not the adventure.

SOURCES OF INFORMATION

A racing cyclist exists in a rather cut-and-dried world of specific events, but the touring cyclist faces such a freedom of choice that it can almost be paralyzing. When setting out to gather the information needed to plan a lengthy tour, where the heck does a rider turn first? My unreserved recommendation is Box 8308, Missoula, MT 59807. That's the address of Bikecentennial, and nobody can help you get to specific sources of information better than its staff can. Write to them and include $1.95 for a copy of *The Cyclist's Yellow Pages,* which is a 48-page resource guide to maps, books, routes, organizations, and group tours—printed on yellow paper, of course. Better yet, get this valuable booklet free (and six others) by sending in your Bikecentennial membership fee. The yearly rate is $15 for individuals, $12 for students, $10 for those aged 60 and over, $20 for the whole family. Other membership benefits include issues of the bimonthly publication *BikeReport* and discounts on all Bikecentennial booklets, route guides, and accessories, as well as other books of interest to tourists. There is also the good feeling that comes from supporting a nonprofit organization that is working hard for the betterment of your kind of cycling.

Several factors must enter into the thought process as you begin to plan your trip. Various types of tours are possible, and I'll discuss some of them later in this chapter, but for now let's assume yours is in the mold of the most common. That is, summer vacation time is coming and you will have a couple of weeks for the ride, which you want to begin and end at your front door. You've found that you enjoy the adventure of camping out but don't really feel the need to have hot meals every day, so you will pack a tent and sleeping bag but no stove or cooking utensils. Occasionally you will spend the night in a motel so you can get a shower and visit a nearby laundromat. Otherwise, you plan to stay at public or private campgrounds in or near state and national forests. Your route will be a big loop that takes you to various parts of the state, including some historical sites and natural wonders that you've always meant to visit but just never got around to.

Once you've decided which areas you'd like to travel through, begin gathering the specific maps and other route information you feel is necessary for creating the itinerary.

Maps

No doubt you are very familiar with the best roads for cycling within 50 miles of home, but you will need some detailed maps in order to make good choices for the rest of the state. Certainly the major state and federal highways are to be avoided as much as possible, and so are secondary roads that include stretches of gravel or dirt. Neither fast, heavy traffic nor flat tires and dust do a happy tourist make. To find the best alternatives, get maps of your state from the department of transportation, local chamber of commerce, a major oil company service station, an automobile club, or a bookstore. You want at least two different maps so that you can crosscheck the information they contain.

Good state maps will tell you many things besides the various types of roads and where they go. The elevations of mountains, passes, and towns will indicate how much climbing a certain route has. Town population figures will give you an idea of the facilities (or lack thereof) you can expect to find. Some maps will show the location of campgrounds, though you will need a camping guide, such as those published by Rand McNally, to find out exactly what each one offers. State and national parks or forests will be identified, and sometimes so will roadside areas for picnickers. Certain roads may be labeled as scenic routes, and points of historical interest may be marked.

To refine what state maps show and perhaps discover usable secondary roads they have not included, you can obtain county maps in the scale of ¼ inch or ½ inch to the mile from the state's department of transportation, a bookstore, or an auto club. Going a step further, topographical maps can be used in conjunction with county road maps to see land contours and specific features. These maps come in several scales, with 1 inch = 4 miles being the best for planning long tours. Given the limited area each map shows and their cost (up to $2 each), it isn't practical to have topographical maps for an entire route, but they can be ordered for specific locales you have an interest in. For a free map index for land east of the Mississippi River contact: Distribution Section, U.S. Geological Survey, 1200 S. Eads St., Arlington, VA 22202. West of the Mississippi River contact: Distribution Section, U.S. Geological Survey, Federal Center, Denver, CO 80225.

For a state-by-state listing of where to write for order forms and price lists for state and county road maps, consult *The Cyclist's Yellow Pages*. You may also be interested in ordering traffic-flow maps, which show the average number of motor vehicles using specific sections of roads during a 24-hour period. (For the most pleasant cycling, Bikecentennial recommends sticking to roads with fewer than 1,000 vehicles per day.) In addition, *Yellow Pages* lists addresses for obtaining bike route maps in the dozen or so states that have them, and there is information about Bikecentennial's national touring network and routing service.

Don't neglect to find out if there are touring cyclists in your locale who have ridden in the areas you are headed for. Their experiences can be very helpful in deciding which roads to use and which to avoid. Get in touch with such riders through bike shops and clubs, especially those affiliated with the League of American Wheelmen.

There is one important point to remember whenever you write

away for information: Be as specific as you can and allow plenty of time for the response. A line like "Send me all the information you can as soon as possible" will probably get you nothing at all. Narrow down your request and make sure to mention that you will be bicycle touring, because it might make a difference—there may be specific literature for cyclists or even a person experienced in handling such inquiries.

Planning the Route

Once you've collected the maps and various pieces of information, you can begin planning the route. Hand in hand with this, of course, is deciding how many miles you can enjoyably ride each day, where you'd like to stay each night, the places you want to spend time sightseeing, and so on.

There are two ways to determine the length of tour, in total miles, that it is practical to shoot for. One is to make a close approximation of how many miles it will take to ride everywhere you want to go, then divide that figure by the number of days you have for the tour. The resulting daily average must be within your ability (and, more important, your desire) or you must alter the route. The second way is to decide the average daily mileage you want to ride, multiply it by the number of days you have for the trip, and then design the route based on that total distance. (When figuring the number of miles you expect to cover each day, be sure to take into consideration such factors as variations in terrain, prevailing winds, prospects for rainy weather, etc., and remember to make an allowance for riding time that is bound to be lost to the unforeseen.)

For riders making their first extended tour with a loaded bike, an average of 50 miles a day is a good goal. This may not seem very impressive until you stop to consider that it adds up to 350 miles a week, 700 for a two-week tour. That's a healthy hunk of distance. In fact, this is a pace used by even experienced riders, such as the Siples of Hemistour fame, who in June's words "kind of ooze along" when on tour. "We are probably on the road six to eight hours and we feel comfortable with 50 to 60 miles—just to the point where you feel like you've done something," she says.

Other riders may just as easily be able to handle 75 miles a day or even 100. Terrain, weather, load, riding strength, mental attitude, personal objectives, the length of the tour—these factors and others must enter into your planning. Never let the pace you set for yourself be dictated by what another rider has done before you; until experience reveals your true capabilities it's certainly better to underestimate your ability than overestimate it. Otherwise you could quickly find yourself pressed into a workaday riding pattern in order to stay on schedule, the pleasures of touring snuffed out by this drudgery.

Daily mileage totals don't have to be consistent, of course, and you should keep this in mind as you search the maps for overnight sites. For example, you may wish to begin the tour with a 75-mile ride just to get out of familiar surroundings as quickly as possible. The next day you can come back with a much more leisurely 40-miler that allows recovery and establishes the flow of the trip. Variations in the distance covered each day will help you out of a physical and mental rut.

When mapping out the roads you will use, select secondary and county roads over federal and state highways whenever possible. Even though the latter may be wider, have a better shoulder, and make a more direct path between places, their drawbacks outweigh these advantages. Traffic will be fast and plentiful, of course, and many times there will be no trees close enough to lend shade and a windbreak. Sometimes, especially in the West, a cyclist has no choice but to use a major highway or even a stretch of Interstate (the law allowing). But if an alternate road is available it is almost always the better choice.

When traveling between large towns it is usually possible to find a secondary road that parallels the major highway. Secondary roads may be quite narrow, and they won't have a paved shoulder, if they have one at all, but traffic is usually light enough and slow enough that this doesn't make them unsafe. Still, a rider on a bike widened by panniers must be prepared to relinquish the pavement anytime traffic conditions become dangerous. An example would be a wide-load vehicle approaching from behind—this is why it is so helpful to have a small rearview mirror that clips to your helmet or glasses. On two-lane roads you must also be alert for a car passing another and coming directly at you. Because of curves, hills, trees, houses, etc., drivers will come upon you suddenly, so be as visible as possible by wearing brightly colored clothes and using a safety flag or slow-moving-vehicle triangle.

These potential dangers notwithstanding, secondary roads are the best choice for touring. The intimacy they provide with the country-side, farms, and villages is what makes a trip by bike so interesting. By using traffic-flow maps you should be able to route yourself around potentially congested areas, and some common sense helps, too. For example, no matter how terrific a county road looks on the map, if it passes a popular recreation area you can bet on heavy traf-fic on weekends. But schedule your ride on that stretch for a weekday and you'll have the road almost to yourself. On the other hand, when nearing logging or coal-mining areas it's best to pass through on the weekend when the monstrous trucks aren't operating.

There can be other considerations in route selection based on the characteristics of the region you are touring in, but as a final general tip keep in mind the need to drink frequently and eat high-carbohy-drate snacks during the course of each day's ride. Whether you will have your main meals in restaurants or buy from grocery stores, plan your itinerary to take you through at least one town every day so you can restock the pantry and water bottles. But just to be on the safe side, always try to keep a day's food supply in reserve. The same goes for water, especially when you are riding in desert regions or in the heat of the summer. As discussed in Chapter 2, steady fluid replace-ment is essential for good cycling performance. Pack a jug of water if you aren't certain it is readily available along the day's route and at the campground you will be using. This is especially important in the West, where drinking water can be scarce and towns far apart.

OTHER METHODS OF TOURING

The solo, self-contained trip may be the essence of bicycle touring but is by no means the only way to go. If you and camping simply don't mix, you can plan a tour as just described but spend the nights in motels, hotels, or hostels. Hostels are dormitory-like and offer inexpensive lodging which usually includes beds and cooking facilities. The hostel system isn't nearly as well developed in the United States as it is in Europe, but there are chains in New England, the Pennsylvania Dutch Country and the Colorado Rockies. For a listing, write to American Youth Hostels, National Campus, Delaplane, VA 22025.

Bikecentennial has been developing a new lodging system called Bike Inns, which are very similar to hostels if not the same facility. They are located along the 4,450-mile TransAmerica Trail and other Bikecentennial routes. For a listing, write to the organization and request a copy of the *TransAmerica Trail Directory*.

Another alternative is to stay with people listed in the *Touring Cyclists' Hospitality Directory*. They have volunteered to provide accommodations for riders in a sort of cooperative agreement—the directory is available to anyone who is listed as offering hospitality to others. Now published by Bikecentennial, the directory contains more than 550 addresses and it continues to grow. For more information contact the fellow who has developed the system: John Moseley, 13623 Sylvan, Van Nuys, CA 91401.

The advantage of spending nights indoors is greater comfort, both after the day's riding is done and while actually on the road. Without the weight and bulk of camping equipment you will be able to cover the miles with less effort and the bike will handle better. Disadvantages include the need for more detailed advance planning and, particularly when staying in motels, greater expense. You may have to make a series of reservations to be assured of having a room each night; regardless, you will be tied to a rather rigid itinerary because of the necessity of ending each day's ride in a town with motels. The self-contained rider, on the other hand, has the freedom to pitch his tent virtually anywhere.

Touring with a Friend

Touring with your spouse or a friend can add greatly to the experience. Or it can ruin it. The plusses include companionship, shared enterprise, a helping hand if trouble strikes, and having someone to relive the trip with after it's all over. However, those memories can

A major consideration when planning a tour is whether to ride solo or with one or more fellow cyclists. You must take great care when picking a partner, because much of the tour's success will depend on how well the two of you are matched on all levels. (*Photograph courtesy of Bikecentennial*)

be sour ones indeed if you and your partner are not well matched in terms of cycling ability and what each of you wants to accomplish on the trip.

The best way to know if you and a certain person can tour together successfully is to ride together often. It always amazes me to see personal ads in cycling magazines which go something like: "Wanted: One companion for tour from Montreal to Seattle by way of Dallas. Male or female. Leaving immediately." I can't think of anything more likely to end in ruin than to hook up with a stranger for ninety days on the road. Instead, you and your potential partner should be well acquainted on a personal level and in thorough agreement on how the tour will be ridden. Compromises will be in order, but neither of you should feel unhappy about any aspect of the trip. If each of you isn't as confident of having as great an experience together as you would riding alone, don't force it.

Partnering with your spouse (or best friend of the opposite sex) eliminates the unknowns at the personal level, but it can create problems because of differences in physical strength between men and women. The man may have to reduce the speed and distance he is capable of so that the woman doesn't overextend herself. A natural way to accomplish this is for him to carry the bulk of the load and for her to ride in front at the pace she is comfortable with.

Family Touring

It is entirely possible to ride even across the country with young children, as has been proved by Tim and Glenda Wilhelm, authors of *The Bicycle Touring Book*. They did it with their 9-year-old daughter riding her own small bike and their 2-year-old son tucked into a trailer. If you have kids yourself or young brothers and sisters, the tour you include them on could be one of their biggest adventures in childhood. Some scouting-type organizations have supervised tours for youngsters, but in general the opportunities for pre-teens are not many outside of the family.

The Wilhelms' advice is not to attempt a family tour unless everyone is behind the idea and everyone gets along well together at home. Weekend camping trips to a park or forest are a good way to begin and also find out if a longer tour is likely to work. Since the whole family can travel each day only as far as the kids are able and willing to pedal, an extended tour that would include difficult terrain or some riding through congested urban areas may not be practical.

The key to keeping youngsters happy on tour is to provide plenty of diversion from the relatively humdrum chore that making forward progress can become. A short break every hour helps a lot, as does the inclusion of visits to places kids like most—amusement parks, zoos, fairs, etc. Other ingredients which contribute to success include giving the children an active role in planning the tour, setting daily mileage goals that are within the capability of the weakest person, and having the flexibility to change the itinerary if it will add to peace and happiness.

Group Tours

There are more than three dozen commercial and nonprofit organizations which offer group tours, and at some point you may wish to give one of them a try. Advantages range from the chance to ride with others for a change to having the routing and logistical details taken care of for you. They also provide the opportunity to pedal through far-off parts of the country and world if you care to transport yourself and your equipment to the launching site.

Group tours utilize the gamut of overnight accommodations—everything from campgrounds to hostels to country inns. Some tours provide a sag wagon for lending aid in case of difficulty and carrying the bulk of the gear so that the cyclists can ride with minimal weight. Most organizations have no age groupings, instead offering tours for novice, intermediate, and advanced riders of any age. Daily distances average about 40–50 miles, usually under the guidance of a group leader who works for the company. Trip lengths range from weekend jaunts to Bikecentennial's ninety-day transcontinental odyssey.

A good way to find out if group touring is something you will enjoy is to take part in organized cycling activities in your locale. Many group rides are held by clubs affiliated with the League of American Wheelmen, a list of which can be requested by writing to the LAW at Box 988, Baltimore, MD 21203. Contacting both the LAW and Bikecentennial is probably the best first step you can take to find out what is currently happening in organized group tours.

When looking into the possibility of joining a commercial tour, be sure to find out everything that could have a bearing on your enjoyment. One important concern, of course, is the cost. Tours that offer such niceties as sag wagons, overnight accommodations in lodges, and restaurant meals will be more expensive than those using hostels and campgrounds—and don't forget to figure in your transportation charges to and from the tour site. Find out things like the age of the other cyclists, their riding ability, the number of miles scheduled for each day, the qualifications and experience of the leader, and whether the group is supposed to remain intact or if individuals can choose their own pace as long as they merge at the day's destination. Make sure you understand who is responsible for taking care of mechanical and medical problems. Check into what happens to your deposit if for some reason you must cancel.

After you've done the homework and decided to sign up, prepare for the tour just about as you would for a solo trip. Try to be in top physical shape, make sure the bike and other equipment is in excellent condition, and pack so that you will have everything you need. Don't be tempted to lighten your load by assuming you will be able to borrow this item or that from another rider. A touring cyclist should always strive to be self-contained, because it creates self-confidence.

Once on the road, be cautious around the other riders until you get a feel for their judgment and bike-handling ability. Several of them—maybe you are included—may not be very experienced riding a loaded bike in close proximity to others. Obey the laws of the road and extend courtesy to everyone. You are a part of the group, so do everything possible to make it a safe, friendly, and enjoyable experience. Not everything that happens during the course of the trip will please everyone, but getting upset about things and asserting one's individuality are not going to help. Always remember that you have chosen to be where you are.

9

INTRODUCTION TO RACING

"On my good rides my mind seems to be ahead of my feet. I feel a peculiar urgency, as if in a hurry to get somewhere and I can't wait for each pedal to turn over . . . boom, boom, boom."

"I love the excitement of a race, the excitement of the field. There's a definite group mentality and you have to sense what the field is feeling. It's nice—it's a form of communication."

"I guess you could say I've become addicted to racing. I can't really stop. If I stopped I would lose all my friends, I'd lose all my pride."

These remarks, made by three U.S. champion cyclists, describe some of the gratifying aspects of bicycle racing. There is a certain pleasure to be had in riding fast and pressing the body to its limit. There's a thrill to being in the midst of a mass of bicycles and riders all speeding along at 30 mph. And there's a real sense of self-worth which comes from hard effort and physical achievement.

People like many different things about bicycle racing, and there's no telling which will appeal to you until you try it. If you have been cycling seriously for a year or longer—that is, getting out on your bike four or five times each week and doing some long weekend rides—you have an adequate foundation from which to begin training for competition. But first you must realize that racing on a bicycle will be one of the most strenuous things you'll ever do. That's why the rewards are so appreciated. Not everyone can handle the demands, but the sport has a place for anyone who is willing to put in the considerable amounts of time and effort required. If you are interested in meeting this challenge, this chapter and the following ones will explain what you need to know for your initial seasons—

how to get started, how to train, and how to ride the various road racing events. But first let's look into the differences between riding as you have for fitness, recreation or touring, and riding to compete.

Being a racer requires some mental and physical abilities that even the above-average cyclist has probably not acquired. If you are a fit rider you can probably hold a pace of 18–20 mph for quite a while. Cruising at that speed is relatively comfortable and it will keep your heart rate high enough to produce the training effect. In terms of stress, though, there isn't much unless a ride lasts more than three hours or there is a lot of climbing.

The racer can also pedal for a long time at 20 mph, but he has an additional ability that sets him apart. He can put on a burst of speed—up to 27 mph or more—for several minutes and then drop back to 20 mph to recover. And he can do it numerous times in a single ride. This ability comes through training, the subject of the next chapter. The point here is that it is a matter of mental as well as physical conditioning. To be a racer you have to develop the willpower to make a hard effort every time it is needed.

In fact, it is the mental aspect that often decides who the successful racers are. For example, often there are riders in the field who aren't really competing. For various reasons they know they can't win, so they race for other goals—for training, for experience, for fun, for the feeling of accomplishment in completing the distance. They may be good cyclists and they may take an active part in the race as it progresses, but when the crunch comes they can't or won't disregard all the painful distress signals their bodies are sending. Other competitors, though, will react in the opposite way—they realize that when the going gets tough it's time to get going. They excel when a challenge is thrown at them, when attacks begin late in the race or a really hard part of the course looms up. This test of a rider's ability to respond when it would be so much easier to let up is what bike racing is all about.

Steve Woznick, many times a national champion in track events, described the confrontation with this mental challenge when he said, "You have to be willing to rip it all apart, even yourself." Other people call it a willingness to suffer, but I'm not sure suffer is the right word. It's really more like plain hard work—hard work which is surely painful at times but which can also be mentally rewarding, even enjoyable, especially when it pays off. When it doesn't . . . well, then it comes a lot closer to suffering.

Training and racing will produce lungs that feel big and open, and leg muscles that are large and strong. This makes it physically easier to ride fast, and it builds confidence. Even when you get tired you will have something left to call on. Former Olympian Rick Ball was talking about this when he said, "You become familiar with the normal signs of bodily distress and you lose your fear of them. You learn that you won't fall off your bike, turn blue, and perish in apoplectic asphyxiation just when your breathing gets frantic or your lungs feel tight or your legs burn a bit." This awareness doesn't come overnight, of course, but develops as you cultivate fitness and realize that you can depend on it to pull you through.

"People who win races are in a class of their own," said Ron Skarin, another former national champion. In the 1970s, Skarin was one of a handful of people who did win races. He doesn't attribute his success to superior natural ability but rather to the kind of mental toughness I'm talking about. "In a race I can open the throttle more than some other guy can," he said. "I have a capacity to suffer more, which has been developed. I wasn't born with it."

The best competitors have both the physical ability to put out extra effort and the courage to use it. To them the only thing that matters is riding as hard as possible to beat everyone else and win the race. The pain is there, but it's worth it. One reason why the winner of most big races seems to come from a handful of riders is that so many others perceive a big gap in ability between themselves and the elite. In fact, it's a very small gap and it's mostly mental.

Government of the Sport

Among the basics you'll need for entering the sport is a racing license from the U.S. Cycling Federation. There are currently no qualifying standards (in terms of riding ability) for getting a license. All a U.S. citizen needs to do is fill out the application and return it with the proper annual fee for his or her age group.

The USCF is a federation of racing clubs, and the best way to get started in competition is to join one of them. A good way to locate those in your area is to ask at a local bike shop. The best clubs have daily training rides and informal weekly races. You don't need a license for these and you could spend your whole first season gaining experience by competing at the club level. But if you plan to enter any sanctioned races during the year you should apply for a license early in the season; it may take several weeks to receive it and it is good through December 31. Your local club or bike shop may have application forms; if not, write directly to U.S. Cycling Federation, 1750 East Boulder St., No. 4, Colorado Springs, CO 80909.

The USCF can also supply the name and address of its district representative who oversees the racing where you live. This person will have a list of all the USCF clubs and races in the area.

Why is it important to join a club? First, meeting and riding with other cycling enthusiasts makes the sport more fun. Second, you will learn faster by being around riders with more experience and ability than yourself. And perhaps most important, many clubs provide coaching, a tremendous advantage for a beginning racer. A good coach can teach you the basics of the sport, help you set your goals, and then provide the extra motivation you need to achieve them. It is possible to become a good rider without a coach, but having one will certainly help it happen sooner.

Your coach, your teammates, and the results in club races will let you know when you're ready to enter sanctioned events. Depending on your age on January 1, you will be in one of these age classes: Midget (8–11 years old), Intermediate (12–14), Junior (15–17), Senior (18–34), Veteran (35–44), Master (45–54), Grand Master (55 and over). Each of these is divided for men and women, and because so many racers are Senior men this class is broken into categories. A beginning rider starts in category IV and then upgrades to category III, II, and I as he gains experience and good results. In many race programs the Senior III and IV riders compete together and there is a separate event for I and II riders.

If you are a first-year Junior, Senior, Veteran, Master, or Grand Master, your license will cost $15 (1982 fee). From the second year onward it is $25. The charge for Midgets and Intermediates starts and remains at $10. For the license fee a rider also receives monthly

Today there is more coaching available than ever before. This group of young riders is part of a development program at the Lehigh County Velodrome in Trexlertown, Pennsylvania.

issues of the USCF's publication, *Cycling USA*, and a racing rule book. The latter is an important document containing regulations about equipment, gear restrictions, clothing, length of races, prizes, conduct of competitors, etc. and is printed in pocket-size format to fit easily in a racing kit. When you first receive the rule book you should go through the section on general racing rules, which tells about the requirements for competing in the various events. The book also contains the USCF's constitution and bylaws, if you're interested in how the federation works.

The USCF is a nonprofit organization and is run mostly by volunteers. The primary unit is the member club, all of which can vote annually for members of the USCF board of directors, a group of twenty-four that meets quarterly to supervise the activities of the sport. Along with a growing number of other national sports-governing bodies, the USCF maintains its office in a building provided by the U.S. Olympic Committee at its headquarters in Colorado Springs, Colorado. In the USOC complex are dormitories, a sports-medicine center, a cafeteria, and classrooms. Current and prospec-

tive national team riders usually spend several weeks of every year there for training camps. It's a beautiful location, right on the edge of the Rocky Mountains, and the winters are mild enough so that riding is possible almost year-round.

As the national governing body of amateur cycling, the USCF is a member of the USOC and is allied with other sports organizations such as the Amateur Athletic Union (AAU) and the International Human Powered Vehicle Association (IHPVA). The federation is also affiliated with the world governing body of cycling, the Union Cycliste Internationale (UCI). This organization does on the world level what the USCF does in America—it makes the rules of the sport, trains and licenses officials, maintains competition records, holds world championships, and so on.

The criterium is the most popular mass-start race in the United States. Starting fields can include as many as 200 riders on courses a mile or less in length through city streets, often riding in groups at speeds of 30 miles per hour. Criteriums are also the most exciting road event for spectators, since the riders make numerous laps and sprint often for special prizes called primes.

Bike Racing's Heritage

Most Americans don't realize how big the sport of cycling is and how long it's been around. In most European and Latin America countries it is a national passion, as popular as baseball and football are to North Americans. Major races are carried live on television, and the best riders are well-paid professionals. The most famous cyclist of modern times, Belgium's Eddy Merckx, is a millionaire and is as well known in Europe as Pete Rose is in the United States.

The oldest, most prestigious road races in Europe are called classics and are one-day events. At the other extreme is the 2,200-mile, three-week Tour de France—that most grueling of all athletic contests. The first Tour was held in 1903, back when the sport began to thrive in Europe and was also entering its golden era in the United States. There were outdoor bicycle-racing tracks in nearly every American city, and even local races drew thousands of spectators. In the 1920s and '30s, indoor six-day races became practically a national obsession in such arenas as Madison Square Garden.

Cycling historians relate the decline of U.S. bicycle racing in the late 1930s to the increasing popularity of the automobile—for one thing, bike racers could no longer command admiration as the fastest thing on wheels. Whatever the reasons, the sport virtually disappeared until, by the early 1970s, there were only a few thousand licensed riders. It was then that the nation's awakening to the benefits of physical fitness combined with the skyrocketing price of gasoline to cause many people to dust off their bikes and begin pumping the pedals again. By 1980 about 10,000 had become involved in racing and there were many signs that another golden era might be in the offing: Olympic speedskating hero Eric Heiden and his sister Beth took up bicycle racing and thereby created much publicity for the sport, heightened by Beth's victory in the 1980 World Road Championship; Sue Novara won her second World Sprint Championship the same year; the hit movie *Breaking Away* featured bike racing and showed millions the excitement of cycling; and big commercial names as diverse as Lowenbrau beer, Mohawk Carpets, and 7-Eleven began getting involved in the sponsorship of major races and racing teams. Everything has combined to make the decade of the '80s a most promising one for competitive cycling in America.

Spectators' Guide to Racing

Even if you never intend to be out there thrashing the cranks, as a cycling enthusiast you owe it to yourself to become familiar with bike racing. The sport offers as much speed, excitement, strategy, and drama as anyone could want, and in most cases it's free for the watching. Though velodromes usually charge a nominal admission fee, mass-start road events can be viewed by everyone able to afford a couple of hours' time. This unticketed and unregimented setup allows a person to pick a good vantage point and stand within feet of riders straining up a hill or sweeping through a corner. Or you can simply stay in the start/finish area, watch the sprints for special lap prizes called primes (say it "preems"), and listen to the announcer's call of the race. The spectacle can be so compelling that it shuts down an entire town, just as it does each Memorial Day in Somerville, New Jersey, and each Father's Day in Nevada City, California. Even residents of New York, Chicago, and Los Angeles halt their frantic pace to stand in awe as the racing cyclists swoosh by.

But do they understand what they are looking at? Probably not, especially if they haven't seen bike races before or aren't within earshot of the announcer. Competitive cycling is a complex sport and often isn't what it appears to be, as indicated by the axiom that says the fellow in front probably isn't winning. In fact, quite often the best rider doesn't win. Factors such as the individual rider's specific strengths and shortcomings, the type of course, weather conditions, team strategies, and mechanical problems all combine with the key factor in cycling—wind resistance—to make the flow of each race different and virtually unpredictable. It's sport at its best.

Not only are such things bound to mystify the new spectator, but

Author Tom Doughty in center. In a mass start event you are closely surrounded by other riders and have a sense of closeness, danger, and speed.

bike racing has a language all its own. Here, for example, are some terms used when describing a mass-start race:

As the event begins, the main group of riders that forms is called the *field, pack, bunch,* or *peloton.* A rider who can't keep up with the field is said to be *dropped* or *off the back.* Those who *attack* and get ahead are *off the front.* Aggressive moves are made with a sudden acceleration called a *jump.* The purpose of an attack is to make a *break-away,* which can be either a solo or a group action. The *break* is said to be so many seconds *up* on the field (which is a corresponding number of seconds *down*). One or more riders in the field may try to launch a *chase* to *bridge the gap* to the break, but teammates of those in the lead can try to thwart this by means of *blocking.* If two or more riders come to the finish line together they will *sprint* for the victory. When a big bunch arrives it is called a *field sprint* and riders may try to provide a *leadout* for a friend or teammate. This allows the second rider to *sit on the wheel* in the *slipstream* of the first rider, then come around him with a high-speed jump or *kick* of his own just before he *throws the bike* at the line.

These and other terms will be used in the chapters which follow, especially in the one on tactics. And at the end of the book there is a glossary which lists more cycling jargon and includes definitions of some of the common types of races. Prospective competitors must of course become familiar with all the terms, and new fans of the sport can gain a good understanding of race strategy from them. After reading the chapters on racing, you will see that a bike race is much more than it appears to the uninitiated, who tend to view it as an unstructured swarm of riders jockeying for position until, almost by lottery, someone happens to cross the finish line first.

Types of Racing

There are three branches of racing, each of which uses a different type of bicycle.

Cyclocross is rare in the United States but popular in Europe in the winter. It requires a combination of riding and running because courses are only partially paved, if at all, and includes obstacles such as steep uphills and stairways which force a rider to dismount and

Cyclocross is a winter event that combines cycling and running. It is a great way to stay in shape and improve bike-handling skills.

carry the bike across his shoulder. Often courses will have mudholes, creek beds, and logs which only the best riders can negotiate on their bikes. The event puts a premium on bike-handling ability and sturdy machines, which are specially equipped for rough treatment and poor surface conditions. Cyclocross is very demanding of competitors and it's a wonderful spectator event which deserves to have more popularity in the United States.

Track racing doesn't get its just share of recognition, either, and the only reason is the relative lack of velodromes in the United States. Certainly this side of the sport doesn't lack for variety, speed, and excitement, and it is ideal for spectators, since all the action is in plain view. Racers take to the steeply banked tracks using bikes which have no brakes or derailleurs, just a single-gear direct drive.

Track racing offers some of the fastest and most intense competition in cycling, and all the action is in plain view of the fans. Track bikes weigh less than 20 pounds, having no brakes and a single-speed, direct-drive gear system.

Among the most skillful cyclists in the world are team pursuiters. Riding only millimeters apart on steeply banked tracks, they reach very high speeds but must still maneuver with utmost precision. This squad of (*front to back*) Ralph Therrio, Paul Deem, Ron Skarin, and Jim Ochowicz competed in the 1976 Olympic Games in Montreal.

On of the most functional—and some say beautiful—pieces of machinery is the track racing bicycle. It has a fixed gear and direct drive so it is not cluttered with cables and levers. National champion Brent Emery can reach speeds of more than forty miles an hour in his speciality, the thousand-meter time trial.

The riding surface is usually cement or wood and tracks can vary in circumference from as small as about 150 meters indoors to 500 meters outdoors, with the most common outdoor size being 333 meters.

Unfortunately, there are only sixteen permanent outdoor velodromes in the United States and not all have an active racing program. It's a shame not only because this limits the chance to attract new fans, but because a velodrome is a great place for youngsters to learn skills under controlled and supervised conditions. If you live anywhere near a track you will no doubt enjoy a visit to watch some competition, take a few laps yourself, and check out the racing program for novice track riders. America's velodromes are located in Kissena, New York; Trexlertown, Pennsylvania; East Point, Georgia; Indianapolis, Indiana; Detroit, Michigan; Northbrook, Illinois; Kenosha, Wisconsin; Milwaukee, Wisconsin; Shakopee, Minnesota; St. Louis, Missouri; San Diego, California; Encino, California; San Jose, California; Carson, California; Portland, Oregon; and Redmond, Washington.

Road racing on multi-geared bikes is the most popular form of cycling competition in America and Europe today. Of the several kinds of road events the most common in the United States is the criterium, a race held on a course that is usually about a mile in circumference. The shortness of the circuit and the fact that it is usually contested on downtown streets makes a criterium the best road event for spectators. The race is easy to get to and competitors come by frequently—Senior men will often ride as many as 50 laps during their events of between 40 and 65 miles. Criterium victory can go to the first rider to cross the line at the end of the last lap, or it can be an event in which there are sprints for points on designated laps throughout the race, with the winner determined by who scores the most points.

As opposed to criteriums, road races are longer, harder, and lonelier. They can be held on a circuit which is ridden several times or on a large loop ridden once, or they can be point-to-point, starting in one town and finishing in another. The distance can exceed 100 miles, and because the riders are out on the road for several hours there is little to attract spectators or sponsors. For this reason and the relative difficulty in organizing an event—marshaling intersections, working with various town governments, providing support vehicles for the riders, etc.—road races have fallen well behind criteriums in popularity among promoters. Most beginning competitors will find that success doesn't come easily in criteriums because of the premium placed on speed and bike handling, while road racing requires lots of conditioning in order to complete the grind and still have something left for the finish.

A road event of a different nature is the time trial. Instead of a mass start, each rider leaves the line at a set interval (usually a minute) and covers the distance alone. A rider can catch and pass another but is not allowed to give or receive assistance of any nature. Once all riders have finished, results are computed and the winner is the person with the lowest time. Time trials can cover any distance or time period, the most popular events in the United States being 10 and 25 miles on an out-and-back course, which helps equalize wind conditions. Time trialing isn't very exciting to watch, but it is the

Road races take riders far into the countryside for distances that can exceed 100 miles through all kinds of terrain.

Beth Heiden concentrates on winning. In 1980 she won the national road and time trial championships and the world road championship in Sallanches, France. In 1979 she was the first woman to ride a 25-mile time trial in less than one hour.

Leader of the pack Connie Carpenter races uphill for another victory. Her first year of serious competition cycling in 1976 saw her win two national championships. In 1976, Connie took the U.S. Road title and went on to the silver medal in road racing in the world championships at San Cristobal, Venezuela. Since then she's earned four national golds and a bronze in the world race.

Sue Novara-Reber holds off Sheila Young-Ochowicz. Sue has won seven consecutive world cycling medals—more than any other U.S. rider, including gold medals in 1975 and 1980. Formerly a sprinter, she's now changing her specialty to the road in preparation for the 1984 Olympics in Los Angeles. Sheila Young-Ochowicz won the sprint title in San Sebastian, Spain, in 1973, making her the first American since 1912 to capture a gold medal in world track cycling competition. She holds a total of five world cycling medals, including three golds. Following a four-year layoff from competitive cycling, Sheila won the sprint championship in Brno, Czechoslovakia, in September 1981.

safest form of racing and thus the ideal event for newcomers to competition.

All these single-day road events are combined to make up cycling's ultimate test, the stage race or tour. Lasting anywhere from two days to two weeks or more, the competition is based on each rider's accumulated time in the individual races (stages), with the lowest total winning. Thus it is possible for a rider to win a stage race without having placed first in any of the daily races. Teamwork plays a big role in this kind of racing, as does constant awareness of the time deficits of all the leading riders. When a break goes up the road, top challengers and their teammates have to weigh the consequences of certain riders' gaining time in relation to their own positions, and respond accordingly.

Often stage races will offer competitions beyond that which determines the overall winner. For example, during the road stages there may be places where hot spot sprints are held. The first riders to cross these lines are awarded points, which accumulate toward a special prize. Then there's the King of the Mountain title for the top climber, decided by points awarded to the first riders reaching designated summits. In addition, an award will be given for the best team, based on lowest overall combined time of the individual riders. Quite often the leaders of the various individual competitions will wear special colored jerseys. These may change hands at the end of each day, depending on point and time totals. The yellow jersey of the Tour de France leader is probably the most coveted piece of clothing in all of sport.

Stage races are the ultimate test of cycling endurance, skill, and strength. While an unknown rider can win a one-day race, coming out of nowhere and never being heard of again, only the best will prevail in a stage race. That's not to say that one-day races are not a good test of talent, but most riders feel that the ultimate accomplishment in road racing is winning a tour. Victory proves a rider's all-round physical and mental ability, that he can do everything and do it well.

And just how does a rider gain this all-round ability? The foundation is laid with a training program, and that's the subject of the next chapter.

10

TRAINING FOR RACING

Training is the way to condition your body and mind to meet the demands of competition. But although there are many different abilities and skills that go into making a complete road racer, there are just two basic kinds of training: long, steady distance (LSD) and intervals. Both are used by athletes in other endurance sports, and even without realizing it you may have been sampling the first technique on your weekend rides.

Long, Steady Distance

LSD requires keeping up a moderately intense workload for an extended period, usually two hours minimum. The effort must be enough to produce a heart rate of about 75 percent of maximum, as discussed in Chapter 3. For most fit riders this means a pulse between 140 and 160 beats per minute. This is not an easy task, especially since the effort needed to maintain this rate must increase during the ride as fatigue sets in.

However, most cyclists enjoy LSD riding. It is almost as simple to do as it sounds, and there is really only one thing which makes it different from recreational riding or touring. That is, you must concentrate on pedal cadence and keep it at race tempo or very close to it to make sure the heart beats at the proper level. Instead of the 70–80 cadence used in touring or when building fitness, the racer on an LSD ride must strive for a consistent 90–95 rpm. Initially this will take some getting used to, and it makes gear selection very important. For example, to achieve a heart rate of 134 beats per minute (70 percent of my maximum) at a cadence of 90 rpm, I find I usually need to roll along in a 42×17. Of course, this is a lower gear and

Long, steady distance (LSD) is important training for increasing cardiovascular capacity and muscular endurance. The key to doing it right is to maintain a consistently high effort for at least two hours, using gears that are low enough and a cadence that is high enough to keep the heart rate at the training-effect level.

workload than what is used in competition. But my legs are spinning at race speed, and this makes them accustomed to the rhythm; the lower resistance allows me to keep it up hour after hour and come back for more the next day. For me and racers I know, gears in the range of 63–72 inches (42×18, 17, or 16) are the best for LSD training.

After you've had some experience with LSD you'll be able to judge your effort level without actually taking your heart rate. (When you need to make a spot check while riding, count the beats for 6 seconds at the carotid artery in the neck, then put a zero after the number to get the rate per minute). In general, if you don't feel as if you want to take a nap after an LSD ride, you probably haven't ridden long enough or at a high enough cadence. On the other hand, if you overdo it you will feel fatigued when you ride the next day.

What does LSD accomplish? It provides just enough stress on your heart and lungs to increase their capacities and develop long-term strength. It builds muscular endurance without much risk of tearing down the body. This means it is possible to ride LSD sessions several days in a row, something that's impossible with the other form of training, intervals. As you continue to put out the same amount of effort, speed will improve and you'll cover more ground in the same amount of time. Your body will process more oxygen more efficiently and become better at using fat as an energy source.

LSD is the groundwork of every training program. It will eventually enable you to ride far enough at a fast enough tempo to stay with the field in a race. But to finish among the leaders you will need more weapons in your arsenal than sheer endurance. When it comes down to it, most races are far from being long, steady distance—they consist of many on-and-off efforts which require a variety of strengths. For example, the pace will be smooth for a few minutes but then a rider attacks. Others accelerate in response and you join the chase. After an all-out effort the guy is caught and things become steady again. But around the next bend is a steep hill, requiring a hard effort of a different type. The way to prepare for this type of riding is with interval training.

Intervals

Interval sessions are shorter than LSD workouts but they are much more stressful. The idea is to simulate the high-speed intensity of racing but to do it in a way that avoids driving the body and mind into long-lasting fatigue. Before adding intervals to the training program, a beginning racer should accumulate at least 1,000 miles of riding at an LSD pace. Then no more than one interval session should be done each week for the first month, after which a second can be included. It is best to allow at least two days of steady, recovery riding between interval workouts. If you enter a race, be sure to count that as an interval session in your weekly training schedule.

A common interval workout is to warm up well, select a moderately high gear, and go at about 95 percent of maximum for 1 minute, change to a low gear and roll along easily for 1 minute, gear up and go hard again for 1 minute, and so on for a total of ten repetitions. The key is to ride at the same speed during each "on" minute. The first few will seem relatively easy, but the last few will make up for it. You should strive for the same amount of work each time, and this means your effort will hit 100 percent of maximum as you get tired. After the ten repetitions you should ride along at a moderate pace for 15–20 minutes to help muscles flush out waste products. Advanced riders will then do another set. But if this workout seems too difficult, you can either reduce the number of repetitions until your strength develops or allow more recovery time between "on" segments. Some riders like to use their heart rate as the green light for when to go again, waiting until it falls below 120 beats per minute. Just remember to keep pedaling during the recovery period to promote blood circulation and simulate the race situation.

Interval training is the way to prepare for the intense, anaerobic demands of racing. Only by conditioning the body and mind to perform beyond the boundary where pain begins can a rider be a successful competitor.

There are many variations to interval training, depending on the length of the effort, the time for recovery, and the number of repetitions. You might go hard for 2 minutes and then recover for 10, repeating this sequence only three or four times. In general, the longer the work period, the fewer repetitions and sets are done. A wholly different approach is to do random intervals patterned after the *fartlek* (Swedish for "speed play") workouts that runners do. This technique calls for a wide variety of pace changes—sprint up a hill, go slow through a school zone, time trial for 2 miles, accelerate to catch an unsuspecting tourist and then ride easily with him for a mile, etc. This type of speed work avoids the regimentation of timed intervals and it can work well if you have the self-discipline to put out enough effort.

A technique I often use to uplift my base of conditioning is to ride intervals using two gears, one considerably lower than the other. For example, I will alternate "on" periods between a 53×15 and a 53×18. This is difficult because in the 15 I have to push really hard. Then, after the short recovery, I have to pedal very fast in the 18. By the end of ten repetitions it's the 53×18 which seems toughest.

Intervals are hard, and most riders hate them. The worst part is thinking about it, knowing it's going to hurt. But you'll probably find, as I do, that once past the first two or three they're not so bad, and after they've all been done it feels good. There's no other workout that can provide the same sense of accomplishment.

The Combined Program

A training program must combine intervals, LSD, and days restricted to shorter riding for the purpose of recovery. A good weekly program for a beginning racer will have one interval session, one LSD ride of about three hours, and four rides which could include some hill climbing, jumps, high-cadence work in low gears, and group riding to work on bike-handling skills, but there must be plenty of easy spinning. Take one day a week off for recovery and use it to do bike maintenance.

As time goes by, the amount of training you need will depend on your goals and competition. If your ambition is to ride low-key club races or Senior III-IV sanctioned events, you can do fine by maintaining a riding program of 60–90 minutes each weekday with a longer ride on the weekend. Midgets, Intermediates, and Veterans can also do well on that amount of training. But if you are an aspiring Junior or have your sights set on being competitive in upper-category Senior races, it will take a minimum of two to three hours of training each day.

The adjoining table lists weekly schedules for ambitious men and women racers over age 16 in the early, middle, and late season. The general training guidelines are basically the same throughout the season and from year to year. What will change is the amount of work accomplished during training rides—how fast and how far you go. These tables are not recommended for riders under 16 because their bodies are not ready for this much stress. Younger riders should shorten the distances and leave out the intervals. Sprints, jumps, and racing itself will provide them with enough variety and high-cadence work.

In Chapter 2 there is advice on how to fit training into a busy daily schedule. But if you simply don't have the time to follow the program outlined in these tables, you will have to cut some corners. Realize, though, that you must compensate for the quantity you are missing by making sure every workout is of high quality. Once you have your LSD base, you should add an extra interval session, since intervals do the most to increase strength and the workouts are relatively short. You will also have to adjust your competitive goals, since training that emphasizes speed at the expense of endurance is more in line with the requirements of criteriums and time trials, not road races.

All athletic training is based on the principle that a body grows stronger in response to stress. Of course, you can't tear yourself down completely and hope to benefit, but neither can you expect much improvement if you don't occasionally push yourself to new limits. Each training ride, whether it is done hard or simply for getting the kinks out, has to contribute toward the goal of better performance.

Weekly training schedules for beginning racers over age 16
(Younger riders reduce distances by about 20% and omit intervals)

	Monday	Tuesday	Wednesday
Late-season maintenance of fitness	30–35 mi LSD or 1½–2 hr.[1] Strive to keep a 70–75% training-effect heart rate.	20–25 mi LSD or 1½ hr. Recovery day of easy spinning in low gears.	40–45 mi LSD or 2–2½ hr. Begin ride at 60% of training-effect heart rate.
Main racing season	30–35 mi LSD or 1½–2 hr. Spin low gears if race was Sunday. Work at closer to 75% of training-effect heart rate if race was Saturday.	Intervals.[2] Vary weekly sessions by using timed repeats, *fartlek*, time trial simulations, hill work, etc. Spin 10 mi before hard work; 5 mi after.	30–35 mi LSD or 1½–2 hr. Recovery day of spinning low gears at 60–65% of training-effect heart rate.
Early-season buildup	20–25 mi LSD or 1½ hr. Depending on extent of weekend effort, spin easily in low gears to recover, or push at 75% of training-effect heart rate.	30–35 mi LSD or 1½–2 hr. Spin comfortably early and late. Include some *fartlek*-type work during mid-ride, such as time-trialing or hill climbing.	20–25 mi LSD or 1½ hr. Recovery day of spinning at 60–65% of training-effect heart rate.

[1] Daily mileage goals are proportional. During first weeks you can ride less; later you will ride more. Strive for an 8–10% mileage increase each week.
[2] Begin including intervals about four weeks before first race. Club practice races and short time trials should be counted as an interval workout.

Thursday	Friday	Saturday	Sunday
30–35 mi LSD or 1½–2 hr. Strive to keep a 70–75% train-ing-effect heart rate.	Rest day. Do bike mainte-nance and pre-pare for big ride of week. Short ride, if de-sired.	50–60 mi LSD or 2½–3 hr. Begin ride at 60% of training-ef-fect heart rate. Pedal continuously (no stops or coasting).	40–45 mi LSD or 2½–3 hr. Recovery day of easy spinning in low gears.
60–75 mi LSD or 3 hr. Begin ride at 65–70% of training-effect heart rate. Pedal continuously (no stops or coasting).	Rest day. Prepare bike for weekend compe-tition. Take a short spin to loosen legs and test bike.	Race one day each weekend or do an in-terval-type workout that simulates competitive riding (best if done with others). On the other day concentrate on spend-ing time on the bike (2–3 hrs) but with the goal of spinning, either to en-hance preparation or to recover from the hard day.	
60–75 mi LSD or 3 hr. Begin ride at 60–65% of training-effect heart rate. Pedal contin-uously.	Rest day. Do bike mainte-nance and pre-pare for long weekend ride or race. Short ride, if de-sired.	Race one day or do a long ride possibly a one-day or overnight trip to explore other aspects of cycling. If racing, use the other day to spin eas-ily for an hour to stay loose for the event or recover after it.	

But just as important as stress is rest. Whether it's a good night's sleep or a nap before or after the workout, successful training depends in large part on feeling that you're ready to go. Just as too much work can produce the symptoms of overtraining, so can the proper amount if there is no consideration given to recovery. Instead of building you up, the physical effort will bring about deep fatigue.

Listen to Your Body

A rider in training must pay attention to the messages the body is sending. For example, during periods when workouts are intense you wouldn't expect any trouble in falling asleep, but sometimes the opposite is true. You can literally be too tired to sleep, and when this happens it's a clear sign that you are overdoing it. Otherwise, be aware of the difference between being tired and being lazy. Sometimes you can talk yourself into an unscheduled day off because you feel a little beat. The best thing is to go ahead and ride. If you're truly tired you will know it within a few miles and you can make the session short and easy. But some of my strongest rides have come when I almost didn't go.

If you find that you are not recovering you should skip the next interval workout. But if you get to the point where you're canceling almost all intervals, then it's time to cut back on the LSD. Even though long, steady distance doesn't feel very hard on the body, it can be. Without realizing it you could be reaching 90 percent of maximum heart rate by the end of LSD rides. If so, it's time to reduce both the distance and effort until your body has regrouped. There have been days when I've found myself in my climbing gear—42×20, or 56 inches—on perfectly flat roads and still been struggling to pedal. When I realize I'm that tired I ride less than two hours and get back home.

This brings up an important point. Despite all the recent developments in sports medicine and exercise physiology, athletic training is just as much art as science. Since most amateur athletes don't have access to jock docs, clinics, or even a coach, you must learn to understand your own body and what it needs. This takes constant awareness and a good deal of experience, of course, but the process can be helped along if you pay attention to a few medical signposts used to assess the effects of training.

One of the most obvious is body weight. Unless you are thin to begin with, your weight will decline as you become more physically fit. Afterward, any big drop is a sign that you are burning many more calories than you are consuming and you must modify training or diet or both. If no corrective action is taken, you'll enter a state of weakness that will negate all the training you've done.

Heart rate is another tip-off. Basically, the lower the resting rate the fitter you are, but heredity plays a part in how low low is. That is, some individuals may never have a resting rate below 60 beats per minute no matter how much they train; others may get down into the 30s. Also, the more fit a person is, the lower the maximum heart rate will be. During strenuous exercise an unconditioned heart can race up to a dangerous 200 beats per minute, but fit athletes rarely have maximums over 180. Their hearts do more work by having a greater stroke volume, not by beating faster.

As a barometer of his riders' daily condition, USCF national coaching director Eddie Borysewicz has them take their pulse twice each morning—once when they wake up and again as soon as they get out of bed. The difference between the two rates should be 10 to 20 beats per minute if everything is going well. In my own case, on a day when I'm fully rested I usually have a pulse of 44 when I'm lying down and 60 when I stand up. Should my second reading be 70 or 80, this tells me I haven't recovered from the previous day's workout, even though I might not feel particularly tired. After you've been training for a while you may be able to dispense with this two-pulse method and use the in-bed heart rate. You can be quite certain that you're not getting enough recovery time if you wake up and find that your resting pulse is significantly higher than normal. If mine is at 50 or even 60 I don't worry too much, but if it gets higher than that I know I have to take it easy.

Once you become sensitive to your body's signals, the way you feel after a few miles on the bike is perhaps the best indicator. You might think you are quite tired and then be surprised that you've got good strength. On the other hand, you might feel fine but discover that the energy just isn't there. Eddy Merckx himself experienced these puzzling ups and downs during the career which made him one of the greatest racing cyclists of all time. The Belgian's advice was to go by how your body feels and not by some preconceived schedule. That is, if you have planned a long or hard workout but the first miles are a real labor, put it in a low gear and spin back home. Save the tough riding for days when the strength is there. But don't fool yourself into mistaking laziness for tiredness.

A training diary is the best way to keep track of your progress as well as your mistakes. Make daily entries of your weight and pulse, and describe your workout and miles ridden. Note how you felt and put down anything unusual that may have a bearing on your recovery, such as loss of sleep for some reason, missed meals, unusual stress at work, etc. Such things can cause problems down the line, and it's important to be able to pinpoint outside reasons for poor performance when you might otherwise fault your training routine. Also note any changes you make to your riding position, alterations in the bike's equipment, etc. This may help you find the cause of, say, a sore knee that develops several weeks after making a minor adjustment that would otherwise be forgotten. In general, the diary should be used to record anything that can have a bearing on riding performance, and this includes racing activity. As each new season begins, you will be able to refer to your diaries from past years and duplicate training that works for you while avoiding that which experience has shown is of little benefit.

Be Honest with Yourself

In order to be a complete racer you must beware of the temptation to neglect the types of training you don't like. It's human nature to think of excuses for avoiding anything that doesn't feel natural or comfortable. But if you always work on your strengths and not on your weaknesses you will become a very lopsided rider. No matter how strong you are in certain areas, racing will amplify your shortcomings—they will show up very quickly when you compete against other riders.

If you are the caboose whenever the pack finishes the race, you'd better get to work on your sprint. If other riders can accelerate away from you like dragsters leaving the line, then it's time to start improving your jump. Not being able to time trial is another serious weakness. All these things are put to the test in competition. Racing will quickly let you know just which areas you're falling short in. Then it's up to you to do the work that brings improvement.

When I started racing I was doing a lot of interval training but not much LSD. The result was that I couldn't last the distance in Senior I-II road races. I'd be all right up to 80 miles, but then it was time to lock up and go home. I corrected this problem by altering my training, but another problem area, sprinting, has been harder to remedy. I'm not a natural sprinter, which is a daring rider with an inborn physical ability for spontaneous reaction and acceleration. In fact, it's very hard for most riders to let themselves release every bit of their power to the pedals. The feeling verges on loss of control, and the instinct for self-preservation makes it easy to hold back. But I began practicing sprinting, and since one of the scariest parts is moving the bike all over the road, I would ride from one side to the other three or four times in 200 meters, making very abrupt changes of direction while still trying to put all my force into the pedals. Sprinting got a lot easier for me after that and my results improved. I became more spontaneous and my fear of losing control subsided. Now I really enjoy being in a sprint.

Another example of a rider who overcame his weaknesses is two-time national road champion Dale Stetina. Sickly as a child, with sinus problems and asthma, Stetina is physically no superman. Most of his good early results came from trying hard and using the skills he did have to maximum advantage. For a long time he lacked the strength to push big gears, and so he concentrated on learning to spin really well. In this way he was able to pedal fast enough to stay with the stronger riders. He also continued to develop his other skills, such as climbing, and the day finally arrived when he proved to be one of the country's most complete riders.

Dale Stetina is the kind of competitor I spoke of in the previous chapter—his success is not just physical but mental. He has the most determination of any rider I've ever known. He can be in a race where physically he is not even in the top ten, but he'll be right up there because he wants to be and he's willing to put out the effort it takes. He has built a reputation for his climbing ability, but a lot of times when we are going over the top he's the guy who is suffering the most. Like anyone else, he has moments when he's really going great, but they're not that frequent. Usually he succeeds because he wants to so badly.

Winter Cycling

If you live in one of the Sun Belt states you're in heaven as far as cycling is concerned. The climate will let you ride all year round, something most northerners find impossible because of the frigid temperatures and icy roads of winter. Even so, I believe that cyclists can benefit by turning to other activities during the traditional off-season from December through February. And that goes for riders in Arizona as well as Vermont.

There are two main benefits to hanging up the bike for a while or at least reducing the frequency and length of rides. One has to do with human nature. A period of reduced activity gives us mental refreshment, a chance to reflect on what we've accomplished and then look forward to the beginning of the new season. Without a break there is the danger that cycling will become part of the humdrum routine that encompasses so much else in life. Second, the hours that would be spent on the bike can be used instead for participating in other sports. Not only does this add variety, but some activities can even improve next season's cycling by contributing to cardiovascular fitness and muscular strength.

Running, cross-country skiing, and speedskating are used by bike racers in the off-season, and they are also excellent complementary sports for the touring cyclist and those who ride for physical conditioning.

While running doesn't do much for the muscles used in pedaling a bike, it is a great way to maintain and even improve the internal fitness gained by a season of cycling. However, if you choose running (or a sport that involves running) as your primary winter activity, it should be worked into your program gradually. Begin to run while you are still using the bike so that you can alternate the activities—

run one day, ride the next, run again, and so on. This will help minimize the muscle and joint soreness that invariably comes when a cyclist's legs begin receiving the unaccustomed forces; it is estimated that when running you land with three times your body weight on each foot. Stretching exercises are also important, especially those for the calf muscles.

Cross-country skiing and speedskating don't require nearly as much break-in time as running and they have perhaps the best transfer of any sports to cycling. Each is a wonderful cardiovascular conditioner and each contributes to strength in the same thigh muscles used to propel a bike, the quadriceps. In fact, many top cross-country skiers—Bill Koch, the 1976 Olympic silver medalist, is one—use cycling in their off-season training, and two world champion speedskaters—Sheila Young and Beth Heiden—have gone on to win world titles in bike racing. However, there are drawbacks to each of these winter sports: You will need quite a bit of skill in order to perform either one well enough to give yourself physical benefit, and there must be good snow conditions or an available ice rink. Another strike against skating is the boredom inherent in doing laps; the adventure in a day of cross-country skiing makes it the more enjoyable sport. Another benefit is the upper-body strength that a winter of skiing will develop.

What are some other good choices? Swimming, racquetball, handball, soccer, basketball—these sports and any others that you enjoy and that will drive your heart rate to the 60–75 percent of maximum which produces the training effect. A weight-training program is also beneficial, but don't expect it to contribute to all-important cardiovascular fitness. Your heart rate might approach the necessary level if you use a circuit training program in which 15–20 repetitions are done with light weights and there is no resting between exercises. But the principal goal of weight training should be the development of total-body strength and stamina so that the rigors of cycling can be handled more easily.

Of course, everyone who really enjoys cycling won't want to go cold turkey for too long. That's no problem for Sun Belt riders, and even up north it is possible to take mid-winter rides when an occasional thaw comes along. But there are other ways to stay in touch

Track cyclists, such as these members of Venezuela's 1979 Pan-Am team, frequently use rollers to warm up before an event. For many years roller riding has also been part of winter training for cyclists who live where weather conditions prohibit riding outside. But while rollers are useful for teaching balance and smooth pedaling, they don't provide enough rolling resistance to make them a very good substitute for actual road riding. This has resulted in the invention of devices such as the Racer-Mate (*see photograph on page 168*).

with the feel of cycling, and you can do it right in the house at any time, no matter how loudly the blizzard is raging outside.

The traditional method has been to use rollers. There are many different brands, but all work the same, having a drive belt that spins the front cylinder as the other two are turned by the bike's rear wheel. Riding rollers is a fine way to develop smooth pedal action and balance, and although your first attempts may result in some wild crashes it won't be long before you can stand up and even ride with no hands. However, as times goes by you'll realize some basic limitations to roller riding: boredom, the lack of enough resistance to stress muscles, lungs, and the cardiovascular system suitably, and insufficient carryover to actual road riding.

Boredom can be overcome to some extent by listening to the stereo or watching television—anything to take the mind off how slowly the minutes seem to pass. You'll have to turn up the sound, because rollers send out quite a rumble (although some new models are advertised as being almost silent), and it is a must to have a fan humming away. Riding in a closed room will have you sweating profusely within 15 minutes, so you'll need to protect the floor under you and also wipe down the bike after each session. During your first riding sessions it is helpful to set the rollers in a doorway, and even after you've become confident in your ability it's good to have a wall within arm's reach. If you do come off, the bike won't go zipping across the room; the wheels will stop spinning instantly and you'll simply tumble to the side. But keep furniture out of the way, and children and pets, too.

An hour is a long time on rollers, and I don't see any benefits to be gained by riding them more than three times a week. Some riders increase their sessions in final preparation for getting back out on the road, but rollers simply can't equal the resistance to pedaling that real cycling provides. Fred Matheny addresses this problem when he says, "Cyclists have tried to compensate for the relatively low rolling resistance of rollers by using big gears, riding on half-inflated clinchers, or cleverly folding a towel under the rear roller. At best these tricks add some resistance, but this resistance does not increase as speed increases as it does on the road. Exercise gained from rollers, no matter how cleverly modified, is not specifically related to road conditions and therefore does not translate effectively to actual riding."

Until recently the only way to ride indoors and really improve pedaling strength and cardiovascular fitness was to use an ergometer. This bicyclelike device is often seen in physiology labs, where it is used for precise testing of work output. A handwheel lets a rider easily adjust the friction band and vary resistance from a free spin to a steep uphill. Ed Burke judges the ergometers made by Monark and Schwinn to be tough enough for serious long-term use, but he notes two drawbacks: Each has to be modified (saddle, handlebars, and pedals) before a rider can achieve the same riding position as on a bicycle, and they cost in the neighborhood of $400.

So it comes to this: Rollers don't provide the necessary physical benefits, and for many an ergometer is too expensive. Invented recently to solve this dilemma was the Racer-Mate, an indoor training device which has earned the praise of many riders, including Matheny, who has used his through the long Colorado winter. Burke has conducted a laboratory test with cyclists at Ohio State in which the Racer-Mate was proved to give ergometer-like benefits. Training-effect data showed that using the device was significantly superior to riding rollers in the same gear combinations.

The Racer-Mate, dubbed a "wind load simulator," consists of a fan-wheel assembly that attaches to your bike's seat post and rides on top of the rear tire. The tire drives two small wheels with curved fan blades, which draw air in and disperse it radially, thus providing wind resistance as well as a cooling breeze. The acceleration of air mass creates a torque on the fan wheels that increases exponentially with speed, just as the wind resistance does when you ride on the road. Once the fan-wheel unit is mounted, the bike can then be ridden on rollers or, with the front wheel removed, on the optional Racer-Mate stand. In either case resistance is adjustable by changing

The Racer-Mate was the first of several new, similarly designed home training devices that provide nearly the same feel and benefits as road riding. The two fan wheels catch air and produce a resistance that increases with the speed of the bike's rear wheel. Riders who already have rollers can train on them using just the fan wheel assembly instead of the whole unit with its stand.

gears and it automatically increases with pedal speed, thus giving the benefits and sensation of actual road riding.

Matheny notes that the Racer-Mate can be used for almost any type of strength- and fitness-building workout, although "it did nothing to alleviate the boredom of attempts to simulate long road rides indoors, but that fault is inherent in the situation, not the device." Since the Racer-Mate is easily attached to the bike in about a minute, it has potential beyond wintertime use, especially for those facing tight weekday schedules. Fred suggests, "It can be used during the season by riders who can get on the road several times a week but are stymied on other days because their jobs or other responsibilities take up the daylight hours. The Racer-Mate can be used year-round to maintain or even improve fitness gained in regular riding."

The price of this invention has risen steadily since its introduction, with the 1982 tags reading $159.95 for the complete unit including stand and $79.95 for just the fan-wheel assembly for use with rollers. The Racer-Mate is available through bike shops or by ordering directly from the company (Racer-Mate Inc., 3016-C NE Blakely St., Seattle, WA 98105).

11

TIME TRIALING

I'll never forget the first bike race I entered. I was so nervous. It was a mass-start event and I was afraid I'd be dropped at the starting line because I wouldn't be able to get my feet into the toe clips. All the other cyclists seemed like gods to me because they went so fast. I couldn't imagine that I was ever going to be able to ride like that.

Anxiety is natural for every rider before a race, so remember this when that sinking feeling hits as you line up for your first event. And realize that if you have done your training properly and are mentally committed to giving a total effort, the chances are excellent that you will be able to hold your own. The other riders are human, not superhuman. Even in the early moments of your first race you will start gaining the self-confidence that comes with putting yourself to the test and meeting the challenge.

Still not convinced? Would you like to get a taste of racing without plugging yourself into a swarming pack of riders? There is a way to do it and at the same time reduce the apprehension that will surround your first mass-start event. It is to ride time trials, and I heartily recommend this as a first step into competition. Since you will be riding alone against the clock, there is almost no danger of crashing and yet you will be able to race as hard as you can. Then, by comparing your times with those of riders who compete in your USCF class or category, you will know when you are really ready to enter mass-start racing. Once you are, your experience in time trials will help you be more at ease and self-assured in that first criterium or road race.

Many club time trials are not USCF-sanctioned, and this allows license-free participation by riders of all abilities. I've seen kids in sneakers on 3-speed bikes riding the same event as 10-speed hotshots in full racing garb. If there are no time trials in your area, a bike shop or club can easily start a weekly series. At the end of the chapter I'll describe how, but basically all it takes is a measured stretch of road and a person with a watch, pencil, and paper. Everything is simplified if the competitors ride out to a certain point, turn around, and finish at the starting line, and this equalizes windy conditions.

The time trial is called the race of truth because performance is determined solely by ability, not by the multitude of things that play a part in the outcome of a mass-start race. Riders commonly start at 1-minute intervals, and rules prohibit drafting or assistance of any kind when passing or being passed. But there is a helping hand, psychologically speaking, in knowing someone is a minute ahead. Like the mechanical rabbit that inspires a greyhound at a dog track, the minuteman gives you something to continually strive for. Aside from that, you're on your own. The only tactic is to pace yourself to ride as fast as you can for the distance.

Time trials can be of any length, but club events are usually 5 to 10 miles, a distance that riders of all ages and abilities can handle. In

Time trialing is racing alone against time and is a way for new riders to test their abilities and experience a sense of accomplishment. This is former national time trial champion Andy Weaver.

sanctioned racing, 25 miles is the standard—this is the USCF championship distance for individual road riders. In addition, the Olympics and U.S. and world championships feature two very different time trials. One is the 1,000-meter event on the track, which takes just over a minute to ride. The other is a road event, the 100-kilometer four-man team time trial, which lasts about two hours.

Just because time trials are simple to explain and straightforward to ride doesn't mean they are easy. Pierre Trentin fainted at the end of his winning 1,000-meter time trial in the Mexico City Olympics. And I remember one of the Soviet team time trialists passing out on the victory stand at the Olympics in Montreal. But although time trials hurt a lot when they are being ridden, they can be very satisfying afterward because of the sense of achievement they provide. You don't have to be somebody who can win the national championship in order to feel this satisfaction, because winning is not the only reward in time trialing. In fact, winning is very subjective. You actually score a victory every time you surpass your previous best effort; the main goal in time trialing is personal improvement.

It's a fact, though, that some racers just hate the event. The reason, I think, is that they don't like concentration. But anyone who is serious about road racing must be able to time trial well—it is an essential skill in mass-start events. For example, if you are attempting to break away, bridge the gap from one group to another, or catch back up after a puncture, you will need to solo at top speed for several minutes. That's exactly what time trialing is. And in stage racing, where often a dozen riders will be given the same time in bunch finishes at the end of road race stages, it is the time trial stages which will either boost or pull down an individual in the overall standings. So if you want to be a good racer you really don't have much choice but to be a good time trialist.

Time trialing is my specialty. I won a gold medal in the team time trial at the 1979 Pan-American Games, and in 1980 the Stetina brothers (Wayne, Dale, and Joel) and I took the first USCF team time trial championship. That same year I lowered the national record when I won the 25-mile Senior men's time trial championship in 52 minutes, 25.9 seconds. In my experiences I've found a few things to pass along which will help you improve your time trialing. Important are warming up properly, getting a good start, establishing a rhythm, passing and turning correctly, and finishing with strength.

Warming Up

In any kind of racing it is essential to be able to make a maximum effort right from the start. This makes a good warm-up extremely important. It should elevate your blood circulation and respiration, loosen muscles, and in general get the body and mind ready for the work that is about to come.

Your experiences in training will indicate how long it takes you to feel supple, relaxed, and thoroughly ready for hard riding. In general, the shorter the race the more important it is to warm up completely. It also depends on how you feel. If you're fresh you can usually get by with a short warm-up, but the more fatigued you are the harder you should ride before the race. The reason for this is partly psychological—when you're tired you don't feel you can go fast. But if you warm up fully and put in some big-gear bursts, you may find the groove where you can perform well.

Before a time trial of 25 miles or less I like to warm up for almost an hour. The procedure starts with a little stretching and then some easy spinning to loosen up. Next move into higher gears and do some jumps to get leg speed going. At about 15 minutes before your start, begin calming down by rolling around easily. Don't get off the bike and sit down, because this would negate most of the benefits of warming up.

The Start

As you complete the warm-up, put your bike into the gear you will use for the start. On a flat course this should be about two shifts away from the gear you plan to ride the race in. Roll up to the line immediately after your minuteman has departed and let the holder get control of your bike. Then reach down and make sure your feet are correctly positioned and your toe straps are snug.

The timer will let you know how many seconds remain until your start. As you sit there try to relax. With 30 seconds to go, take a couple of deep breaths. At 15 you should have a good grip on the drops of the bars and your right crank arm should be at the two-o'clock position, ready to receive the first thrust. The timer will begin the countdown with 5 seconds to go, and at "three" you should rise out of the saddle and hold yourself tensed and ready. As soon as you hear "one," start forward. Stay out of the saddle until you get to the point where you can't pedal any faster in your starting gear. Sit down and shift, then get out of the saddle and accelerate again. What you are trying to do is achieve a faster speed than you actually plan to maintain. Why? Because when you sit down for the final time you will automatically slow down a little.

When you are in the saddle for good and pedaling at race tempo you must start concentrating. Breath deeply from the diaphragm and keep a low position with your hands on the drops, but look out from under your eyebrows regularly to check for anything dangerous on the road ahead. Don't tell yourself to go easy at the beginning so you can go hard at the end. Instead, try to determine quickly the fastest speed you can maintain for the whole distance and what you need to do to achieve it. This will depend on your physical strength, the gear you are using, and the cadence at which you are turning it. You must constantly monitor and control all three of these factors in order to produce your best effort.

After I sit down the final time I'll sometimes shift immediately into the biggest gear I think I can use. The excitement of the race usually helps me push this ratio for a while before I start feeling that I'm bogging down. As soon as I notice that my muscle power isn't giving me the speed it was, I shift quickly to the next-lower gear.

Since you are not allowed to draft or pace other riders in a time trial you must immediately pass anyone you catch. USCF rules stipulate that when you draw within 25 meters (80 feet) of someone you have to move 2 meters (7 feet) to the side and make the pass with that much room to spare. After passing, keep your line instead of pulling back over, which would force the other rider to alter course or be in violation of the no-draft rule. You should pass people quickly and decisively; if you dangle on a rider's flank and he notices you, he'll probably start picking up the pace and you might never get by.

An individual time trial is a simple, safe event, the main tactic being to parcel out your strength so that you have used every bit of it when you reach the finish. At both the start and turnaround, get out of the saddle after each shift to build speed quickly, then settle into the strongest tempo you can sustain for the distance.

Handling Hills

If the course is flat, the only times you must get out of the saddle are during the start and the turnaround, though sometimes it helps to stand up for ten pedal strokes midway through each leg to stretch muscles. But on hilly courses it will be necessary to get out of the saddle frequently to maintain tempo. On short, rolling hills it is often enough to stand up and sprint over the top without shifting. When approaching a climb that is steeper or longer, stay in your gear and stand up as you roll into it. When your cadence begins to drop, sit down, shift, stand up and sprint. The purpose of the sprint after shifting is to regain momentum. If you change to a lower gear and don't make any extra effort, you will slow down considerably.

The Turnaround

As discussed in Chapter 5, the ability to ride in a straight line is a skill that takes some work to master. It is very important in time trialing because pushing big gears can cause a wavering path and the loss of precious seconds. Other than this, about the only bike handling required in a time trial comes at the 180-degree turn at the halfway point. Use your cornering skills and move to the far right of the road to set up for the widest possible arc around the pylon or person in the center of the road. If the course is open to traffic, the turnaround point may be just a mark on the pavement with perhaps an official standing nearby to check your number, call out your time, and help you watch for cars. Don't forget to look behind you before swinging across the road.

Just before the turn is a good place to take a breather. First, shift to the gear you will need coming back out. If you have been riding in your 13 or 14 cog, for example, you should probably shift up to the 16. Then coast or pedal easily a few seconds, slowing to a speed at which you can negotiate the turn. Concentrate on your line around the marker and put weight on the outside pedal. Coming out of the turn is like starting the race all over again. Get off the saddle, spin it out, sit down, shift, stand up again, and go on accelerating until you have regained the rhythm and speed that you had before.

The Finish

The last half of a time trial is the easiest place to make up ground on other competitors, because their concentration and energy will be faltering. This is the point where you'll start seeing riders ahead of you like ducks at a shooting gallery. Get aggressive. If you have confidence in your training and ability, you can gradually pick up the pace and advance several notches in the final standings.

The reason you shouldn't try to save energy in the beginning to use in the final miles is that you'll usually have something left anyway. Employ that strength now. You've had the door four-fifths of the way open for the bulk of the ride, so with about 5 miles left, go ahead and throw it open all the way. Then in the last mile take it right off the hinges.

In the ideal time trial—the very best one you could ever ride—you would cross the finish line at maximum speed and not be able to pedal one stroke more. Of course that doesn't happen, but when you can reach the finish and honestly feel that you couldn't have gone any faster, you have ridden a good race. So during the last minutes you should gradually pick up the pace and enter the final mile throwing caution to the wind, giving it all you've got and hoping to make it to the end. If you blow up you can always soft-pedal the last

100 meters, but my experience has proved to me that it is always possible to make it—you always have a little bit more if you dig down after it. Remember that many times only a handful of seconds will separate you from another rider. The effort you can produce when you seem to have absolutely nothing left can make all the difference.

Cool-down

A time trial ridden right is a very hard effort. It will leave your leg muscles swollen with blood, and this can produce soreness and stiffness for several days if you don't go through a cool-down. Basically, this means to keep riding so that circulation is maintained. After crossing the line, shift into a low gear and spin easily for about 15 minutes. There's not much else to do after a time trial anyway—usually all the riders must be in before officials will compute and post the results. When you do get off the bike, cover your legs right away to keep them warm. You'll feel a lot better the next day and recovery won't take as long.

All the foregoing was written with a 25-mile time trial in mind (the USCF championship distance). But the concepts are the same for other distances—changes in length only change the rhythm of your ride. For example, if the race is shorter you can increase your physical output, starting stronger and using a bigger gear for the bulk of the ride. Since you're not riding as far, you can pedal with more intensity. In longer time trials you have to portion your strength and speed over the additional miles. But whatever the distance, the goal is still the same—to use up 99 percent of yourself by the time you reach the final mile.

Team Time Trials

Team time trialing is perhaps the best way to learn basic bike-racing skills, combining as it does the intensity of the individual time trial with the precision required when working with others. It requires riding just inches away from another wheel, staying steady when bumping other riders, and a constant awareness of how they are holding up under the effort—all necessary in mass-start racing.

Teams consist of two or more riders, and as one takes a turn pulling hard in front, the others get a brief rest in the slipstream. This sharing of the workload produces a faster average speed than in individual time trialing even though race distances are usually much greater. The standard in championship competition is 100 kilometers (62 miles), and it is usually ridden in just over two hours by the best four-man teams.

Form is very important in the team time trial. The better the riders blend together, the faster they can go. It works like this: After taking his pull, the front rider swings off just enough so the person behind doesn't have to alter course in order to pass by. He decreases speed slightly and begins to drop back, all the while staying as close to everyone as possible—the closer together the riders are, the more windbreak for all. When it's being done right, riders will frequently brush hands or shoulders as they pass each other. The new rider in the lead takes his thirty pedal strokes (that'll cover about 200 meters) and then moves over to let the next person come through. It's not possible to stay in front much longer than that because speed will begin to drop. The rider in second position is the speedometer—he must tell the leader if the pace is too slow or too fast. Any changes in speed must be made smoothly to prevent disruption of pedaling rhythm, gaps between riders, and wasted energy.

As you can imagine, a lot of practice is needed in order to have a smooth-working group. Teammates also have to study each other's pedaling style in order to know how close to ride and be able to spot signs of fatigue. Finally, there must be some chatter; each rider must keep others aware of how he is feeling as the race progresses. It all means that there are a great many things to attend to in team time trialing, but the rewards are multiplied, too. There's a wonderful satisfaction in working with others to reach both a common goal and a higher level of performance than any rider can achieve alone.

How to Organize a Time Trial

It's a great advantage to be able to ride in a time trial series. For one thing, it will tell you if your training program is working—when you add intervals to your program you should see your times go down as the hard work helps you build strength. Regular time trialing will also reveal shortcomings in your mental makeup and condition you to produce sustained solo efforts. Finally, a weekly event serves as a good speed workout. You will exert yourself more than when training alone, thanks to the competitive situation.

If there is no regular time trialing in your area, a single event or series can easily be organized. Often something will develop informally when a few cyclists agree to meet once a week to ride a given course. Pretty soon others hear about it and join in, and before long the event is a local institution. The people who participate regularly take turns helping with the timing, or nonriding friends or spouses pitch in. Sometimes a local bike shop gets involved and provides some manpower.

The most important element for any time trial is a safe course. Although time trialing first became popular in England as to way to have bike races on public highways, a closed course is always best. It doesn't have to be out to a turn and back again; a loop course is fine as long as the riders can be accounted for. Before opting for the open highway, look for a place where traffic is limited or prohibited, such as public parks, industrial parks after work hours, or even an old airstrip. If you can't find a closed course, try for one where you can marshal the traffic—that is, post people at each end to slow down cars or even stop them briefly while a rider is starting, turning, or finishing. Try to get your community officials to recognize the event and perhaps a police officer will be assigned to the start-finish area. And speaking of police, don't ever plan a race on public roads without letting them know about it. Some states have rules against racing on the highways, but often a time trial will be permitted because it doesn't produce a large group of riders that will clog the traffic lane.

It's best if the course has no intersections or right-angle turns— places which can produce dangerous confrontations between drivers and riders. Ideally, the road should be flat or slightly rolling and have a good surface with a wide shoulder. The turnaround should be in an area where there is good visibility fore and aft. Five to 10 miles is a good distance for a weekly event; some clubs throw in a 25-miler once a month.

It's certainly possible for a time trial to be run by one official

Sample Time Trial Start Sheet				
Rider name	Start time	Finish	Elapsed time	Rank
J. Brown	1:00	39:43	38:43	5
T. Green	2:00	33:09	31:09	1
R. Yellow	3:00	36:21	33:21	2
D. Blue	4:00	41:19	37:19	4
F. Red	5:00	38:50	33:50	3

armed with a watch, pencil, and paper. But it's better to use two watches—one as a backup—and two to four officials. Make up a start sheet along the lines of the one shown here. If the officials don't know everyone by sight it's helpful to have cloth numbers pinned to the riders' right shoulders.

The officials should start the watches 1 minute before they want the first rider to leave the line. There needs to be one person acting as timekeeper and another as recorder; the latter can double as holder for the start if no riders will be finishing until all have started. Otherwise, a different person will need to serve as holder. As the first minute ticks off, the timekeeper gives the countdown to send the first rider off, and then does the same on each minute for the succeeding riders. Again, if riders will be finishing before all have left, there need to be two people involved with the watches.

It's good to have someone stationed 30 yards down the road to shout out the shoulder number of each finishing rider. The recorder lists that number and then the time the timekeeper calls when the competitor crosses the line. When all riders have finished, it's then a simple matter to calculate each one's elapsed time on the course. For example, the first person left on the 1-minute mark, so his riding time is what the clock read when he finished, minus 1 minute. The time for the rider who started second is the clock time minus 2 minutes. And so on. It is ideal to assign shoulder numbers of 1 through whatever to riders in the order they will start. Then all you have to do is subtract the rider's number from the clock time to find his race time. Should a rider miss his starting position for any reason, leave the place open and assign him to the rear of the line. Don't move the others up to fill the gap. Doing so could cause confusion in figuring results, and it will foul up riders who are out warming up and have already been told the precise minute they'll start.

Finally, don't forget to give a copy of the results to the local newspaper. The sports department may even welcome a short article or an occasional photo. This is a good way to give recognition to the competitors and perhaps bring more riders out for the series. It also authenticates the racing in the eyes of the community, which is important for a couple of reasons: It adds to motorist recognition of cyclists as serious athletes so there will be a safer riding environment, and it opens the door to town support when the day arrives for the club to put on its first mass-start race.

Local time trials are fun and rewarding for all types of riders. A fitness-minded or recreational cyclist can get as much satisfaction out of them as an Olympic hopeful who covers the distance minutes faster. Even the slowest rider on the course can justifiably feel like a winner when he breaks his former best time. That's why I recommend time trialing for everyone. It's not just a way to get started in road racing, it's a worthwhile event in its own right and one which is bound to gain in popularity among fitness-conscious Americans in the years ahead.

12

TACTICS

When defining the word "tactics," Webster couldn't have done a better job in terms of mass-start bicycle racing: "The art or skill of employing available forces with an end in view." Unlike in time trialing, where there is nothing you can do to win but ride faster than everyone else, there are various means to the "end in view" in criteriums, road races, and mass-start events on the track.

Before getting down to specifics, it's important to understand this: Basic to race tactics is the ability to use the same riding skills and drafting techniques discussed in Chapters 4 and 5. A high-speed, competitive situation does not change the fundamental methods of bike handling; racing simply makes a rider's control more critical in terms of safety and performance. Thus it is important to continue developing the basic skills already outlined and then to add sharpness and spontaneity by participating in group training rides and club practice races. There is nothing like this kind of experience to help you handle your bike confidently when you move into sanctioned competition.

Riding in the Field

The whole idea of tactics is to never use energy unwisely but to deploy strength and ability where they will do the most good. Minimizing wind resistance is crucial to good performance, which makes drafting an important part of most tactics.

Every mass-start event begins with a field of riders. No matter what happens later on, there is almost always an identifiable main group throughout the race. In your early career you'll probably spend a lot of time in this group, but even so you should be trying to accomplish the most you can with your developing strength. The first consideration when riding in any pack, no matter what its size, is to get as much windbreak as possible. Stay on the wheels of other riders in the area most sheltered from the wind. When the field goes around a turn or the wind changes direction, you much change your position too. By working at this you should be able to remain with the pack until the end of the race and possibly be fresh enough to go with an attack, launch one of your own, or at least not be kicked out the back when the field sprint winds up.

If you expect to take an active part in the race you must be near the front of the field at all times. To be really effective you should be within the first fifteen riders; if you're past thirtieth position you won't be able to recognize or respond to important moves. The problem is that up front is where most of the other riders want to be, too. This means they will constantly be moving up the sides of the field and getting ahead, so just to stay even you must constantly be trying to work your way forward.

The best way to move up in the field is through the middle, not on the left or right. Taking to the outside uses more energy, because you are exposed to the wind. Don't wait until you find yourself near the back and needing to pass half the field to regain a good position—make it a habit to immediately move up and fill any hole that opens in front of you. It's like a game of checkers. It takes practice to squirt confidently through the gaps, but it's also fun. You can see, though, that something so seemingly simple as riding in the field takes quick reactions, bike-handling skill, and constant awareness.

Sometimes your task will turn from reacting to what's happening up front to trying to hang on to the back. If you have a particular weakness that might cause you to be dropped, there is a tactic you can try to reduce the possibility. Suppose, for example, that you're a relatively weak climber and there's one big hill on the course. You're not having any real problems staying with the field, but you know that if you lose contact on the ascent you'll never be able to catch up. As the hill approaches, prepare yourself mentally by expecting to hurt—this will help keep you from giving a less-than-total effort. Then work your way forward so you'll be at the very front when the road begins pitching up. Climb to the best of your ability and ignore other riders as they start going by. At the summit you may well be at the back, but at least you'll still be in contact. If you had begun the hill in the middle or rear of the field you would have been dropped. In fact, the danger isn't over yet, because the summit of a climb is a traditional place to attack. You should try to put the mental and physical distress aside, accelerate over the top, and quickly regain a position in the front third of the field. Be ready to hit the big gears and go with any serious moves.

Attacking

If no one gets away and several dozen riders arrive at the finish together, the stage is set for one of the sport's great spectacles—a field sprint. Can you imagine what it's like when fifty riders all go for the line at once? Talk about a lottery! Even if you are the best sprinter in the race your chances of winning are pretty poor. In a big field you can easily get boxed in by several slower riders and never be able to use your top speed.

To avoid field sprints and thus improve your chance of placing well, you must get rid of some of the riders. This will happen to some degree thanks to attrition, crashes, and mechanical problems, but you can help matters with well-timed attacks. When done correctly, some riders will be unable to respond and others will be too discouraged. Attacks should be made in a gear that allows quick acceleration but won't let you spin out too quickly. For a flat road something on the order of 53×14 or 15 will fill the bill.

Obviously, an attack is more likely to work if it comes at a moment when others are unlikely to chase, but it is surprising how many riders make attempts which have little chance of success. When the field is going hard, for example, don't bother to try anything. You may get a gap, but it won't be big enough to enable you to stay away. Instead, attack at a time when the pace is slowing down. As mentioned, the top of a climb is a good spot because riders are tired and won't feel like chasing. Or wait until just after the field has chased down someone else's attack. You can tell when the pace is easing up after a big effort—instead of being strung out, the riders begin bunching up.

When attacking the field, do it from about five or six riders back. Don't jump off the very front, because the riders behind will automatically chase you; you're the leader, so they follow. Instead, surprise them by accelerating and blowing by at a speed they can't instantly match. A gap will open and some of them may be too disheartened to even give chase.

You can also attack in the first miles of a race or the last—it depends on how you are feeling, your strength as a solo rider, and how you think the field is going to react. It's fine to have a general plan for when and where to make your move, but be ready to toss it aside if another opportunity presents itself.

An attack can be made to try to get away alone or to help improve your chances by reducing the number of riders in the group.

The Breakaway

It sure is thrilling to break away alone and speed to the finish for a heroic victory. But unless there's just a short distance to go or you are much stronger than your competitors, your chances of staying away will be better if you have some help—several riders can take turns against the wind using an echelon or pace line, just as in a team time trial. The breaks that work best usually consist of four to six riders, and the reason they succeed is that they are more efficient than the field. They won't hit the same top speeds as the pack, but they won't have the slow spots either.

Sometimes there will be a rider in the breakaway who won't take his turn at the front. He may be trying to slow it down for the benefit of teammates left back in the field, or he may be tired and saving energy for the finish. Whatever his reason, he just sits at the back drafting everyone else. This can ruin a potentially successful break, because as the other riders get tired and realize that they are simply towing him to possible victory, they'll start sitting up too. Before long the field closes in.

There is a technique to get rid of a rider like this, but it requires some cooperation. The idea is to take turns putting him off the back. If he is on the tail end of the pace line and you are directly in front of him, let a gap start opening between you and the rest of the group. When it gets to 50 meters, sprint back up as hard as you can. He'll have to work extra hard just to come close to keeping your wheel, and as soon as he is back to the group another rider takes a turn dropping him back. If the hanger-on is really tired he'll soon be gone for good; if he's simply been playing it lazy, he'll get the message to start doing his share of the work.

Bridging Gaps

What if a break takes flight and you're not with it? Should you try to join in, and, if so, when? The answer depends on your assessment of the breakaway's chances for success. You have to determine by looking at it whether it contains good riders, whether they're working together, whether it's a serious attempt, and whether they're ca-

When a breakaway starts gaining distance on you and the field, you must decide whether to try to bridge the gap. This is where time trialing ability pays off.

pable of staying away. For example, if the field is doing 28 mph and a little break blasts off at 30, you might as well save your energy. The chances are good that it will not make much ground and will soon be swallowed by the field. Or if you see that a few riders aren't taking a good pull, then you know the attempt will probably fail.

But if the break looks smooth and is definitely building up time on the field, you'd better get moving. The lead may be 10 seconds, then 15, then 20 . . . don't wait any longer than that. It's almost impossible for a solo rider to cross a 30-second gap to a serious break. To launch your chase, attack as if you were making a break yourself—after all, that's exactly what you're doing. Then put your head down, call up all the reserves of strength built by your interval training and time trialing. If someone has gone with you, do it like a team time trial. Once you make contact, start sharing the work as soon as you can.

Teamwork

Detroit's Roger Young, a former national track champion and very fine criterium rider, has said it's almost impossible to win a major race without help. He was referring to the fact that in a big event there are so many good riders all watching each other that the odds are against any individual move's succeeding. This is especially true when you're as famous as Young, the "Motown Motor"—everyone knows how fast and crafty he is, so they all look for his wheel at the finish. Yet in spite of being a marked man he goes on winning races. How does he do it? Teamwork.

Until now the tactics I've discussed have been for how you can improve your own chances. But if you have teammates or good friends in the race, you can also do things to help them. Why would you want to? Perhaps you realize you don't have the starch to do much in the race, but your friend does. Or maybe he got into the key breakaway and you didn't. Perhaps you're both in the break but he's a better sprinter. As long as your own odds of winning are next to nothing, why not give him a hand? The purpose of having a team is to maximize one another's chances of doing well. Often teammates will share their prizes after a race in recognition of the fact that it was the sacrifice of some that helped others finish in the money.

The most common way to help a teammate is by blocking in the field when he's in a break. After all, the fewer the riders in his group, the better his chances of winning. Blocking can be done in several ways. You can go to the front of the field as if to help the chase but actually slow down the tempo. Or if you're leading through a turn you can go very wide and slow, even braking before entering it. Such forms of blocking are negative and they can backfire—you can use so much energy trying to monitor the speed of the field that when a chase is launched you'll be unable to do anything about it.

By sitting up and pedaling easily at the front of the field it is possible to help the chances of a teammate in a break. If someone in the field suddenly attacks to try to overcome your blocking, get on his wheel but don't pull through and help his effort.

Probably the most effective way to block is to cover the break. This means that each time someone attacks and tries to go up to the leaders, you immediately get on his wheel. Don't take any pulls, just go along for the free ride. One of several things will happen: The attacker will give up and drop back to the field because he doesn't want you along; or he will be unable to bridge the gap without help; or he'll decide that being in the break is the most important thing and he'll tow you right up to it.

Teamwork can be just as important at the rear of the pack when a rider is delayed by a flat tire, mechanical problem, or crash. Once off the back by a minute or more, it is hard for a single rider to regain the field. Even if he succeeds, he may be so drained of energy after the long chase that all he can do is hang on for the rest of the race. But teammates can help turn such calamities into minor accidents. Two can go to the front to keep the speed of the field under control as one or two more drop off to pick up their stricken friend and pace him back into contact. Scenarios like this are everyday occurrences in road racing, especially in Europe, where there is such emphasis on team riding. For example, the great Bernard Hinault suffered a half-dozen delays due to punctures and crashes in the grueling Paris-Roubaix classic in 1981 and still was able to win the race.

The Sprint Finish

Field sprints are just incredible. Everyone is out of the saddle at 30 mph, riding elbow to elbow and tossing their bikes to and fro with no apparent regard for the possibility that there could be a horrible crash at any moment. It looks chaotic and it's all over so fast that it's hard to realize what happened. But every sprint is different. There are definite moves to be made and various tactics which come into play. To do well you need a combination of mental alertness and quick reflexes, plus a solid foundation of training and experience.

A sprint starts with one or more riders getting off the saddle and jumping to top speed. The person who goes first is said to be leading out. The others try to get in his slipstream, picking up speed and waiting for the moment to make their own bids. As the finish line

Successful sprinting takes strength, quick reflexes, and lots of experience.

approaches, several different riders may come to the front briefly, only to be passed by those slingshoting from behind.

The technique of standing up and jumping to high speed is practiced during interval training. This high-gear work also will show you which ratios give you the best acceleration and staying power. For in-the-saddle sprinting, low-gear intervals and downhill spinning will condition you to pedal at cadences beyond 120 without excessive bouncing. This demands both coordination and relaxation, because when your legs are moving that fast your brain can no longer keep up—there's just no way you can mentally guide each foot through a smooth circle.

When training with others, take turns leading out and trying to come around. Use road signs as finish lines and start the action from about 200 meters out. Prepare for the jump by shifting to a slightly bigger gear, then get out of the saddle. Let yourself go and put as much power as you possibly can into the pedals. Bend over the handlebars slightly and lean the bike from side to side. This technique allows maximum force to be exerted, because you are thrusting directly at the pedals. If your cadence gets too high you'll have to sit down, shift, and get up again.

Tactics for the final sprint depend partly on the course and road conditions. Therefore, it is important to be familiar with the finishing stretch. While you're warming up, go to the line in the gear you will use for the sprint and pedal about forty revolutions back up the course. Forty revolutions in 53×15 covers a distance of just under 300 meters, the area in which the most explosive part of the sprint will take place. Find something along the sidelines to identify the spot and, if it's a criterium or a circuit race, make an effort to notice it each time you go by. Being aware of the distance to the line will help you avoid mistakes in timing when it comes to sprints for points, primes, or the end of the race.

As you scout the finish line, notice which way the wind is blowing. For an into-the-wind sprint you'll need a smaller gear than you normally use. Try not to be the one to lead out; make your move as late as possible to avoid having to break the wind. If there is a tailwind you can jump much earlier and use a bigger gear. In a crosswind, if it's coming from the right, plan to finish on the far left side of the road so you will have shelter from other riders but no one will have any behind you. However, if you come into the finishing stretch with a lead, get on the right side to take advantage of the wind barrier formed by the spectators. If someone else leads out in a crosswind, pass him on the downwind side to use a little less energy.

In a criterium you should start getting ready for the sprint with about 3 laps to go. Tighten toestraps, empty the water bottle, and try to compose yourself. Breathe deeply and get into the frame of mind to really go for it. If it's shaping up as a field sprint, move toward the front at this time, because you may not make it later—by the last lap the pace will be picking up and everyone will be fighting to keep or improve his position.

Various factors determine where you should be on the final lap. If you have a good jump and are able to come off a wheel with authority, and if taking chances doesn't bother you, it's best to be in fifth to tenth position. The shorter the finishing straight, the closer to the front you need to be. For example, if it's only 250 meters to the line after the final turn, then you should try to be between third and fifth place at the corner. For an even shorter straight the best situation is to come through the turn in first or second place.

When you don't have much of a sprint, a good strategy is to lead out the whole last lap. The rest of the riders will be happy to have you breaking the wind for them, so go ahead and roll along at near maximum speed. The really fast, explosive guys will get past you near the line, but you'll still get a pretty good placing if you muster up whatever acceleration you can.

The best sprinters have two valuable assets: a good kick and a high maximum speed, called "top end." Top end is especially important in a long, wind-up sprint, the kind which happens often in road racing when the finishing stretch is several miles in length. In this type of sprint, riders launch attack after attack, trying to escape and solo to the line. The field's response is to continually chase them down, with the result that the overall speed gets faster and faster. Before long, many riders will become drained of energy as the ones with the high top end continue to accelerate. The rider who can choose the right wheels to follow and hold his position without doing any hard accelerations is usually the one who wins.

Since every sprint is different, there's no teacher like experience. As time goes by you will develop your own sprinting techniques and strategies, based on your abilities. What's more important—and this is true for all parts of the race, not just the sprint—is that you be alert at all times and anticipate what other riders are going to do. If you just ride along in your own little world you won't notice what's happening until it's too late. Then you will have to compensate by using valuable energy that could have gone for offensive instead of defensive moves. Watch the other riders. Is their pedal action deteriorating? If so, maybe they're getting tired and you can try to break away. Is someone shifting into a higher gear than everyone else is using? He's probably about to attack. Get on his wheel before he has a chance to jump and you'll be able to go with him.

You may have great natural ability and an ideal training program, but without awareness and good tactics you can't reach your potential as a racer—you can't use your weapons to their best advantage. There are so many variables in a mass-start race that only by playing your strengths against the other riders' weaknesses are you likely to beat them. You must analyze each part of each race after it happens and ask yourself how you could have done better.

It may seem unfair to be beaten because someone outsmarts you or teams up on you, but remember that it works both ways. If you learn your tactical lessons well and use them at the right time, you can place higher in races than riders who have greater physical assets and are better trained.

13

INJURIES

Even though cycling ranks right along with running and swimming as a sport with excellent health benefits, high-mileage riders are no strangers to injury. Besides the various minor aches and pains that daily physical exertion can bring, serious cyclists must deal with problems which have the potential to reduce riding time or even force a layoff. Here is a look at some of these afflictions and how to deal with them.

Leg Problems

Leg injuries are the most common in cycling. They can be internal (involving muscles, tendons, and ligaments) or external (abrasions caused by a fall). Internal injuries can be further divided into two groups: direct and indirect. The difference is in whether the problem arose suddenly or whether it developed and worsened over a period of time.

Direct internal injuries include (1) contusions resulting from a fall in which the muscle and tissue is crushed between the pavement and the bone; (2) strains to muscles or tendons due to violent contraction or forced movement past normal range of motion, again usually due to an accident; (3) sprains to ligaments due to a wrenching action that does not actually cause a fracture or dislocation.

In the event that you suffer any of these three injuries, cycling physiologist Ed Burke recommends immediate application of ice for 30 to 45 minutes. "This cold therapy should be used twice daily," advises Burke, the chairman of the U.S. Cycling Federation's Medical Committee. "When the ice is removed, a light foam-rubber pad should be placed over the injured area and secured with an elastic bandage wrap. The leg should be elevated. The objective is to have light compression on the area to help discourage swelling and internal bleeding. At no time should heat be applied to an acute injury."

Depending on the severity of the contusion or strain, the skin may turn black and blue and range of motion may be quite limited. There will be a degree of pain, tenderness, and swelling. Burke advises continued ice treatments until all signs subside and full range of motion returns, which can take from three to seven days. As things improve you can begin light flexion and extension exercises and later some easy cycling, but nothing that forces movement past the point where pain is felt. In severe cases see a physician to rule out the possibility of a fracture.

Indirect internal injuries include bursitis, tendinitis, tenosynovitis, shin splints, and chondromalacia. All are caused not by falling off the bike but by how it is ridden.

Bursitis is usually caused by overuse. Bursae are small sacs which contain the synovial fluid for lubrication of joints. There are eighteen bursae in the knee, and they can become inflamed by pushing a big gear, pedaling from an incorrect position, or riding without leg cover in cold weather. Proper treatment requires rest from cycling, ice application for its anti-inflammatory action, and use of mild heat and massage after a few days.

Tendinitis is the name for tendon strains caused by repetitive movement. Of the various types of tendinitis which can be encountered by cyclists, three are more prevalent than the rest: patellar, Achilles, and popliteal.

- Patellar tendinitis occurs to the tendon which connects the kneecap (patella) to the lower leg bone (tibia). It is caused by overuse of the quadriceps muscles on the front of the thigh.
- Achilles tendinitis involves the tendon which connects the calf muscle (gastrocnemius) to the heel bone (calcaneus). Injury can result from improper saddle height or bad pedaling technique.
- Popliteal tendinitis usually results from a too-high saddle which produces a continuous locking and unlocking of the kneecap. This causes the popliteal tendon (rear and outside of the knee) to rub against the lateral collateral ligament, which connects the femur and fibula. This produces inflammation of the tendon, the ligament, and/or the bursae between them.

The treatment of all three tendon injuries is the same: rest, application of ice, and local massage and heat after inflammation has subsided. And, of course, you should take another look at your saddle height and make any necessary alterations.

Tenosynovitis is inflammation of the synovial membrane of a tendon. In cyclists this occurs most frequently in the ankle area where the Achilles and peroneal tendons lie. Causes of this injury include improper foot placement on the pedal, biomechanical foot defects, and poor pedaling technique. Treatment includes rest from riding and application of ice or immersion in cold water. Once inflammation has subsided, mild heat and massage can help complete the healing. Use heel lifts in your shoes when you begin to ride again so that movement of the Achilles tendon will be limited.

Shin splints involve the flexor muscles located in the front of the lower leg. The irritation takes place at the origin of the sheath which connects the two bones there. Probable causes include faulty foot alignment on the pedal, overuse stress, and arch problems. Treatment calls for icing sessions of from 20 to 30 minutes on the entire front and inside edge of the shinbone. Arch supports and stretching may help, as will the use of aspirin to relieve pain and inflammation. But healing of this particular injury is usually slow.

Chondromalacia is just one of a number of knee injuries cyclists can suffer but it is probably the most disabling. Known as "runner's knee" because of the toll it has taken in that sport, chondromalacia is the result of a tracking abnormality as the patella glides up and down in the groove between the femur and tibia bones when the knee is bent and straightened. This results in actual disintegration of the underside of the kneecap and the cartilage surfaces. Symptoms start with deep knee pain and a grating or crunching sensation. Once this is felt it is time for immediate action.

"Chondromalacia is a difficult problem to treat, and there is no satisfactory cure for it," Burke warns. "Therefore, it is important to recognize the early signs in order to prevent progression to a chronic injury and arthritic condition. Check your saddle height and shoe-cleat position to make sure the problem isn't being caused by incorrect adjustment. It does not take too much toe-in or toe-out to stress a knee and cause an injury. Orthotics (supports worn in shoes) can often improve chondromalacia if it is caused by foot abnormalities.

"Treatment includes staying off the bike, aspirin, and application of ice to the knee for periods of 5 to 7 minutes. Once the pain is gone and the problem that caused it has been corrected, you can begin strength-training exercises for the quadriceps, hamstrings, and calf muscles to help make the knee more stable. Strong quads are especially important in the proper tracking of the patella."

The common denominator in treating a knee injury or any problem with leg muscles, tendons, and ligaments is to get off the bike as soon as pain arises. A couple of days off may be all that's needed to avoid a serious injury. I know it's hard to resist trying to "ride through" what seems to be a minor problem, but it makes more sense to miss a couple of days now than a couple of weeks—or months— later on. The second step is to apply ice, which will limit the blood flow and metabolic processes in the area, thus reducing swelling and giving you early control of the situation. Additionally, aspirin will help alleviate inflammation and pain. Gentle stretching can be helpful when done immediately after the ice treatment. Better yet, if you make stretching a part of your daily routine there will be less chance of injuring muscles and joints in the first place.

Before riding again after an internal leg injury be sure you have made all necessary corrections in terms of saddle height, cleat position, and foot support (see Chapter 4). Take short rides in low gears to allow a gradual strengthening of the injured area and to give everything else a chance to become accustomed to any alterations in riding position. It is wise to always ride in long tights when the air is cool, or at least coat knees with oil, petroleum jelly, or the like.

Road Rash

Most external injuries to the legs and other parts of the body come in the form of "road rash." This descriptive term might sound humorous, but you'll not be smiling when you catch some. You won't be sleeping too well for several nights, either, as you search in vain for a

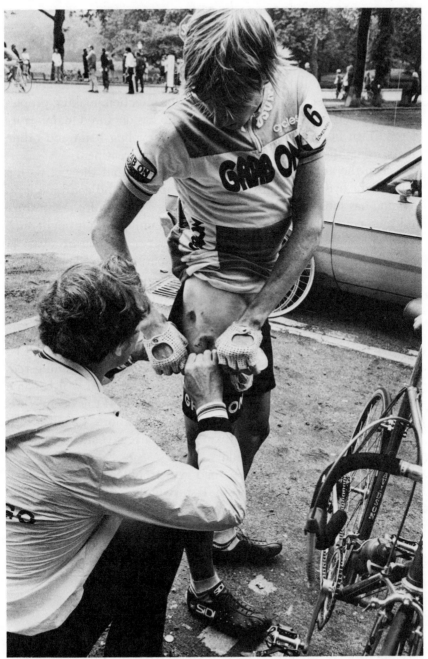

Road rash is the most common product of a fall. Legs are always susceptible, and this is one reason why racers keep theirs free of hair—it makes cleaning and medicating an abrasion easier. Notice that this rider is wearing an undershirt, which gives the jersey something to slide against to help avoid losing skin on the back and shoulders.

comfortable position, one that won't have you sticking to the sheets.

A slide along the pavement will result in missing skin and exposed blood vessels, and that's problem enough. But the penetration of dirt and foreign matter increases the chance for infection, making proper cleaning and treatment a must. Burke, who has doctored many cases of road rash in his work with the national cycling team and other racers, offers the following advice for effective treatment.

"Clean the area with soap and water and get out the grit with a brush. Pour hydrogen peroxide over the abrasion and continue until foaming has subsided. Use some sterile gauze to dab off the moisture and then cover the raw area with a petroleum-based ointment such as Neosporin to keep a scab from forming. A scab is nature's way of providing protection from infection, but nature didn't know about cycling. During riding a scab can be reopened before healing is complete, which will only prolong the problem. If the abrasion is on a joint, a scab will limit range of motion.

"Place a nonsticking sterile pad over the ointment. Change the dressing daily and watch for signs of infection. If it occurs it will be apparent within two to seven days, with the wound becoming red, swollen, hot, and tender. Lymph glands near the area will become swollen and painful, and you may develop a fever. If this occurs, it is best to see a doctor to stave off further complications. Regardless, if you haven't had a tetanus antitoxin shot in a few years, get one no later than 24 hours after the injury.

"Some precautions will keep road rash troubles to a minimum," Burke continues. "Wear a cotton T-shirt under your jersey. In the event of a fall, the jersey slides over the shirt and your abrasions may not be as widespread. Keeping legs shaved will help minimize the amount of skin lost and aid in the healing process. You will find that cleaning and bandaging the wound is much easier without hair present, and chances of infection will be less."

How to React in a Crash

Although talking about the treatment of injuries that result from a crash isn't a cheerful subject, it's almost certain that sometime, somewhere, somehow, you will take a fall. Just as baseball players get beaned and football players are leveled by clothesline tackles, crashing is an unpleasant but inevitable part of cycling. It shouldn't happen often and there is a lot you can do in terms of common sense and defensive riding to see that it doesn't. But go down you will, sooner or later.

What to do during a crash has been the subject of numerous articles in cycling magazines. Most writers make it seem as if you have all the time in the world to ponder the predicament, decide the best way to fall, and then do all the right things with your body. Hogwash. No matter what the cause, crashes usually happen so unexpectedly and so suddenly that you are on the way down before you know it. That's why it is so important to protect yourself with a helmet, gloves, a T-shirt under your jersey, and even by keeping your legs shaved. These safeguards can help you get back up with a lot less damage. And when it comes to a helmet, it might make the difference in being able to get up at all.

Besides road rash and contusions, probably the most common injury resulting from a crash is a broken collarbone. This is caused by impact in the shoulder area and often occurs because the rider has kept hands on the bars in a futile attempt to regain control. American pro racer Jacques Boyer has noted a lower incidence of broken collarbones coming out of crashes in Europe, and he says the reason is the initial reaction of those riders when falling. Over there they try to dive away from the bike, not hang on. A falling rider will attempt to land on his stomach with arms outstretched and the bike trailing behind. This considerably reduces the chance of a broken bone and keeps the bike from contributing to other injuries.

Saddle Sores

There is another abrasion that can cause even more discomfort and disability than road rash. It is the chafing that occurs to the part of the anatomy where everything in cycling hinges, the crotch. This saddle soreness has plagued even the greatest cyclists—Eddy Merckx, for instance, was known to have tried innumerable saddles in his attempt to find relief—and it is often a problem for riders getting in their first long miles each new season or suddenly increasing their weekly totals. The raw tenderness is bad enough, but almost crippling are the open sores and boils that can develop. Until you've had to have a saddle boil lanced you only think you know what pain is.

Overcoming saddle soreness is sort of a Catch-22. The more you ride, the higher the risk of skin injury caused by friction and pressure; but riding is the best way to build tolerance to what is vividly called "the trauma of the saddle." Discomfort will be nearly impossible to remedy if you don't wear cycling shorts with a chamois-lined crotch, if you have a poorly shaped saddle, or if the saddle is set at an incorrect height or angle. Once these contributing factors are neutralized, the following Burke advice will do some good.

"As with most skin infections, scrupulous attention to body hygiene can prevent many problems," he says. "Shorts should be washed with mild soap after every use to remove chamois lubricant and sweat. Clean the groin with rubbing alcohol, which serves as an antiseptic and will toughen the skin.

"To keep friction to a minimum, the chamois should be softened and lubricated before each ride. Some riders like to rub in a water-base product like Noxzema because it is easy to remove. Others prefer a product like petroleum jelly or Kucharik's Chamois Fat. Frank Westell, the well-known British trainer, has his own formula of Vaseline, lanolin, cod-liver oil, and vitamin E. Should you develop broken skin, there are various over-the-counter medicated ointments available at pharmacies which can be used to help retard bacterial growth and the chances of infection."

Muscle Soreness

General muscle soreness and tightness throughout the legs is often the reaction to big increases in mileage. But it can show up anytime after an unusually hard effort—a tour into hilly terrain, a time trial, or some form of intense training. Riders often blame the soreness on the buildup of lactic acid, but Burke cites a different cause.

"Within an hour after a hard ride which produces lactic acid, 99 percent of the lactate has been removed from the working muscles and converted into other products," he states. "The soreness is actually due to microscopic tears to new muscle cells that were used for the first time by the hard effort. Fluid moves into the cells and causes swelling, which is sensed as soreness and mild pain. This is perfectly normal, and mending of the injured cells can be helped along by rest and some easy riding. Massage will remove the fluids from the swollen cells and stimulate the lymphatic system to remove metabolic waste products."

A degree of soreness in the back, neck, shoulders, and arms is not unusual in the early season or when you ride beyond normal limits. It is usually the result of muscle fatigue from supporting the upper body and holding up the head. All the involved muscles will be strengthened by cycling itself, and the incidence of soreness will diminish as the season progresses. You can help things along by toning upper-body muscles through weight training; even simple push-ups do a lot to condition the arm and shoulder muscles used when cycling. Many riders have found daily sessions of bent-leg sit-ups just the thing for preventing lower-back pain.

Of course, proper riding technique is essential to minimizing fatigue. Try to change your hand position frequently, going from the tops to the drops to the brake levers and all points between. This will create slight alterations in upper-body position and help delay muscle fatigue and stiffness. When on tour, hop off the bike every hour or so to walk around and stretch. Above all, ride relaxed. A tense muscle fatigues quickly, so keep hands, arms, and shoulders loose.

Numbness

Tingling or even numbness in the hands, feet, and crotch is sometimes experienced, and this is reason for some concern. The usual cause is compression of nerves between bones and the handlebars, shoes, and saddle. If allowed to continue it can result in a long-lasting problem; some riders have reported a numbness in their fingers which stays with them weeks after its onset.

If you experience hand numbness it is likely to be located in the pinky and fourth finger. You can usually prevent it by adding extra padding to the handlebars, wearing cycling gloves with padded palms, and changing hand position frequently. Hand discomfort affects enough riders that several companies now market special handlebar wraps which provide added cushioning.

Crotch numbness is quite unsettling the first time it happens, and it's something you won't want to happen again. Usually it is the result of improper saddle position, particularly when the nose of the saddle is too high. This results in excess pressure when you lean into the handlebars. Some moderate, short-lived numbness in the area seems to occur after most long or hard rides in the low working position, but it shouldn't be felt in other types of cycling. If you wear chamois shorts and use a saddle containing a layer of high-density foam, there should be sufficient padding to prevent nerve compression.

Feet that become numb or feel as if they are on fire can be helped by inserting foam insoles into the shoes and/or by wearing thicker socks. You may have to keep toe straps a bit looser, too. Shoes that are too small can cause foot distress by restricting blood flow in capillaries. Riding in soft-soled shoes like those made for tennis or running can result in discomfort because of pressure from the pedal cage. That's why cycling shoes have soles of wood, hard plastic, or steel-reinforced leather.

Fatigue

"Exhaustion and overtraining should be main concerns of the serious cyclist. That feeling of fatigue in the last few miles is just as crucial as any injury, yet many riders fail to realize that this can be the result of too much training rather than too little. The desire to improve can make cyclists try too hard in a small space of time instead of pacing and building their effort. They go too far with the adage 'What doesn't destroy me makes me strong.'"

Even the most experienced racers occasionally suffer from overtraining. It is a problem that can hit any rider who is anxious to improve his ability either to tour long distances or to compete more effectively. There is a rather fine line between the amount of stress to which a body can adapt and grow stronger, and that which will result in deterioration.

If there is one thing good about overtraining it's that it will let you know when it is beginning to happen, usually in enough time for you to back off and avoid big problems. Among the warning signs are:

1. Headaches, sniffles, fever blisters, and similar signs of lowered resistance and physical depletion.
2. Mild leg soreness which persists from day to day.
3. A lethargic, I-don't-care attitude toward everyday life and cycling itself.
4. The desire to quit during races or any difficult effort.
5. Loss of body weight.

A good way to evaluate the stress of cycling on your body and thus safeguard yourself from falling victim to overtraining and staleness is to keep a record of your pulse rate. Each morning before getting out of bed, count your pulse for 15 seconds. Then count it again after you get up and move around for a couple of minutes. Do this daily and record the difference between the two rates. If there is a sudden increase in this number it is a sign your body has not recovered from yesterday's ride. If so, cycling should either be suspended for that day or done less strenuously."

If the signs of overtraining are not recognized and heeded, it may take you weeks to recover and return to sound fitness. The best way to deal with the problem is to avoid it altogether, which you can do by following these recommendations:

1. Put in eight to ten weeks of steady endurance-type riding before going into anything more strenuous.
2. Do not fail to get enough sleep.
3. Eat a diet which supplies all the basic nutrients and is about 60 percent carbohydrate.
4. If it is possible, take a short nap after an afternoon workout.
5. Should your cycling interest call for heavy training, remember that the appropriate pace is what your own body can handle, not what others dictate.
6. Monitor yourself for signs of overtraining and recovery from the previous day's ride, as noted above.
7. Several days before a big race or tour, taper off your training. This will build both mental and physical strength and help ensure that you'll get a maximum benefit from all the work you've done.

Where to Get Help

If you can't cope with an injury using the advice in this chapter, seek professional medical help. But more than that, try to make it a doctor who is experienced with the physical, psychological, and emotional differences between athletes and sedentary individuals. Even better, make it a doctor who is also an athlete.

Find such people by calling the trainer at your local high school or college and asking for names of physicians experienced in treating athletic injuries. A medical school should also be able to give you some names, as will the nearest chapter of the American Medical Association. If there isn't one listed, contact the main office at 535 N. Dearborn St., Chicago, IL 60610. Should your injury involve bone or muscle, contact the American Orthopaedic Society of Sports Medicine, 430 N. Michigan Ave., Chicago, IL 60611, to find the closest sports orthopedist. And if it is a foot problem, ask the above sources for doctors in your area who are members of the American Academy of Podiatric Sports Medicine.

14

THE BIKE AND ITS PARTS

There's an old saying in cycling that goes like this: "It's not the bike, it's the motor." Take it from a guy who has ridden extensively on more than a dozen of the world's finest bicycles, it's true. Despite what you might be told by a salesman in a bike shop or what you will read in advertisements, no bicycle is going to automatically make you a faster or more proficient rider. It's the motor that counts, and the motor is you.

The role of the bicycle is to let the motor function. Any bike, no matter how fancy or expensive it is, that doesn't allow you to pedal from the correct position is not as good as a cheaper model that does. Further, no bike can ever be a substitute for proper training and conditioning. I've seen many races, especially lower-category events, where the winner was on a bike worth a third as much as those ridden by the first guys to fall off the pace. The difference was the quality of the motor, not the machinery, and that's a valuable lesson for everyone involved in any aspect of cycling.

Nevertheless, it is a special feeling to own and ride a high-quality bicycle. We're fortunate today because there are so many fine brands to select from. Leading bike manufacturers in the United States, Europe, and Japan are producing full lines which include lightweight, multi-geared models ranging in price from less than $200 to more than $2,000. I'll come right to the point and perhaps shock you a bit by saying that anyone who is serious about cycling and is ready to make an ongoing commitment to the sport should spend a minimum of $400 for a bike. That kind of money will buy a well-constructed frame with above-average components throughout. It'll be a bike that can meet the requirements of all the riding you're likely to do

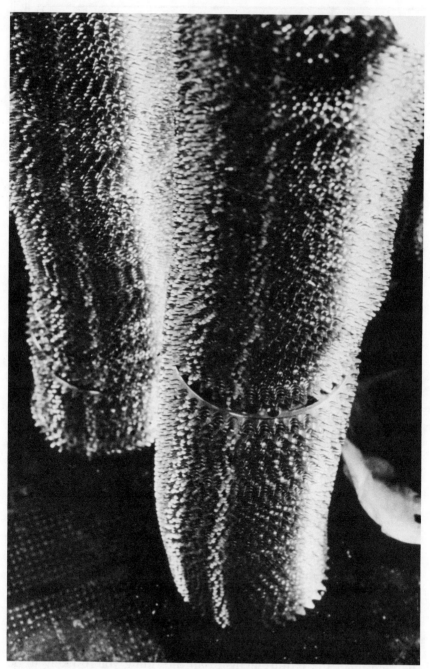

(Photograph courtesy of Franco Varisco)

(with the exception of upper-category racing). Sure, you can spend less, but be warned that cycling is a sport that can capture your very soul, leaving you quite dissatisfied with yourself when you realize how much more bike you could be riding if only you had added a bit to your initial investment.

The trick, as I see it, is to spend enough to make sure you get all the bike you need—nothing less, but also nothing more. Once you reach a certain point, the law of diminishing returns takes over. Since the motor is the vital thing, paying a lot more for small improvements in components or a reduction in overall weight of a pound or two just isn't worth it. The only person who might be justified in breaking this rule is the racer who specializes in an event where the competition is evenly matched. In this case the bike could possibly produce the winning edge, but I still think it's better to invest more effort in training than more money on equipment. However, there are several components on which extra money is wisely spent, as we shall see below.

I might get some arguments, but I really believe that serious cyclists should ride nothing less than a 10-speed bike. The weight difference and versatility compared to 3- or 5-speed models is significant and well worth the bigger price tag. Also of great importance is the fact that the quality 10-speed bike will have a frame that is light, responsive, and strong enough to stand up to many thousands of miles of riding.

Frames

The frame is the heart and soul of a bicycle. More than any other single component it determines how a bike is going to ride—how it will corner, accelerate, behave when going up or down a hill, handle rough roads, and even stop. The frame is also the most expensive component, which is why I suggest a $400 minimum investment in a bike. After all, a top-quality handmade frame and fork assembly (properly called a frameset) will carry a price tag of $425 and up. If you are buying a complete bike for that price or less, you are actually paying relatively little for the frame itself. This could well cause you

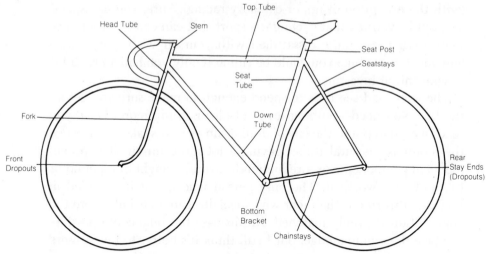

Diagram of main parts of the frame and related components.

to wonder: How can there be such a big difference in the cost of frames when they look so much the same?

There are two main reasons. First, the cost of the material used in construction. The cheapest bikes have frames made with steel pipe—thick, welded tubing that is very heavy and lifeless. As price goes up, so does the quality of the tubing, with the better frames being made of steel alloys produced specifically for bicycles. One of the most widely used and respected is Reynolds 531, a manganese molybdenum alloy. The seamless construction of Reynolds tubes is common to all the top tubing manufacturers, though the composition of the alloy usually varies somewhat. But whether a frame is made from England's Reynolds, Italy's Columbus, France's Vitus, or Japan's Isiwata and Tange, you can be confident that the tubing has an excellent strength-to-weight ratio and ideal riding characteristics. In fact, for all practical purposes these brands are identical, even though you might hear claims that one or another is somehow superior. I've ridden bikes constructed from most of the major tubings and I really can't tell the difference, save for the manufacturer's decal on the frame.

The second reason lies in how the tubes are assembled. It stands to reason that the more handwork that goes into the construction of a frame the more expensive it will be. The frames found in inexpensive bikes are simply welded together on an automated assembly line, but higher-quality tubing can't be handled in this way. It is too thin and will become brittle if overheated, so with few exceptions all good lightweight frames are brazed together by hand and the tube intersections are reinforced with lugs. These fittings are often quite ornate and are precisely sized to allow each tube to enter and be solidly sealed with the brazing material, usually bronze or silver solder. This produces a joint much stronger than welding could, and it allows the use of very thin-walled tubes for overall frame lightness.

Top-of-the-line frames go a step further, using very light and expensive double-butted tubing. These tubes are drawn about half as thin throughout as they are at the ends where they fit into the lugs. This ensures all the thickness that's needed for brazing while keeping overall weight to the bare minimum with no real loss in strength.

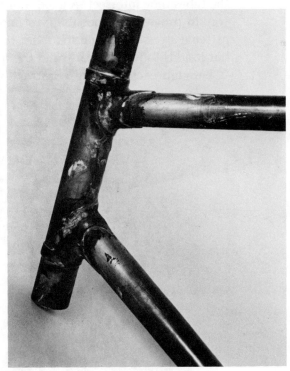

The head tube area of a frame under construction. The fittings at intersections of tubes are called lugs. The brazing material, usually bronze, is heated until it runs into the thin space between the tubes and lugs, thus making a solid bond and giving a frame extra thickness and strength where it is most needed. Most frames built without lugs are simply welded together. This requires much thicker and heavier tubing, resulting in a heavy bike and a lifeless ride.

Lugs can be quite thin and ornate and still do their job. These have cutouts that help reduce weight and also allow the frame builder to see that the brazing material is spreading throughout the surface between the lug and tube.

Since the difference in diameter occurs inside the tubes it's not possible to tell if a frame is double-butted simply by looking at it—the manufacturer's decal on the seat tube will say if it is, as will the price. Something else you can't see is whether the tubes have been mitered, which is the process of shaping tube ends to fit flush against the tubes they intersect. A good frame builder will take this step as a way to prevent any possibility of movement under the lugs during extreme stress. Mitering increases the cost of the frame, of course, but it adds to its durability and the quality of the ride.

Through each stage of construction a frame manufacturer faces

The glossy paint covering a quality frame would make it impossible to tell the type of tubing used if manufacturers didn't supply decals with this information.

decisions about the quality and expense of materials. For example, the lugs and the bottom bracket shell can be pressed steel or the more costly cast steel. The same goes for the fork crown, which might also be forged. There are various makes of fork tips and rear dropouts to choose from. These alternatives and the basic selection of the tube brand and weight combine to determine a frame's final cost. When it's all brought together in a frame factory the end product will give good quality for the money and be totally adequate to meet the needs of most riders. When it's all brought together by an experienced custom builder doing each phase of construction himself, the result should be as good a frame as money can buy.

Not everybody needs a handmade frame, of course, not even someone who races full-time or tours thousands of miles a year. The rider who should look into a custom frame is the one whose skills have surpassed the capabilities of stock production bikes (rare), who requires certain brazed-on fittings (common among serious tourists), or who has a peculiar build (the most legitimate reason). Someone who is so tall that the largest production bikes can't fit, or someone who is unusually proportioned in the relationships of torso, arm, and leg lengths, should go the custom route. A savvy frame builder can alter angles and tube lengths to compensate for a person's unusual proportions, letting him or her ride in the correct position. Basketball star Bill Walton, at 6-foot-11, is a cyclist who had no choice but to order a specially designed frame. When you think about it, the extra money spent with a custom frame builder is a small amount to pay if

With four tubes meeting at the crank area of the bike, the bottom bracket shell is by necessity thick and strong. The threads are to accept the crank's ball-bearing cups.

it buys efficiency and comfort. There's also the satisfaction of knowing that you've got a bike that will let you perform just like the perfectly proportioned fellow beside you. It's just another way that the bicycle works as an equalizer.

But if like me you fall into the normal range of human design, a custom frame is a luxury, not a necessity. You can purchase a standard bike made by a reputable manufacturer and expect no problems in achieving the proper riding position, as long as the frame size is correct. How to determine that is discussed in Chapter 4, but here's the point: Unless you know that all your effort will be going into racing and you need a competition machine just for that, you can feel confident that a bike in the $400 range will be fine for any type of riding you will be doing. Modern designers have developed nice compromises between the rigid and highly responsive racing bike and the traditional long and flexible touring bike. They're putting eyelets on the dropouts so that racks and mudguards can be attached if desired, yet with relatively upright frame angles and a moderate wheelbase these bikes handle well and ride comfortably for all-round cycling enjoyment. Sure, there are plenty of arcane aspects of frame geometry that can be considered—things like fork rake, trail, bottom

Modern manufacturers are producing frame models that are satisfactory for a wide variety of riding. Eyelets on top of the dropouts make it easy to attach racks and equipment for a tour; take off the gear and the same bike can be used for recreational racing.

bracket height, chainstay length, etc.—which help determine in fine degrees how a bike rides and handles. This is why it is important to work with a knowledgeable dealer who understands your needs and can match you with an appropriately designed bike.

While the traditional man's frame (correctly called the diamond frame) is certainly the best design, there are riders of either sex who may require what has come to be called a woman's frame. The top tube of a diamond frame is a hindrance to a woman who has occasion to ride while wearing a skirt, and it's just as much a problem for any-one who commutes in an overcoat or similar apparel. The top tube can also present difficulties for the very short rider or the older one who isn't as dexterous in swinging a leg up and over. Fortunately, there is a solution that doesn't make a rider sacrifice very much of the diamond frame's strength and stability. It's called the mixte frame, and in Europe, where it originated, it is ridden by both sexes without social stigma. In fact, it is some times referred to as the uni-sex frame.

There is one major difference between the European mixte frame and the design which American and Japanese manufacturers have for years produced for women. It is the reason a mixte rides very much like a diamond-frame bike while its cousin tends to be weaker, slug-gish, and flexible. Whereas the traditional women's model has a sin-gle tube that slopes down from the head tube to the seat tube and stops there, the mixte has a pair of small-diameter tubes which run straight from the head tube all the way through to the rear stay ends. Both tubes are attached to the seat tube as they pass by. The result is a firmer and more stable frame, and this superior design is now be-ginning to be copied by many non-European manufacturers.

I've never seen a mixte frame ridden in sanctioned racing, and only rarely have I seen one under a serious tourist. The diamond frame is certainly the better design for any rider having a choice be-tween the two, but if for any reason you must ride a mixte, don't feel that your cycling performance will be greatly impaired.

As a final word on frames, accept no substitutes for steel-alloy tub-ing like those brands mentioned above. As of this writing no other material has been developed that works as well, even though the 1970s saw a number of high-priced innovations, including the use of titanium and graphite. I've ridden enough of these radical departures to find that they simply aren't as good as steel, either in riding characteristics or in value for the money. Many riders obviously agree— most of these frames are no longer being made, and those that are have a very limited share of the market. The unconventional materials have thus far proved satisfactory only for small frames or those used by relatively light riders, mainly because they tend to be too flexible.

Of course I realize that you probably own a 10-speed bike that you've been riding for a while and are quite comfortable with. You may have paid about $150 for it and now you're wondering if you really need to trade up to that $400 machine I'm advising all serious cyclists to own. After all, it is the motor that counts, so what advantages could you expect to gain?

Everyone who puts in time on a bike will improve his or her riding skills. At first the bike is way ahead of you—it has more performance

When shopping for what is commonly called a woman's bike, this is the frame design to look for. It is known as the mixte or unisex. Originated in Europe, it features twin tubes that run from the head tube to the rear stay ends, being attached to the seat tube on the way. This construction gives the bike much the same lightness, strength, and rigidity as the conventional diamond frame, and allows short people or those who ride in dresses, overcoats, etc. to enjoy good performance. (*Photograph courtesy of Peugeot*)

potential than you can handle—but as the miles go by and your skills develop, the average low-cost 10-speed can actually start restricting your development as a rider. Suddenly you can't descend a winding hill or swoop through a corner as swiftly as you'd like to. You realize that your bike can no longer answer the demands you are putting on it. This is when you need a better machine, one that will let you use your new skills and promote further improvement. The confidence that a quality bike gives will let you do those little extra moves which lead to more cycling enjoyment.

Components

When going bike shopping there is much to consider beyond a frame of proper size and design. Each bike on the showroom floor will be fitted with components made by specialized companies around the world. It is never the case that a single manufacturer produces the frame and then each component needed to make it into a complete bicycle. That's why the 1980 Raleigh Super Course, for instance, has a frame made in England of Reynolds 531, brakes and rims from Switzerland, French pedals, and derailleurs from Japan. Bicycle companies select components with the final price of each particular model in mind and, it is hoped, to give the customer the best quality for the money.

One other reason a serious rider will buy just a frame—in addition to those mentioned above and the desire for precise workmanship and a fine finish—is so it can be built into a complete bike with components of his or her choosing. It takes quite a bit of riding experience and technical knowledge to make such decisions, and someday you might wish to go that route. But it isn't necessary in order to have a bicycle that meets your general requirements. In fact, if you do have a strong preference for a certain component and a new bike you are looking at has something different, a shop will usually make the switch for you.

Everyone who races or tours long distances will of course want components with proved reliability. It's a frustrating experience to have a breakdown on the road, and you can reduce the chances greatly by sticking to the major brands of equipment. Two of these,

Campagnolo and Shimano, are favored by the majority of serious riders.

Campagnolo components are produced in Vicenza, Italy, and are standard equipment on many of the world's fine bicycles. For years Campagnolo has been unchallenged as the leader of the component industry; in fact, company founder Tullio Campagnolo was the first to patent a rear derailleur, in 1933, and since then there have been 133 other patented products. The company has expanded into the automobile, motorcycle, aeronautic, and aerospace industries, which gives you some idea of the talent behind the man. Now in his 80s and still active, Campagnolo was an amateur racer from 1922 to 1930, and during that time he began studying ways to improve the bicycle's mechanical performance. He constructed the prototypes of his derailleur in the rear of a hardware shop in 1930, fashioning all the parts by hand, and by 1933 he was able to open a small business. The rest is history. Today production is spread among four factories, and ground was broken in late 1979 for a huge new industrial plant to meet the ever-growing demand for Campagnolo products. More than 70 percent of the components are exported to approximately a hundred countries.

What makes Campagnolo such a valued name among serious cyclists and the great majority of the world's racers is the extremely high quality of design, manufacture, and performance. In general the parts look so good, work so well, and last so long that the sky-high prices are justified in the minds of many enthusiasts. The most prestigious thing any rider can say about his or her bike is that it is "full Campy," which means everything that can be Campagnolo is Campagnolo. Nowadays that results in a price tag of about $2,000 if the equipment is Campagnolo's finest (the Super Record line), which is about four times what a full-Campy bike cost in 1970. To help keep itself in the market with those not so wealthy, Campagnolo has developed lower-priced (but still far from cheap) components and equipment groups, such as the Nuovo Gran Sport line. What's remarkable is that each alloy and chromed-steel piece that Campagnolo produces is finely finished no matter where in the product range it falls. The company obviously takes great pride in the reputation for craftsmanship it has earned.

In my own experience I have ridden Campagnolo's top equipment extensively and have few complaints. The front and rear derailleurs work very well, though there are other brands which are quicker, if not as durable. The hubs, crankset, pedals, seat post—all have given me dependable service under severe use. The headset . . . well, nobody is perfect. It looks great, but I've yet to have one that didn't begin to rotate roughly due to indentations from the ball bearings within the first couple of thousand miles. Thanks to the aura around the Campagnolo name, though, almost all American and many foreign frame builders will install a Campy headset because it signifies "the best."

Until recently, Campagnolo was virtually unchallenged at the top of the component industry. Although there are other good parts manufacturers in Europe, none has really come close to the universal respect Campagnolo has gained. None has equipped so many top cycling teams and been ridden by so many of the sport's finest riders. Maybe it is the motor, but a Campagnolo-equipped bike has been the kind most motors have chosen to power. In the 1970s, however, a new star rose in the East, and though it is only just beginning to make serious inroads into Europe, it is promising to give Campagnolo a real run for the money in the quality component industry.

The name is Shimano. Founded in Japan as Shimano Iron Works in 1921, the small company produced only one-speed freewheels for many years. The head of the business was Shozaburo Shimano, who found himself on the ropes several times because of the economic depression of the late 1920s, the Second World War, and various shortages of raw materials. However, by the time of his death in 1958, his Shimano Industrial Co. Ltd. had diversified into the production of a number of components and at one point was even making frames and complete bikes. Still, Shimano was a name hardly known outside Japan and there was no indication that within twenty years it would become a world leader in the component industry.

A turning point came in 1962 when under the presidency of first son Shozo the company developed its cold-forging technique. The process allowed the use of pressure—360,000 pounds per square inch—rather than heat for forging. This resulted in products of greater strength, uniformity, and precision, and opened the door to automation. Younger brothers Keizo and Yoshizo joined the business, and these developments soon had Shimano looking toward supplying the huge U.S. bike industry. Early overtures were rejected because of traditional ties with European component companies, so Shimano got a foothold by outfitting Japanese bikes being exported to America.

The tactic worked. By 1969 all eight of the largest U.S. bicycle manufacturers were placing orders with Shimano. Under the leadership of Yoshizo, Shimano American Corporation was begun, and it cultivated good business relationships while keeping the factory in Japan attuned to the needs of the U.S. market. He has done the same as head of Shimano Europe, with the result that the company is truly international in scope and lays claim to being "the world's largest maker of quality bicycle components." Like many modern Japanese companies, Shimano has become known for craftsmanship, innovation and value. Its top-of-the-line Dura-Ace EX and AX components are the most technologically and aerodynamically advanced components available. These components offer an array of innovations which are proving to be the pacesetters of the component manufacturing industry.

My basic thinking when it comes to selection of components is to choose those which have proved to be strong enough and reliable enough to last over the long term. You do get what you pay for in bicycle components, but not every rider needs the utmost in strength and wearability. If your riding is mainly for fitness, commuting, short touring, time trialing, and the like, there is really no need to go into the expense of the best Campagnolo or Shimano equipment. Rather, you should look for a bike—or upgrade your present machine—with their less expensive models or with components made by other established companies in Europe and Japan. Under all but severe use you will find that their performance and durability is more than adequate to meet your needs, and savings can be considerable. For instance, a SunTour Cyclone rear derailleur, which comes in models for racing and touring and costs about $25, shifts as well as anything on the market. Compare that to the $90 price of the Campagnolo Super Record derailleur, or even the $55 for the next model down,

Aerodynamic may be the word for cycling in the '80s, as indicated by this oval-tubed frame equipped with prototype Shimano Dura-Ace AX components. Note how even the water bottle has been streamlined and how brake cables are channeled through the handlebars. In 1981 almost all bike manufacturers and frame builders were beginning to construct frames with tubes flattened to reduce wind resistance. (*Photograph courtesy of Shimano*)

Introduced in 1981, Shimano's Dura-Ace AX line of aerodynamically designed components is the latest advance in the quest for efficiency. Frontal area and turbulence-producing protrusions have been significantly reduced. (*Photograph courtesy of Shimano*)

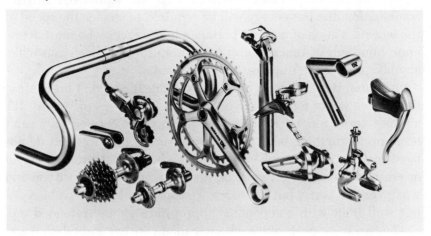

the Nuovo Record. A SunTour Cyclone may not hold up as long under really hard use, but you could buy three of them and still not reach the cost of one Super Record.

In the remainder of the chapter I will discuss some important things to consider about each major component that goes into making a complete bicycle. I've kept my eyes and ears open over the years to learn what works best for other riders as well as for myself. While brand names can sometimes indicate a difference in quality and performance, it's often the case among major companies that the difference is slight and of virtually no consequence. Therefore, I'll refer to components in general terms and use company names only when I have a strong preference for or against a specific item.

Tires and Rims

You can't have a bicycle without them, and yet many riders don't seem to realize how critical wheels are to how it will perform. Taken as a unit, the wheel—hub, spokes, rim, and tire—is the component that can most affect a bike's riding characteristics, next to the frame itself. Wheels help determine how well a bike can corner, accelerate, handle rough roads, and carry loads, not to mention how efficiently it simply rolls along a flat, smooth road. Wheels represent rotating weight, the most important kind in cycling—the lighter the rim/tire combination, the less energy will be required to change the speed of the wheels. This is of great importance to the racer who must accelerate hundreds of times in a criterium, and light wheels can make any bike a lot more responsive and efficient.

Of course, there is such a thing as too light. It wouldn't make sense to sacrifice safety for the sake of saving a few grams of weight. It's also not very economical to keep replacing rims because they can't stand up to anything but a smooth road surface, or tires that do not have enough tread to make it through an occasional patch of gravel or crushed glass. Wheels must be strong enough to support you and whatever you carry, but that doesn't mean they have to be heavy— just well built with components appropriate for the intended use.

The two basic types of wheels are called clincher and tubular, and until recently the former was synonymous with high weight, low performance, and inexpensive bikes. Today, however, you'll find clinchers on many models in the $400 price range. But instead of coming in the previous standard size of 27×1¼ inches, many of the new "low profile" models have widths of 1⅛ or even 1. Additionally, recommended air pressure has been upped from about 60 psi to 90–100. The result is a tire with considerably lower rolling resistance and quicker handling characteristics, yet one that is not overly fragile or expensive. Prices for these clinchers are generally less than $10, with tubes less than $5. A flat is still repaired by patching or replacing the tube, and this is a simple and inexpensive operation. When these lightweight, high-pressure clinchers are matched with a good alloy rim, the result can equal the performance of many tubular wheels at a considerable savings.

Tubular tires (also called "sew-ups" because the tube is permanently sewn inside) are more expensive than clinchers, and some racing models cost even more than automobile tires—$50 is not an unusually high price anymore. Other models designed for utilitarian use can still be found for $12 or less, but often these are very heavy and poorly constructed, making them no bargain at all. I recommend going up a bit into the $15–$20 range for a tire to be used for general riding and training. Tubulars suitable for road-racing events will generally be priced from the low $20s to the high $30s, while those $50 tires are mainly superlight models for track racing and possibly some road time trials.

The advantages of riding on tubular tires are real enough that many serious cyclists are willing to put up with the extra expense and maintenance. For a long time we had no choice, because no clincher could come close to matching a tubular's performance. With its tube completely enclosed, a tubular can be inflated as high as 140 psi (some racing models), and this plus its narrowness and lightness provides markedly reduces rolling resistance. Rims for tubulars are always light alloy for increased efficiency and responsiveness, with different weights available to meet a rider's needs. But tubular rims, like the tires themselves, are more expensive than their clincher counterparts. They also tend to be less durable, though this can be overcome to a great extent if rim weight is correctly matched to riding conditions.

If you intend to race, I recommend that you have a pair of tubular wheels. They should consist of low-flange quick-release hubs, 14-gauge spokes, a rim in the 290–330-gram weight range, and 260-gram cotton tires. This combination will make strong, reasonably light, general-purpose racing wheels for all but the heaviest riders. If you weigh more than 180 pounds you should probably go up a bit on the rim weight, though you can get by fine on 260-gram tires if you'll be riding on mostly smooth roads.

Recently some competitors have been doing quite well on the new high-pressure, low-profile clinchers. This may be the trend of the future, especially for the lower-category riders and those in the older and younger age groups. There are two reasons. First, many of the better-quality new bikes suitable for road racing are coming with these wheels as standard equipment instead of tubulars. Second, the

Tubular tires have the tube sewn inside, while clinchers are open and the tube is separate. In recent years, tire makers have made great strides in clincher design, with the result that models now exist that are virtually identical to tubulars in width, weight, and tread design. Some riders are even racing on the new high-pressure, narrow-profile clinchers.

weight and performance characteristics of these clinchers are in line with the average tubular. This allows a rider to compete on stock equipment with little or no disadvantage, while avoiding the expense of buying a pair of wheels just for racing. My only note of caution is that the new clinchers don't yet appear to have the rubber compounds and tread designs to equal the road-holding ability of tubulars. This is a consideration in criteriums, but in most road races it would make little difference.

If touring is your main interest, certainly clincher wheels are the way to go. There are now tire widths, weights, and tread designs to meet virtually every road and load condition. Riders who tour with a weighted bike and are apt to encounter a wide variety of road surfaces will probably find that 27×1¼ tires on alloy rims yield fewer flats, more comfort, and greater stability. In less demanding conditions, lighter and narrower tires should hold up well and improve handling and rolling efficiency to such an extent that it's worth the somewhat harsher ride. Rim-weight selection for clinchers is not as great as with tubulars, but it really doesn't matter for touring, since strength and durability take precedence over lightness. Several companies are now marketing a foldable clincher tire which can easily be packed for emergencies along with a spare tube, compact repair kit, and several spokes. When outfitted like this, you will be able to take care of most wheel problems within minutes, an advantage once held only by the rider with tubulars.

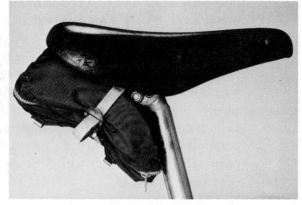

Carry a spare tubular tire or a fold-up clincher and its tube (depending on your type of wheel) under the saddle using an old toe strap. Whether you use a special pouch made for the purpose or something less fancy, like a plastic bag or old sock, it is important to protect the tire from the elements.

Changing over to wheels built with alloy rims and lightweight, high-pressure clinchers is the first thing that can be done to make any older bike more efficient and responsive, especially if it now has steel rims. The one rider who may find that a lighter rim/tire combination is not an advantage is the commuter who must travel debris-laden, poorly maintained city streets.

Tire tread is an important consideration, and there are designs for all types of special conditions. In general you can do very well on a mixed tread. This features a center with ribs in the direction the tire rolls. On either side of this relatively smooth section there is a band of herringbone tread which provides grip and traction when cornering. Many tubular and clincher models are designed along this line, and some clinchers have a raised center for less road contact during straight-line riding and thus lower rolling resistance. But when it comes to a full array of tread patterns, rubber compounds, sidewall constructions, and casing materials for special uses and racing events, tubulars still lead the way.

Two useful accessories for wheels are tire covers and tire savers. Covers, which can be purchased or fashioned from old tires, protect rims and tires from scuffing while they are not being used, and from the weather when the bike is being carried on the outside of the car. (The best carriers are those that mount the bike on the roof or trunk top; avoid bumper racks, because a bike can be flattened in even a minor accident.) Tire savers are inexpensive, lightweight wire devices which attach to the brake bolts and rest lightly on the wheels. They help knock off anything a tire picks up and are especially useful in conditions that make it unsafe to keep taking a hand off the bars to brush away debris. Tire savers may cause a faint buzz that some riders find annoying, but they do help prevent punctures and, therefore, situations that can result in a crash.

All tubular tires and some tubes for clinchers have a Presta valve, which lends itself well to inflation with a hand pump. The much smaller diameter of a Presta valve compared to the Schrader (the same type used in car tires) permits a lightweight, frame-mounted pump like the Silca to inflate a tire to the required 90-plus psi. High pressure is more difficult with Schrader valves, but the Zefal alumi-

Tire savers mount easily to the front and rear brake bolts, providing cheap insurance against punctures to expensive tires.

num pump with the thumb-lock head can do the job. Such frame pumps are not intended for everyday use but for emergencies on the road—plastic models especially won't hold up long if used every time air is needed. It's best to have a floor pump at home; the handiest models feature a built-in pressure gauge and heads for both Presta and Schrader valves.

Wheel covers are a good way to protect tires and rims from damage during transit. They can be put on wheels still on the bike, providing protection from the elements when the bike is carried on a car rack.

When buying a frame-mounted tire pump, it is nice to get the type, such as Silca, that comes in various lengths so it can be mounted on a bike without any hardware. Metal pump brackets add clutter to the bike and can mar the finish.

Hubs and Spokes

Quality hubs are fashioned in one piece from alloy to produce strength, lightness, and precision. They are fitted with a hollow axle and quick-release system that permits a rider to install, reposition, or remove the wheels without a wrench. All manufacturers make quick-releases that look and work about the same; in fact, most brands are interchangeable. The parts are usually steel for strength, but even so the force used to firmly lock the wheel in the frame has been known to snap the lever. If that happens to you, consider replacing the quick-release with Campagnolo's. Many racers ride on Campy hubs, and in all my years in the sport I've seen only one guy manage to break a lever.

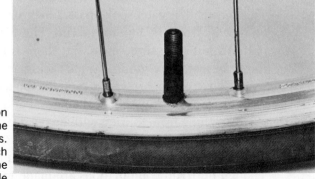

The Presta valve is found on all tubular tires and some tubes made for clinchers. Since its opening is much smaller than that of the Schraeder valve, it is possible to achieve high pressure in the tire using a hand pump. The Presta valve must be screwed open, as shown, before air can be added.

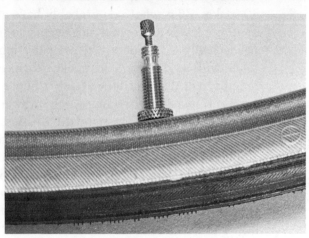

The key decision when considering hubs is the flange size—high or low. A high flange lets the wheel builder use shorter spokes, which results in a slightly stiffer wheel. There are advantages to this in cornering, but on any rough road surface you'll feel quite a bit more vibration, especially if you ride a stiff frame. I like the greater comfort of a wheel built around a low-flange hub, and it seems like most quality bikes now come equipped this way. There's another advantage, too: A low flange gives the spokes a better line to the rim, so there is less chance of breakage at the hub end. I've also found that my low-flange wheels stay in true better than my high-flange.

Almost without exception, the wheels you are riding now or that come on a new bike will be built in a three-cross spoking pattern. This means that each spoke passes over or under three other spokes on its way from the hub to the rim. There are four-cross wheels and patterns less than three-cross, but there is nothing to gain by riding these. In fact, only in some track racing and smooth-road time trials would a two-cross or even a radially spoked wheel be safe. A standard three-cross provides all the lateral and vertical strength needed for everything from touring with heavy gear to taking a fast downhill corner in a criterium.

One other variable in a wheel is the number and type of spokes. Though hub/rim combinations are made to accept 24, 28, 32, 36, or 40 spokes, 36 is what you probably have and definitely want. Again, anything less is for certain race events on smooth surfaces, and 40 are needed only for tandem wheels or touring wheels when very heavy loads will be carried. The spokes themselves are made in various lengths to fit the multitude of hub/rim possibilities, and they come in several thicknesses, or gauges. Any rider my size (about 170 pounds) will do well to stick to standard 14-gauge spokes, which are fairly thick, and avoid those which are butted—that is, drawn thinner through the section between the head and the threads. These are okay for lighter riders, and there may not be much choice with a new bike, since so many seem to come with butted spokes. Of the three types of spokes—plain wire, plated, and stainless steel—I prefer the last, especially those made by the Swiss company DT. Chromed or nickel-plated spokes look real nice, and I've used those made by Redaelli with good results. Union is another top brand.

If there is one thing you don't want to skimp on, it's spokes. A good hub, rim, and tire won't make much difference if the spokes are prone to breaking. There are few things more frustrating than to be enjoying a ride miles from home and suddenly hear that ping and feel that wobble that means a spoke has just snapped. It's one of the most common parts failures, but it shouldn't be. Take care to see that the spoke gauge matches the diameter of the hub flange holes, and that the quality of the spokes is the best you can find. You can often talk to a racer about brand-name suggestions, because for us a spoke that breaks in competition can cause all sorts of bad things to happen, including crashes. We avoid unproven brands of spokes.

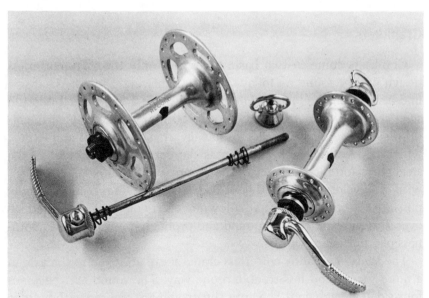

It is easy to see the difference between low-flange and high-flange hubs. The quick-release skewer passes through the hollow axle and allows a wheel to be installed and removed without tools.

Spokes can have a uniform thickness, *top,* or they can be butted, *bottom.* A butted spoke is thinner in mid-length than at the ends. This reduces weight while retaining strength where most stress takes place, at the head and threads.

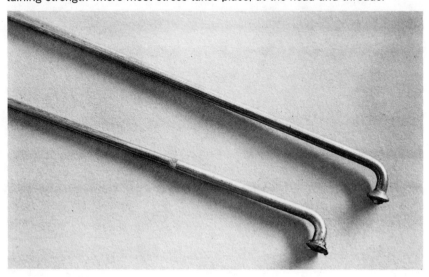

Cranksets

Cranksets come in two basic types, but only the alloy cotterless design will be found on today's quality lightweight bikes. What you find instead on the low-cost models and quite a few older bikes is a steel crankset with arms held onto the bottom bracket axle with cotter pins. These pins are made of soft metal and can wear and loosen, which is one drawback. Another is the considerable weight of the steel parts and the tendency of the stamped-out chainwheels to come with or develop wobbles. If your bike has a steel crankset it's usually possible to replace it with an alloy model. If you do you will reduce overall weight by about a pound and probably improve the smoothness of front gear changes.

The arms of an alloy cotterless crankset are attached to the axle in a more secure and less trouble-prone way. The round axle becomes four-sided at each end. The arms slip on and are secured with bolts or nuts which thread directly to the ends of the axle. This is far superior

A cotterless crank is the superior design and is found on all quality bikes. The round axle becomes four-sided at each end, fitting the square hole in the crank arms and attached with a nut or bolt.

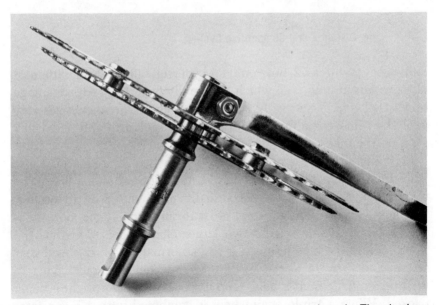

Most steel cranksets use cotter pins to attach the arms to the axle. The pins have a flat face to match the flat on the axle and are hammered in and then secured with a nut. Since the pins are soft they can loosen and permit movement. In most cases a steel crankset can be replaced with an alloy cotterless model, which will reduce weight and improve performance.

to the cotter-pin system and it is the manner in which the best cranksets are designed. Good models also provide protection inside the bike's bottom bracket, where the grease and ball bearings can be contaminated with dirt and metal filings which filter down the tubes. Usually this protection consists of a plastic cylinder that extends through the bottom bracket from cup to cup.

Crank arms come in a standard length of 170 millimeters, because this is best for the rider of average size. But 6-footers and those of us even taller can benefit by going up to 172.5mm or 175mm, because this lets us take advantage of our leg length to increase leverage on the pedals. The result is a longer power stroke and the ability to turn big gears just a bit easier. Crank-arm lengths less than 170mm are available for very short riders, and cyclists like Bill Walton can go as long as 180mm.

The cranksets on standard 10-speeds usually have 52 teeth on the large chainwheel and 42 on the small. Again, this is the case because these sizes have been found to best suit the needs of the average rider. They are fine for everything except upper-category racing, where the norm has become a 53-tooth chainwheel. You can certainly get by with a 52, but you'll find yourself out of synch with most of the riders around you, which can be disconcerting. An advantage of most alloy cranksets is that you can change chainwheel sizes very easily by removing a few small bolts; the crank arm and pedal stay right on the bike.

Most manufacturers offer a three-chainwheel crankset for those who ride in very hilly terrain or who tour with a loaded bike. The third chainwheel on these sets usually numbers 36 teeth or less, which gives a very low range of gears to supplement the more standard ratios available on the two larger chainwheels. This lets the rider operate the bike just as if it had a normal 10- or 12-speed gear system and then go to the smallest chainwheel to avoid having to walk up a hill, no matter how steep it is or how much weight is being packed. When a triple chainwheel is combined with a 5-cog freewheel it produces a 15-speed bike; if it is matched with a 6-cog it produces an 18-speed bike. No one should ever need or use such a system for racing—the extra weight of the crankset and the finesse needed to shift and align the front derailleur make it a disadvan-

Those who cycle in mountainous terrain or who tour with heavy gear can benefit from using a triple chainwheel. The third wheel can be as small as the one shown here, if needed, to give a range of gears so low that a rider should not ever be forced to get off and walk the bike.

tage—but it's something serious tourists can benefit from. A few new bikes come with a triple crankset as standard equipment; otherwise, it can cost $100 or more to change over from a double to a triple.

Despite a common appearance there can be important differences among the various brands of alloy cotterless cranksets, and this is reflected in the wide range of prices. Some models can be found for as low as $30, while Campagnolo's best goes for about $200. What you can expect to gain by going up in price is greater precision in the bottom bracket movement, truer chainwheels, harder and longer-lasting alloys, and a better finish. Shimano is currently offering a nice range of cranksets and has come up with several innovations in tooth design to promote smooth shifting between chainwheels.

Freewheels and Chains

The freewheel has seen quite a bit of innovation in recent years. At one time all freewheels were very much the same in design and material—steel units with 5 cogs of various sizes. Then the 6-cog was introduced, followed by the 7, and alloys and titanium began being used in top-of-the-line models to reduce weight. This has resulted in a remarkable price range for freewheels, with standard steel units selling for around $10 while models employing the lastest technology cost up to fifteen times as much. For most riders, I suggest staying in the $10–$20 range and looking into the various steel models made by SunTour, a Japanese company which offers good quality for the money in all its components. Only the most serious racer might find it worth the great expense to save a few ounces by using an alloy freewheel; those weighing this advantage must also consider that alloy cogs will wear down faster than steel.

If you currently ride a 10- or 12-speed bike, SunTour has made it possible to go up to 12 and 14, respectively, with a minimum of fuss. It used to be that increasing freewheel size by one cog meant you had to install a longer rear axle, re-dish the rear wheel, and spread the frame to make it fit—all at some cost to the pocketbook and the bike's strength. However, SunTour's Ultra 6 and Ultra 7 freewheels are designed to fit frames made for standard 5- and 6-cog freewheels, respectively, with no alterations. The only other equipment needed is a SunTour Ultra 6 or Sedisport chain, both of which are slightly narrower than standard so they can work in the reduced space between each cog.

Another great new idea in freewheels is the Shimano Dura-Ace EX Freehub. If you find this component on a new bike it is a big plus; if you want a rear wheel with maximum strength and also need to change freewheels or individual cogs frequently to meet the demands of touring or racing, the Freehub is ideal. Basically, this system incorporates the freewheel with the hub to reduce overall weight. It allows the wheel to be constructed with minimal dishing (the spokes from either hub flange are tensioned almost equally, adding to wheel strength), and a 6-cog Freehub will fit frames made for standard 5-cog systems. Best of all, cog sizes can be changed very easily. The smallest cog unscrews to let the others slide off the splined body, allowing replacement with the best sizes for the day's riding. A similar design in a freewheel alone is made by the French companies Maillard and Cyclo, whose kits include everything needed to do the work.

There are many different brands of chains, and some include design modifications that are supposed to make shifting quicker and smoother. I think the best model for the money (about $8) is the French-made Sedisport. It is a bit narrower than the usual derailleur chain, so it fits thin freewheels as well as standard models. It's light, it shifts very well, and it'll last a long time if you keep it clean. I also like the performance and long life of the more expensive Shimano Dura-Ace EX chain, though it does not work well on thin freewheels. The ability of a chain to resist wear is important, because a worn chain can lead to deterioration of the teeth on the freewheel and chainwheel and cause poor gear system performance. All considered, I think the Sedisport is the best chain available.

Saddles and Seat Posts

There hasn't been the bicycle seat invented that will be comfortable the first time it is used and each time thereafter. It's easy to see why. Something more than half a rider's weight is supported by the saddle, where small movements from pedaling action and changes in position cause friction, heat, and moisture to build up. Add road bumps and the general narrowness and hardness of most saddles and it's no wonder why riders will sometimes swear that the thing is a product of the Spanish Inquisition.

It needn't be that bad, and there are three things you can do to ensure it isn't. The first is to have a saddle that is wide enough for proper support during the kind of riding you do most. During training and racing the tendency is to stay low on the bike and put more body weight on the handlebars, less on the saddle, which can be relatively narrow for less hindrance to leg movement; when touring, a more upright posture is used, and this makes saddle width more critical for long-haul comfort. Next, make certain the saddle is properly positioned and that your overall riding posture is correct (see Chapter 4). Once these first two matters have been attended to, you simply have to accumulate what is called "saddle time." The more you ride, the sooner you'll condition your sit-down area to accept the discomfort that is almost always there when first attempting to put in serious mileage. The day will come when you can ride for three or four hours without even noticing the saddle. Of course, it is essential to wear a good pair of chamois shorts; if you're in cut-off jeans or something similar, don't blame the saddle for your distress.

While some riders swear *at* saddles, you can find others who will swear *by* almost any type that is made. Traditionalists like 100 percent leather, such as the models made by Brooks and Ideale. Track riders and some time trialists favor pure plastic for its lightness. The majority of riders, however, prefer something of a cross between the

The Brooks Professional is a leather saddle favored by traditionalists who do not mind the uncomfortable hours needed to break it in. That is a drawback for most leather models, but once a saddle is softened and molded into the body's unique shape, a rider will keep it for years.

two—a plastic saddle covered by leather, with a thin layer of high-density foam sandwiched between.

I recommend the last for several reasons. This type of saddle needs no break-in period, it will always hold its shape, the foam helps cushion and dampen road vibration, and the leather top will absorb moisture. That's important in keeping you from slipping around, especially when you're pedaling hard, but a good saddle will also allow you to slide to a new position without having to actually lift your rear end. Some tops are suede leather, and this grips too well when new, though with use the texture improves by matting down and becoming almost shiny. Among the brands of leather-covered plastic saddles favored by racers, who are apt to sit on them for 10,000 miles each year, are the Italian-made UnicaNitor and TTT, and the Avocet RS, my favorite.

All-leather saddles are generally considered too heavy for use in competition, but they have long been a favorite with tourists. The big advantage of leather is that it will actually conform to a rider's shape, something no other type of saddle can do. With proper care a leather saddle can become so comfortable and last so long that it's not unusual for a rider to transfer it to each new bike he or she buys. A drawback is the length of time required to break in the thick, unyielding surface of the quality brands—it can take about 2,000 miles of riding to get the job done. To help the process somewhat, presoftened models are available from some manufacturers. One such Ideale saddle was ridden by John Marino when he set the U.S. coast-to-coast cycling record of 12 days, 3 hours, 41 minutes in 1980 (since broken). He credited the breathability of the leather for keeping heat down and saddle sores away as he pedaled an average of 230 miles a day.

As for all-plastic saddles, don't confuse these—or any of the types thus far discussed—with those things found on inexpensive bikes. Cheap saddles, whether they be rock-hard plastic or thin leather that soon sags, have probably been responsible for more unhappy newcomers to cycling than anything else. These saddles have an actual cost of $5 or less, while a basic plastic saddle that is made with some quality, such as UnicaNitor's, will cost about $15. That's about half the price of a good all-leather or leather/foam/plastic model. All-plastic saddles are not favored by many tourists, but they are some-times ridden by racers in short events in which lightness is more im-portant than comfort. The material cannot breathe, which increases the chance of heat buildup, nor can it absorb moisture and thereby prevent slippery sitting. Most brands have ventilation holes, and these plus the thinness of the plastic allow the saddles to flex and provide at least some softness.

A saddle that obviously has a lot of bounce or cushion should be avoided. If it feels soft as a pillow in the bike shop it is going to work against you on the road. It'll absorb some of your energy, hinder proper pedaling by letting the hips roll from side to side, and con-tribute to the bouncing which creates friction and then saddle sores. Also, thickly padded saddles may have extra width, which will cause your thighs to chafe. A saddle doesn't need to have much padding, if any, to be comfortable. The most important factors are shape, flexi-bility, and position.

Still, some riders just can't seem to find comfort on conventionally shaped and constructed saddles. Others aren't able to bank enough saddle time during the week to cope with the demands of long week-end rides. Realizing this market, various manufacturers have intro-duced "anatomically designed" saddles. These feature special sec-tions of extra foam and a plastic base that is thinner in certain areas for greater flex and weight distribution. The idea is to cushion those parts of a rider's pelvic structure which are most susceptible to un-comfortable pressure. Sella Italia and Avocet are leaders in this field,

(Photograph courtesy of Avocet)

marketing several models for touring and racing. They also have saddles designed specifically for a woman's bone structure. These are shorter and wider than men's saddles, and they apparently work well. My wife, for instance, likes her Avocet much better than any other saddle she has ridden. Women have in the past always had to make do with men's saddles, but these new models give them a better shape to suit their anatomy.

The undersides of saddles look similar, but there are some things to consider. If it is a leather saddle it should have a tension bolt in the nose. This will allow you to adjust the saddle's flex after it is broken in and perhaps develops more softness than you prefer. Some plastic-base saddles also have this feature, though it is really just dead weight because they don't break in. Tourists and commuters will find it handy to have a saddle with small metal loops at the rear for attaching a seat pack, but these are lacking on most of the new models. You can easily add them yourself for less than $5. Racers might be tempted to spend extra money for a saddle with lightweight aluminum or titanium rails, but I caution against it. Hard riding and road shock put a lot of stress on any saddle's undercarriage, and nonsteel rails have been known to break, especially under riders who weigh more than about 150 pounds. In 1978 one of the strongest U.S. riders in the Junior World Road Championship had to leave the race when his lightweight saddle snapped, a real shame considering that it was

A tension bolt under a saddle permits adjustments in firmness. This is a feature all leather saddles should have, because their tops tend to sag gradually during their lifespan.

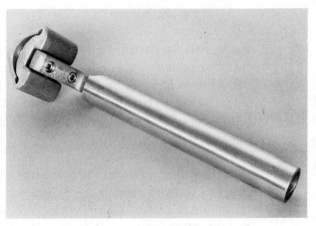

A micro-adjusting seat post is a must for all serious riders. All brands look and work about the same, allowing you to make minute adjustments to the saddle angle and ensuring that it will hold the position you leave it in.

saving him only 3 ounces compared to the same saddle made with steel.

Essential to a good saddle is a seat post which will let you establish proper position and then keep it. By far the best design and the only type I recommend is made of alloy and fitted with a clamping/adjusting assembly which can hold the saddle in any position desired. If you feel the nose should go up or down by a couple of millimeters, this type of seat post, commonly referred to as "micro-adjusting," will let you move it with precision. There are now a number of companies making such seat posts and they work essentially the same, the main difference being price. The S.R. Laprade model is an excellent buy at less than $15, as opposed to Campagnolo's Super Record model which lists for more than three times as much. The extra money buys a nicer finish and 2 ounces less weight, but in terms of performance there is little gained. When shopping for a seat post, remember that seat-tube diameters vary considerably among bike brands and models, so take along your old post to make sure you buy the proper size.

Brakes

Centerpull or sidepull? That is the question when it comes to brakes for lightweight bikes. My answer: sidepull, without a doubt.

Not everyone will agree with that, and anyone who has not been involved with cycling for several years will probably be surprised. After all, sidepull brakes were once standard equipment on most of the world's inexpensive bikes and they gained a deserved reputation for poor performance and adjustment problems. The mark of better bikes was centerpull brakes, so much so that in the early 1970s bike shops found it virtually impossible to sell 10-speeds that were fitted with sidepulls. Customers just didn't want them because they were equated with inferior quality.

Today it's almost the opposite, and for good reason. A modern sidepull will outperform the best centerpull, and the reason is that so many of the new models are designed after the brake recognized as the industry's best—Campagnolo. While everyone else was temporarily touting centerpulls as the superior brake, Campagnolo stuck by its sidepull and proved through racing that its performance was unbeatable. The testing ground included 50-mph descents in the Alps, through switchbacks in the rain, and a brake that does the job there can handle anything you or I will demand of it.

Cheap stamped-steel sidepull calipers with flimsy levers are still around, but they're nothing like the models you'll find on quality bikes or in your local dealer's showcase. The good sidepull is made of finely finished alloy, it'll have a thick cable that resists stretching, the alloy levers will be covered with rubber hoods for hand comfort, and somewhere in the system—usually on the forward caliper arm—there will be a release lever that opens the brake to allow easy wheel removal and installation. (In the Campagnolo brake and some similar designs, the release can be opened any amount necessary to allow for the wobble in a damaged wheel, and the brake will still operate as usual. This is a nice feature for racers and tourists alike.) Complete sidepull brake systems range from around $35 for quite satisfactory Dia Compe and Weinmann models right on up to the Campagnolo Super Record for more than $150. Campagnolo copies made by Dia Compe, SunTour, Galli, and Modolo, plus Campy's own Gran Sport model, range from about $60 to $120.

As for centerpulls, Mafac, Zeus, Shimano, Weinmann, and Dia Compe all make models which work pretty well, given their basic deficiency of design. Certainly any of these centerpulls would be a better choice than a cheap sidepull, and you may not have an option at all if the frame is designed expressly for touring—the distance from the brake mounting position to the rim may be so great that

In contrast to a sidepull, a centerpull brake has more cable and hardware. This allows stretching and flexing in the system, which detracts somewhat from its responsiveness, though quality centerpull brands should be quite adequate for all uses including lower-category racing.

quality sidepulls simply won't reach (extra clearance is sometimes provided so that heavy-duty clincher tires and mudguards can be used). But whenever possible, a good sidepull brakeset should be selected instead of a centerpull, which has more parts, more weight, and more flex in the system when you squeeze the lever. This results in a sponginess that works against your feel for applying the proper pressure. By following a cable to its brake you can understand why. After leaving the lever it must eventually pass through a hanger and then into the assembly that carries the transverse cable, which is connected to each caliper arm. Once the lever is squeezed and the pads touch the rim, further hand pressure is partially lost because of

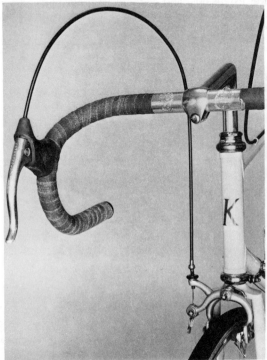

The simplicity of a sidepull brake: The cable goes directly from the lever to the caliper arms, allowing precise response during braking and giving the rider a good feel for how much pressure to apply.

flex in the hanger, brake arms, and cables. With a sidepull brake, the cable goes directly from the lever to the caliper arm—there are no other parts involved—and therefore brake response is more precise.

The brake pads themselves can contribute to a system's sponginess, but pads must not be so hard that their grip is diminished. You'll find various rubber compounds, colors, and shapes of pads—the ones with several "feet" are supposed to let water through for better braking in the rain, though I've never been able to tell the difference. The good brands all work quite well, and Campagnolo's pad material is excellent. In combination with the entire system it allows a rider to feather the levers lightly to adjust speed, yet when really clamping down there is a predictable range of stopping power before a wheel is skidded. Another fine pad material is made by Mathauser, which specializes in replacement pads and pad/shoe assemblies for most brakes. These work very well in all conditions, and they're a good way to improve the performance of any brake—even some Campagnolo owners have gone over to Mathauser's deluxe model, which features a finned aluminum shoe to promote heat dissipation.

All brake levers look about the same, but upon close examination you'll see definite differences in the bends of the handles. This is im-

So-called safety brake levers should be avoided. No good brakeset or bike will come equipped with these lever extensions, and neither will a quality bike have stem-mounted gear levers. Such equipment works against responsive operation of the bike and it tends to foster bad riding habits.

portant, because it means some handles will be closer to the bars than others, making them easier to reach and operate if you have small hands. The shape of the lever top can also vary, as can the design and thickness of the rubber hood. Since you'll be riding on the levers frequently and since the ability to brake properly is so important to safety, make sure the lever design fits your hands well. Levers which have holes drilled in the handles are mainly for show and a bit of weight saving; levers that have extension arms under the top of the handlebar should be avoided. Dubbed "safety levers," they are anything but—they cannot possibly give you the braking control of the lever handles themselves and they promote bad riding habits. These devices are never found in quality brakesets.

Gear System

The gear system can make the operation of a bike seem smooth, precise, and efficient, or just plain frustrating. You may have a full understanding of how the derailleurs operate and complete mastery of the techniques for shifting them, but it's all for naught if you can't count on the gear system to respond exactly as you want it to. If the movement is slow, if the feel is imprecise, if the derailleur adjustments won't hold, a lot of the enjoyment in cycling will be lost. After all, one of the great satisfactions in bicycle riding comes in using the gear system to amplify your strength, to ride at speeds and for distances that your body can achieve in no other way.

The two major Japanese component companies, Shimano and SunTour, have led the way in gear-system development in recent years. Both make an excellent line of derailleurs, with models found on many bikes assembled in Europe and the United States as well as Japan. Their light alloy construction, advanced design, and smooth movement through the shifting range leave them virtually unmatched by European brands, which were once the standard of the industry. Among other commonly available derailleurs only Campagnolo can equal the performance of the top Shimano and SunTour models and beat their durability. But, of course, Campy's quality comes at a price—at about $60 the Nuovo Record rear derailleur is almost twice as expensive as the best Japanese models (and the cost of the partially titanium Super Record is closing in on $100). Campagnolo has recently introduced its lower-priced Nuovo Gran Sport and 980 models, but it is yet to be determined whether these can perform as well as their Oriental competition.

As a set, it's hard to beat the Shimano Dura-Ace EX derailleurs for quickness and precision, though the SunTour Superbe and Campagnolo Record systems are very close. One advantage to going with Campy is the availability of spare parts and the satisfaction of knowing that the equipment has hundreds of thousands of miles of race-proven performance behind it. But Shimano and SunTour have also made inroads in European pro cycling, and there are many U.S. amateurs using this equipment—lower cost with no real sacrifice in performance is the primary reason why. Each company also makes long-cage rear derailleurs to handle the wide-ratio freewheels needed for riding in mountainous terrain and touring with a loaded bike.

There isn't much practical difference in the look or operation of the shift levers that go with these good derailleur sets. All are made to fit on the downtube of the frame, and that's what is important. Downtube levers are in the most convenient location for a rider to reach, and they require the shortest lengths of cable and the least amount of cable housing. All these factors combine to give the best feel for shifting. In contrast, many inexpensive bikes attach the levers to the handlebar stem, and some expensive ones put them in the ends of the bars. Either location is awkward and unsafe. When levers are on the stem it's hard to shift when bent low in the working position, and your knees could hit them and cause an unexpected gear change when you are pedaling out of the saddle. If your bike is equipped this way, it's inexpensive and simple to change over to downtube levers. You'll notice immediately how your hand naturally hangs at the right level for shifting, and how crisply the derailleurs respond to lever movements.

Bar-end shifters should also be done away with—and don't be suckered into buying them by fancy ads that tout their supposed advantages. The cable and housing lengths are so long that much of the feel for what is happening at the derailleur end is lost. To make matters worse, the levers are intended to be shifted by sliding the hands to the ends of the bars and using the last two fingers—not quickly or precisely done. During racing, especially criteriums, it's quite easy to get a sudden and potentially hazardous gear change from a rider brushing by. There is one thing that's good about bar-end levers, however, at least in the set made by SunTour. They come with thick braided cables which are very flexible and stretch-resistant. I use these with my regular downtube levers and they work great.

Pedals

If you are going to invest extra money in some of your bike's components, the pedals are one smart place to do it. There are two reasons. First, a quality pedal will have hardened bearing races and the internal precision needed for rotation with minimum drag. This is a big factor in a bike's efficiency—just imagine how many times you'll be turning each pedal on a single ride, let alone for the years that a good pair should last. Hand in hand with this is the pedal's weight. Top models will have alloy cages and bodies, a big advantage over heavy steel pedals, because it's all rotating weight, by far the most important kind in cycling. Any revolving part takes less energy to accelerate and keep moving if it is lighter, an important consideration in rim and tire selection as well as pedals.

Like many of its other components, Campagnolo's road pedals have drawn the sincerest form of flattery—imitation, primarily by Japanese companies. This design is intended for use with cleated cycling shoes; if soft-soled shoes such as sneakers are worn, uncomfortable pressure from the thin edges of the pedal cage will soon be felt. The cage will have slots or threaded holes for toe-clip attachment,

Campagnolo's road pedal is widely copied, but beware of those that have not included that helpful tab for toeing the pedal over when it hangs upside down because of the weight of a toe clip and strap.

and there should be a small tab to help your foot roll the pedal over from the upside-down position caused by the weight of the clip and strap. It's hard to believe that a manufacturer would leave off such a helpful little piece of metal, but some do.

Avocet sells several lightweight, quality pedals ranging in price from about $25 to $50. At the top of its line is an interesting platform design with a body made of very light high-density nylon. Platform pedals are more comfortable for those who frequently ride in sneakers or wide street shoes, and they also work well with cleats. The Lyotard Type 23 is an all-steel platform pedal that costs about $15 and is a good choice for a second bike that will be used for commuting or short jaunts when it is impractical to wear cycling shoes.

The standard road pedal (sometimes termed a "rat-trap" pedal) can be found in all-alloy beginning at around $25 a pair and climbing all the way to the Campagnolo Super Record with titanium axles, which lists at a whopping $175. While there's no need for most riders to even consider spending that much, certainly a $50 investment in pedals is not extravagant. Since the cleat/pedal combination is the primary link in the transfer of your power to the bike, this must be as efficient as possible. With durability another key factor, it makes sense to go for the best pedals you can afford.

The same goes for toe straps, but not necessarily for the clips. That is, "best" in terms of toe clips usually means they are made of aluminum alloy, a dubious benefit considering the beating they take. Aluminum simply won't hold up as well as steel, and, in fact, some

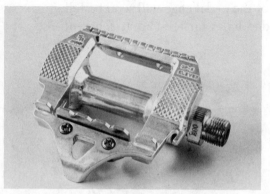

A platform-type pedal can be used with cleats, but it provides more comfortable foot support than normal road pedals if you frequently ride in sneakers or other soft-soled shoes.

brands are badly deformed by any force at all, such as being pressed against the ground when the bike is parked. Not only that, but after a couple of bendings and straightenings they tend to break. Avocet, Christophe, and Cinelli now produce alloy clips which will spring back to shape and resist cracking, but at about $8 they cost twice as much as standard steel clips, which can last for years through all kinds of hard knocks; often you'll replace them because they get rusty, not because they break. Clips come in short, medium, and long, with the proper size being the one that puts the ball of your foot directly over the pedal axle.

Go for the best toe straps you can find. A strap that stretches or a buckle that won't hold is bothersome, and it could be dangerous. Any strap will work while you're just riding along, but when you really have to pull the pedals around during an acceleration or climb and a foot pulls out, it can make you lose control. The way to avoid it is to use straps that are made like a sandwich—two strips of leather around nylon. You can easily see this by examining the sides of the straps; if they appear to be one solid piece of leather, don't buy them. The laminated straps cost about twice as much, but they'll still be less than $10 and should last several years. Also, their buckles will grip securely and let you make minute adjustments in tightness—cheap straps have a way of feeling either too tight or too loose. The traditional name in quality toe straps is Binda, but a number of companies, such as Avocet, are now making good ones. Just look for the sandwich-type construction.

When buying toe straps, pay a little extra and get a model with laminated construction. The center layer of nylon will prevent the leather from stretching and possibly letting your foot pull out during energetic pedaling.

Handlebars and Stems

At last, components where elegance can be considered before performance—but there's a catch. In handlebars and stems, the maker of the most race-proven equipment is also the maker of the most beautiful. That's Cinelli of Italy. Cinelli bars and stems have long graced the world's finest bikes and have naturally spawned imitators, right down to the bars' double-thick center section with detailed engraving. Since the sleek Cinelli stem has also been widely copied, there are now many bikes around with that certain classic look. But Cinelli is still Cinelli.

The stem is critical to proper riding position and bike handling. Extensions commonly range from 70mm to 140mm, the correct size being determined by personal body dimensions (see Chapter 4). Stem length, on the other hand, is relatively standard and quite short, because there needs to be only 2 or 3 inches of stem out of the headset when frame size and rider are properly matched. One other size consideration is stem diameter, which is basically determined by the

Cinelli bars are available in various widths and shapes and are the state of the art. The center section is adorned with detailed engravings.

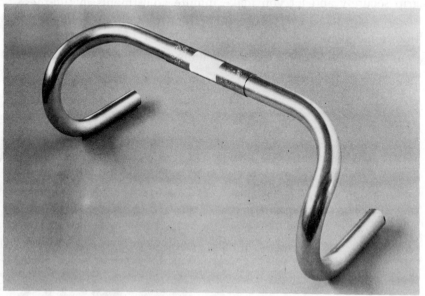

Cinelli stems come in extensions from 7 to 14 centimeters to let riders achieve their best position on the bike. As with the bars, the sleek lines and softly polished alloy provide a classic look.

frame's country of origin. Frames made in Japan, England, and Italy usually take stems with a 22.2mm diameter, while most French frames require 22mm.

There is freedom of choice in one aspect of stems, and this involves the method by which the bars are tightened into position. Cinelli, TTT of Italy, and Shimano have introduced streamlined models which remove the binder bolt from underneath the front of the stem and substitute an internal clamp. These are priced about $15 higher than their standard models and those of other good companies, such as Japan's Sakae (S.R.). The aerodynamic stems look great, but whether they really reduce air turbulence, and whether the reduction is of any significance, is questionable.

Cinelli makes four models of beautifully finished aluminum handlebars for road riding. All are very close in weight, but there are important differences in shape. Model 64 is the most popular, having a bend that allows comfortable riding on the top as well as the drops,

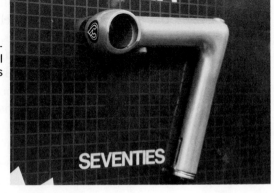

Cinelli and other companies have introduced stems that use an internal clamp to hold the bars. The sleek lines may even help lessen air resistance.

SEVENTIES

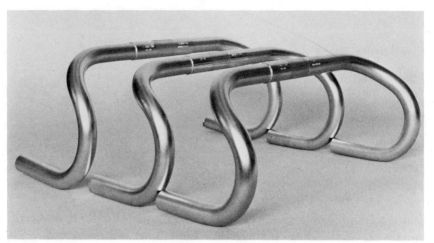

Handlebars come in various widths and drops and can have slight differences in overall shape, as shown by these three Cinelli models.

which are relatively shallow—this bar suits tourists as well as racers. Model 66 takes the same shape and expands it in all directions to better suit large riders, while Model 63 falls between the two in terms of drop. Model 65 is recommended for competition only because, like a track bar, it begins its forward curve from the center and is not designed to be ridden on the tops. All these bars come in 38- and 40-centimeter widths and Model 66 adds a 42. The general rule is that the width of the bars should equal the width of your shoulders, but whatever feels best is the most important consideration, just as with the overall shape itself. Realize, though, that a bar on the narrow side might cause you to hold your arms in a manner that could restrict your chest expansion.

As with stems, S.R. makes bars that have all the gleam and style of Cinelli but don't cost quite as much. S. R. World bars and stems are now found on many quality bikes, especially Japanese makes, and they are a good choice for upgrading your own cycle. If your main interest is touring, you should take a look at the Randonneur bar made by S.R. and others. This model, which is standard equipment on some new bikes, features tops that slope up from the center before curving into the drops, allowing a more upright riding position. Riders with short arms or torsos might find this shape more comfortable than the more common Maes-type bar with flat tops.

For safety and comfort, handlebars must be covered and plugged.

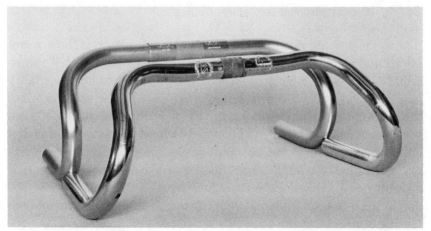

A Randonneur handlebar, *front,* features an upward slope to give more hand positions on the tops. Tourists may prefer this shape instead of the standard Maestype bar with flat tops, *rear.*

The latter is necessary to prevent the ends of the bars from cutting into your body in the event of a crash, and it is best accomplished with rubber or plastic plugs held in place by an internal expander. The bars are wrapped to give a better grip and help cushion hands against road vibration. The traditional material is cloth tape with adhesive on the back, and this is still the easiest and most economical thing to use. If one layer isn't enough for comfort, just add another, always remembering to wrap it from the ends toward the middle so your hands won't push against the overlap and make it separate. There are also handlebar coverings made of leather, rubber, foam, and other materials, which can be used if you find that you need more than average shock absorption for hand comfort. Some top-of-the-line handlebars from Europe are coming with a stitched-on leather covering that is comfortable and looks classy, though it can be slick when wet if you're not wearing gloves. Also, if you crash and tear it up, you're out of luck—it can't be replaced since it's factory installed.

Headsets

The headset is one component that really takes a beating and is quite susceptible to failure. In fact, after buying a new bike the headset will likely be the first (and maybe the only) major component that wears out and needs replacement. A main reason is the amount of dirt and water the front wheel throws at the bottom half of the assembly. This will enter conventionally designed headsets, contaminating the grease and accelerating wear. Also, by the very nature of the headset's function it can fall prey to deterioration caused by road shock and faulty adjustment. The headset must allow the bike's front end to turn smoothly, yet just a bit of looseness or tightness can add to the bearings' tendency to pit the races and cause rough rotation. It all adds up to a dilemma that plagues even Campagnolo, whose $60 Super Record headset tends to wear out just as quickly as models costing a fifth as much.

Conventional headsets that I've had good success with are the Edco and Shimano's Dura-Ace EX. But I think the future in headsets lies in some of the technology recently introduced. For instance, Avocet now has a model in the Super Record price range that is sealed against entry of dirt, has special crossed roller bearings for better load distribution, and is said never to need maintenance. Chris King also makes a very good sealed-bearing headset, which is machined from aluminum and is the lightest on the market. Those who already have a Campy headset can eliminate the most troublesome parts by going to the Jasik sealed unit (about $25) to replace the lower cup, crown cone, and bearings. Since the top bearing race isn't subjected to anything close to the amount of grit that hits the lower one, a sealed top is a luxury, not a necessity.

Many riders consider the headset a throwaway item and will simply use one until it becomes too rough or sticky, then make replacement with another of moderate price. In the chapter on maintenance I'll tell you some ways to prolong headset life by keeping dirt out, and a trick for reviving a shot headset for hundreds of more miles of use.

Sealed-Bearing Components

Every component that contains ball bearings, and even one that usually doesn't, is now available with sealed bearings. This doesn't mean the parts will be maintenance-free, only that they won't need as much routine cleaning, lubrication, and adjustment. As time and miles go by, even sealed bearings will wear and need replacement. Often this means you'll have to send the part back to the manufacturer instead of dealing with the shop at which you bought it. Personally, I'd rather be able to take care of any bearing maintenance in my own garage workshop, but there are three places where I think sealed bearings are advantageous—in the bottom of the headset, in the bottom bracket, and in the wheels of the rear derailleur. These parts are often exposed to dirt and water and they are in general bothersome to maintain.

In addition to making one of the best sealed headsets, Avocet also markets a sealed bottom bracket. Other popular models include Phil Wood, Edco, and the French-made Stronglight. Of course, all good conventional bottom brackets are semi-sealed; they will have a sleeve, usually plastic, which extends from cup to cup to protect against any contaminant coming down the tubes. Since the bottom bracket is the lowest part of the frame it tends to collect dirt, metal filings, water, etc., and a sleeve does a pretty good job of keeping this stuff out of the works. But it can't do anything to prevent dirt from entering through the axle opening in each cup. This is where a sealed-bearing system really pays off. Another advantage is that the sealed units will not come out of adjustment and contribute to excessive wear on the bottom bracket parts. A sealed bottom bracket will cost from about $40 for steel to $90 for lightweight titanium, as opposed to around $20 for a conventional unit.

Sealed bearings are also an advantage in the jockey and tension wheels (pulleys) of the rear derailleur. Actually, it's rare to find bearings here instead of bushings, and that's probably because the wheels are exposed to so much grit, water, and dirty chain lubricant. Normal bearings would require frequent cleaning and maintenance, even though they would allow the wheels to turn more efficiently—there is a surprising amount of drag that can occur as the chain winds around and through them. Several years ago the Bullseye sealed-bearing pulleys were introduced to solve this problem. They will fit any derailleur, and the manufacturer claims they rotate with one-sixth the friction of conventional pulleys. I don't know about that, but there's no doubt they are great for staying clean inside and rolling smoothly no matter what you put them through. Additionally, they can easily be opened for inspection and regreasing when necessary. The drawback is that Bullseyes cost almost $20 a pair and I've found that their aluminum seems to wear faster than the plastic of stock pulleys.

Hubs were the first component in which sealed bearings were used. Several brands have come and gone, but others, such as Avocet, Phil Wood, and OMAS, have won a share of the market. Of all sealed equipment, however, I think sealed hubs are needed least. The reason is that conventional hubs of good quality hold adjustment well, roll efficiently, and aren't unusually susceptible to entry of grit or water. And if the lubrication does become contaminated it is a relatively easy operation to clean and repack the bearings. This is discussed in more detail in the chapter on maintenance, but I'll point out now that only for use in the most severe conditions are sealed-bearing hubs, at about $70 a pair, worth buying. The same goes for sealed pedals, which are also quite expensive and offer no real advantage except in an extraordinarily wet, dusty, or sandy environment.

Note of Caution

Throughout this chapter I've used the words "aluminum," "alloy," and even "titanium" in connection with components. In fact, there is very little plain old steel in a quality bike anymore, and where there is it seems as if somebody has come up with a lightweight substitute. OMAS and Arnold Industries, for example, make alloy nuts, bolts, and other small items to replace their steel counterparts in brakes, stems, derailleurs, cranksets, etc. The idea, of course, is to help lighten the bike—and your wallet. I don't think anyone will really benefit from using such parts, but most are harmless if you have the money to waste. Realize, however, that quality component manufacturers design their equipment and select materials with strength and durability in mind. I'd certainly think twice about replacing a steel part with alloy if it must bear weight or withstand stress.

Another way to save weight is to shave down, cut out, or drill holes in parts. My advice: Don't do it. Many manufacturers now produce components which have already undergone this type of lightening

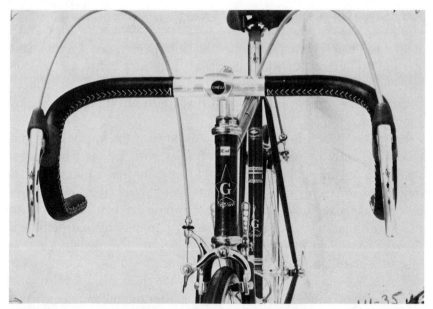

Although some of the world's best bicycles, like this Italian-made Guerciotti, feature drilled-out levers, brakes, chainwheels, etc., such artistry is best left to knowledgeable craftsmen. Many a component has been ruined in a basement workshop or broken during riding because of the misguided belief that a few grams less weight can really make a difference.

work, which was once restricted to bike shops and the basements of bike freaks. It doesn't make sense to risk fracture and failure by trying to make your own modifications—certainly the few grams of weight you eliminate won't make a bit of difference to the bike's performance, unless it's in a negative way. When it comes down to it, the best way to lighten a bike is to reduce the weight of its motor.

EQUIPMENT FOR TOURING

Bike magazines are full of beautiful displays of racks, packs, and panniers, but most bike shops aren't. Dealers quite understandably carry a limited selection, and this narrows the choice for riders in search of just the right equipment for the type of touring they intend to do. This really isn't a problem, though, because most major manufacturers produce a full assortment of gear for everything from one-day outings to weekend excursions to transcontinental trips. If you cast your lot with the product line of one of these companies, you really can't go wrong. Among the top names are Cannondale, Eclipse, Kangaroo, Karrimor, Kirtland, Touring Cyclist, and Veloci-pac. Some bag manufacturers offer racks designed for their products; otherwise, the racks made by Jim Blackburn are light, strong, and functional.

Frames designed for racing can also be used for touring, but not as conveniently or comfortably as frames with longer wheelbases, shallower angles, and eyelets on the dropouts for attaching racks (brackets can be bolted to frames that don't have eyelets). It is always best to take your bike along when shopping for bags and racks to make sure that everything you intend to purchase fits correctly and that the bags don't interfere with the wheels or your pedaling action when they are loaded.

There are several types of bags made for the touring cyclist, and which one you should have is simply a matter of how much gear you need to carry. The rule of thumb, of course, is to travel as light as possible so that there is minimal effect on bike handling and your own expenditure of energy. *Bicycling* magazine, which consistently publishes valuable articles for the touring cyclist, gives the following tips for bag selection:

- Riders on extended tour who will be carrying quite a lot of gear, such as camping supplies, should use rear panniers. These are a matched pair of bags that attach to a rack mounted around the rear wheel. Panniers come in various sizes, and it is best to buy them no larger than needed—too much weight in the rear can cause poor handling and wheel problems.
- To help balance the bike, at least a third of the total load should be carried up front in either a handlebar-mounted bag or front pan-niers (attached to a front-wheel rack). The choice depends on weight—handlebar bags affect bike control least when holding less than about 6 pounds; if more weight than that needs to go up front, front panniers should be used either instead of or in addition to the handlebar bag.
- Front panniers should be able to be mounted on the rear rack, too. This versatility allows them to be used as the main bags on short tours as well as for shopping or errands around town.
- Since safety is a primary concern, bags must stay securely in posi-tion until you wish to remove them. Then they should come off eas-

ily. A handlebar bag should be supported by a small rack of its own or a suspension system that prevents sway and bounce. The same goes for a small bag made to fit under the rear of the saddle. The panniers and any bulky objects in them must not be able to get into the spokes; there should be stiffness of some type to help the bags keep their shape.

- Features to look for in a handlebar bag include a transparent map case on top, a wide opening on the side facing you while you are riding, a method of attachment that doesn't interfere with the brake system or your hand positions on the bars, and a shoulder strap for carrying the bag when off the bike.
- Bags should have wide openings and be easy to pack. You can choose panniers with a single large compartment or several individual chambers, but the latter will cost more.
- Most bags are now made of nylon instead of the traditional canvas, a benefit because they are lighter and more flexible. However, for durability it is important to have a fabric weight of 7 or 8 ounces per square yard. (You can determine this by checking the label on the bag or by asking the store owner or inquiring of the manufacturer.)
- Examine the inside seams of bags closely and count the number of stitches per inch. Eight or more makes a durable seam, and a double row of stitches adds strength. Corners and stress points should be reinforced with some kind of sturdy material.
- Zippers and other closures should work smoothly and not leave gaps where water and dust could easily enter.
- There should be easy access to the main compartments of rear panniers when a sleeping bag or tent is tied on top of the rack. Panniers should separate so they are easy to transport and can be used individually when needed.
- It's good to have bags that are treated to repel water, but there aren't any which are actually waterproof. Seams, flaps, and zippers will leak, so plastic bags will have to be used to protect items you don't want to get wet.

Tents and Sleeping Bags

It is difficult to give specific recommendations on camping gear because so much depends on individual preference and usage. In fact, it is smart to rent or borrow the equipment for your first camping tour. In this way you won't spend a good deal of money only to find that what you bought doesn't really meet your needs or, worse, that camping out isn't what you want to do after 100 miles on the bike. Plenty of riders prefer the comfort of a motel as their reward for a long day of pedaling, and I admit I'm one of them.

Turning again to the expert advice in *Bicycling* magazine, here are some tips for choosing the right gear once you've decided to become a self-contained tourist.

- First, carefully decide how much camping you want to do and the type of weather conditions and temperatures you'll encounter. This will help you make the correct choice of sleeping bag and tent so you won't be carrying more weight and bulk than necessary. It's smart to pay extra for quality; good equipment that is taken care of properly can last a lifetime.
- The more suitable tents are for bike camping the more expensive they tend to be, so expect to pay $100 or more. Look for an external waterproof fly and breathable sides to minimize condensation. It should be a simple design with enough room for you and all your gear. Since there are lightweight alternatives to conventional 4-to-10-pound tents (including nylon ponchos or tarps, plastic tube tents, Gore-Tex bivouac sacks, etc.), it's good to check out several systems before making your choice.
- A sleeping bag should also be selected with temperature in mind so you won't wind up with excess weight and bulk. Man-made fillers are cheaper than down and, though heavier and less compact, offer the advantage of maintaining warmth when wet.
- A sleeping pad must be used under the bag (and a plastic sheet under the tent). Pads are made of foam—closed-cell is preferable to open-cell because it insulates better and won't absorb water. Or you may use an air mattress. These are comfortable and compact, but don't help much when the temperature drops below 50°F.

Cookstoves

When it comes to cooking food on tour, especially when the route keeps you in the vicinity of stores and restaurants, probably the best advice is to forget it. Though various types of small, lightweight, one-burner backpacker stoves are available and they work satisfactorily, they are a piece of clutter that you'll probably find you can easily do without. Also, there is a certain amount of danger involved in using and transporting their fuels, and there may be a problem finding refills. By not carrying a stove you will also not have to fool with cookware. Instead, plan your diet around raw fruit and vegetables, nuts, breads, cheese, a few canned foods, etc., and have a hot meal at a café occasionally. Buy whatever eating utensils you do need in a compact kit for easy storage.

WHERE TO BUY EQUIPMENT

Finally, a word about how and where to purchase frames, complete bikes, components, and accessories. If you live in a good-size town or city, it's very likely there will be at least one bike shop which deals in the kind of quality equipment that serious riders need and want. Often such shops are owned and operated by dedicated cyclists who have a firsthand knowledge of the demands of the sport and which bikes and components fill the bill. A conscientious shop won't

A speedometer/odometer is handy for the racer in training and the tourist. This IKU unit mounts to the handlebars and is driven by the bike's front wheel.

carry products with flaws in performance or durability—after all, the owner depends on satisfied, long-term customers for his livelihood. He will often go out of his way to help you obtain just the right equipment for your type of riding. For instance, if you are looking at a new bike but prefer a different type of saddle and pedals, a dealer will usually be happy to make the exchange and give you full allowance for the unused new parts. If you are in search of a new frame, he will likely have contacts within the industry to find just what you want if it is not presently in the shop—and if you're not certain what is best for you, his knowledge can help clear up the questions. Yes, I'm very high on building a good relationship with a quality bike shop. It's a great advantage to have a place to go for information on all the aspects of your cycling, from repairs to clothing and even riding techniques.

But not everyone is lucky enough to have a quality local shop. For many riders in rural areas or small towns the alternative has become lots of reading to gain needed information and then purchases from mail-order businesses. There are large companies and even individual shops across the country which print retail catalogs. These are often loaded with helpful technical information about equipment—such as comparative weights, types of metals used, interchangeability with other components, etc.—and the good catalogs feature everything needed for the serious cyclist, including clothing and shoes, tools, small spare parts, books . . . you name it. You'll also be apt to see all the latest innovations in aerodynamic, ultralight, and sealed-bearing equipment, which is slower to show up on dealers' shelves.

Something else that most mail-order catalogs and advertisements feature is prices lower than you'll usually find at bike shops. This happens because the big companies can buy in large quantities and often directly from the factory, which means their cost is less. Even though you must pay for shipping, the prices are still attractive—if you also don't mind waiting a week or more for delivery and taking the chance that the item is temporarily out of stock. For those without a nearby shop, mail order is a fine alternative, but it seems to me that it's worth paying a little extra to do your business locally whenever possible. You'll have the benefit of expert advice, you'll be able to take the item home with you on the day you want it, and if a problem develops you'll have an easier time getting things worked out. You'll also be supporting people who are making their livings by working for cycling in your community, and that's nothing to be taken lightly.

15

MAINTENANCE

Tom Schuler is one of America's best racing cyclists. He was a cohort of mine on the 1980 Olympic team, and a year earlier he was top point scorer in the 21-event National Prestige Classic series, the country's major season-long competition. Tom, like all riders in the upper levels of cycling, rides more than 8,000 miles a year in training and racing. And, again like most of us, he'd rather be pedaling his bike than working on it. "I don't adore my bike or anything," he'll tell you, adding with a chuckle, "If I could afford to, I'd definitely have a live-in mechanic."

Tom's attitude points out a dichotomy in cycling. On the one hand a person can truly love to ride a bicycle, so much so that he or she will spend several hours every day doing so. But when it comes to daily, weekly, or even monthly maintenance sessions to keep the machine running smoothly and efficiently, dedicated riders sometimes come up short on enthusiasm. That's the way it is for me. Maintenance is not one of my favorite activities, but I do enjoy having a bike that works well. I've found that I can never be confident that it will unless I do the job myself.

For every rider with an outlook like Tom's and mine, I venture to say that there is someone who enjoys cycling because of—not in spite of—the mechanical aspect. These are the folks who love to tinker, love to experiment, and who look forward to their next crankset overhaul as eagerly as their next century ride. They are known in the sport as equipment freaks. Their love of the bike is all-encompassing, and, I must admit, it is an enviable attitude to have. When it comes down to it, without a certain mechanical mastery over the machinery under you it is impossible to realize the bicycle's full potential for performance.

"Hold it," you may be saying. "I have a tough enough time remembering which way to turn the knob to open a door . . . I need my neighbor's help when I want to replace a light bulb . . . I'm on Daylight Savings Time all year because it's too complicated to change the clocks. . . ." Fear not. I'm convinced that if you can ride a bike, you can just as easily learn to do all the basic maintenance procedures to keep it in top-notch condition. It doesn't matter at all if you've never been mechanically inclined or if you perceive yourself as a total klutz when it comes to which end of the screwdriver to use. I've known plenty of riders who surprised themselves by becoming good bike mechanics, and then were pleased to discover how much confidence this gave them to venture into other "impossible" areas of life.

The great thing about a bicycle, mechanically speaking, is that it's simple and it's right there in front of you—very little of it is out of sight or touch. It represents a very limited universe. All brands of components—brakes, cranksets, freewheels, pedals, etc.—are similar in design and function no matter where they are made around the world. Once you learn how to clean, lubricate, and adjust your bike's rear derailleur, for instance, you'll be able to work confidently with any other brand. Sure, there is plenty of specialized knowledge and there are arcane tricks of the trade that go into making some guys the kind of mechanics who can be entrusted with the national team's machines at the world championships or Olympics, but remember that they began just as I did and just as you are now. And that's by reading about the subject, then getting their hands into their bikes.

It is beyond the intent of this book to go fully into all aspects of mechanical work. Indeed, there are already several books as thick as this one that cover only maintenance and repair. Some are quite good, and I encourage you to refer to the bibliography for some titles if you have the ambition to become a truly expert mechanic—or even a frame builder. Personally, I've found that a great way to learn maintenance is to watch experienced mechanics at work, and I've been lucky enough to look over the shoulders of the country's best. I encourage you to make friends with the pro mechanics at your local shops or with club riders who have ability in turning a wrench. When using a book to learn mechanical procedures, do so with the bicycle right there in front of you. By making it a three-way conversation you'll quickly learn the specifics about your own machine and the book's information won't seem difficult to understand.

There are several benefits to doing your own routine maintenance. First, of course, you'll save money. It's not uncommon for a bike shop to charge $12 or more for an hour's worth of work, and that's in addition to the cost of any parts. For some jobs it might be economical to go to a pro mechanic—namely when special tools and ability are required, such as for the installation of a headset or crankset or construction of a wheel—but why pay for brake and derailleur adjustments, hub overhauls, and routine power-train maintenance? These jobs are as simple as fixing a flat tire, and they needn't cost you anything more than a few minutes of your time.

By knowing how to do your own work you will be able to attend to your bike's needs as soon as they arise. You won't be restricted by a shop's hours and you won't have to give up your bike for several days until the work is done. In fact, you'll be able to anticipate when maintenance is needed and do it well before the time when actual problems arise. This will add greatly to the life span of your components as well as their day-to-day reliability.

As your mechanical knowledge grows, you will be less apt to find yourself stuck in the middle of nowhere with a problem that might ordinarily seem insoluble. For example, even the best-maintained bike can fall victim to a broken cable or loss of a nut or bolt because of road vibration. Let's suppose you're riding in hilly country and during one of your many shifts with the rear derailleur the cable suddenly breaks or pulls out of the fixing bolt. That's real trouble, because it means the derailleur will automatically hold the chain on the freewheel's highest gear (smallest cog). You don't have any tools with you, so with 20 miles of hills to go you'll either have to do a lot of very strenuous pedaling, or dismount and walk, or thumb for a ride . . . or you can conduct a short roadside search for the tab off a pop-top beverage can. When you find one, use it to unscrew the rear derailleur's high-gear adjustment screw so you can remove the tension spring. Then reinstall the screw fully so that the derailleur will hold the chain on one of the larger cogs (lower gears) and give you easier pedaling. You still won't be able to shift the rear, but by using the front derailleur you'll have a 2-speed bike with a low enough

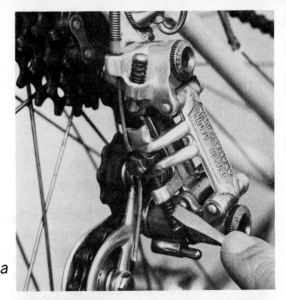

a

Mechanical knowledge can pay off at any time. For example, if the rear shift cable breaks when you are far from home, you will not be left stranded or suffering in a high gear if you are familiar with how a derailleur works. Use a screwdriver or something that will suffice to remove the derailleur's high-gear adjustment screw so you can take off the tension spring (*a*). Then reinstall the screw (*b*) and run it in far enough to hold the chain on one of the lower-gear cogs (*c*). Now you can pedal home with less strain and even handle some hills.

b

c

gear to handle the hills and get back home without great difficulty.

Two things determine how much maintenance and repair a bike will need. One is the overall quality of the components and the other is the kind of use you put on them. Of course, it is no surprise that the equipment on a bike in the $400 price range should work better and last longer than that on a cheaper model. But this will only be true if it is maintained on a schedule that corresponds to the number of miles the bike is ridden and the conditions, in terms of weather and road surfaces, that are encountered.

In the early part of the year it is common for racing cyclists to average 50 miles a day as we build our fitness base for competition. Often this means riding in spring rains or at least on roads wetted by showers or snow melt, and it requires almost daily bike maintenance as well as frequent repacking of the bearings in the crankset, headset, and hubs. All this extra attention, I think, is the reason why many racers come to look at maintenance as a necessary evil rather than something that adds enjoyment to the sport. In fact, quite a few competitors will use an older bike with second-line components for early-season training just so they can get away with minimal upkeep. But for the vast majority of riders, routine maintenance needn't be a daily chore. Instead, it can be an enjoyable and rewarding session that brings cyclist and bike closer together once or twice a month, a session that results in an efficiently working machine and a confident rider.

Let's look into this mechanical aspect of the sport, first by describing how to set up a repair area in your home or garage and then by detailing the maintenance and repair procedures that should be within the ability of even the least technically minded rider.

Bike Repair Area

The best place to set up your repair area is in the garage or basement. Riders without either might choose a spare room in the house, but this is not as good, because of the grease and grime associated with bike maintenance and the odor of the solvents and lubricants you'll be using. Some riders don't seem to mind their home looking and smelling like the inside of a bottom bracket, but usually that's because they live alone or with other bikies.

Your area should be outfitted with a pegboard for hanging tools within easy reach, a sturdy workbench, and some means of supporting the bike in a way that lets you turn the crank and spin the wheels. There are several ways to manage this. I use the cheap method and simply attach ropes to the handlebars and saddle, tying the other ends to a rafter in my garage workshop. The advantage is that I can raise the bike to any height I want, while the drawback is that the bike tends to swing. Other inexpensive supports can be fashioned by attaching a couple of V-notched 2×4s to the bench or wall so that they cradle the bike's top tube, and by rigging a wall attachment for a bumper-mount car rack (in fact, this is the best use for such a rack; bikes should be transported on top of or inside cars, not out where they'll be crushed in the slightest traffic mishap). The other alternative is to buy one of the various home-repair stands now on the market. These range from simple bottom-bracket supports that hold just the rear wheel off the ground, right on up to expensive shop-quality models that let you position a bike at any angle through 360 degrees.

Tools

The tools you'll need depend mainly on how deeply you become involved. The ultimate goal of many cyclists who discover a love for the mechanical side of the sport is to own as many Campagnolo tools as possible, if not the complete kit, which costs in the neighborhood of $1,000. As with everything else Campy, the tools are expertly crafted, finely finished, and incredibly durable. And, of course, they have spawned imitations—totally acceptable ones in most instances, especially for the casual mechanic. However, you'll not need many speciality tools to begin with, and those used for routine work are relatively inexpensive.

First, the general tools which you may already own or can purchase at any department or hardware store. This list will get you started, and later I'll be mentioning a few additional tools which can help make certain jobs go easier.

- 6-inch crescent wrench
- 14-inch crescent wrench
- screwdriver with a small tip
- needlenose pliers with a wire/cable cutter
- 8-ounce ball-peen hammer
- metric combination (box/open end) wrench set
- channel-lock pliers
- small flat and rattail files
- punch
- 5mm, 6mm, and 7mm Allen wrenches

To these add the following basic bicycle tools, which are sold by most shops or can be purchased through mail-order companies:

- chain rivet extractor
- spoke wrench
- third-hand brake tool (helpful but not necessary for sidepulls)
- tire levers (only if you have clincher wheels)
- cone wrenches (one pair of 13/14mm, one pair of 15/16mm; spend extra to buy Sugino or even Campagnolo because cheap sets don't last)
- Y-wrench (combines 8mm, 9mm, and 10mm sockets)
- freewheel remover for brand on your bike
- crank bolt wrench (only if you have cotterless crankset)
- tire-patch kit

This is the tool assortment needed for general repair and maintenance. With it you can do all the procedures described in this chapter.

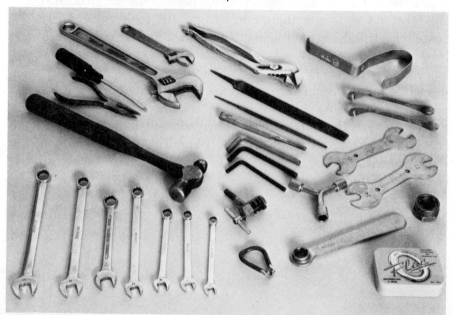

You'll also need an assortment of rags, old newspaper, containers for cleaning solvents, and some lubricants (noted below).

General Cleaning

Whoever said that cleanliness is next to godliness must have been a bike rider. A clean bike not only looks good, but it will work better and last longer than one which is covered by dirt and sludge. But as every serious cyclist also knows, cleanliness is next to impossible without an ongoing maintenance effort.

I've mentioned that a big help to the 10-speed bike mechanic is that most of the parts are right out in the open where they can easily be attended to. There are two sides to this coin, though, because the exposure of the components also means they can catch everything that's bad for them—mud, sand, water, dust, etc. Lubrication will be contaminated and turned into goo, sand and grit will coat the chain and cause excessive wear to the power train, rain will wash away the smooth operation of brakes and gears. Even worse, if these natural enemies are not removed from the bike quickly they can work their way into the ball-bearing movements inside the pedals, headset, crankset, and hubs, causing major (and expensive) problems.

There are two schools of thought on how to care for your bike either after a rainy ride or following the general buildup of grime. I fall into the group that many racers on the circuit belong to but that some equipment freaks are aghast at. That is, give me a can of Gunk, an old toothbrush, a hose, and 10 minutes, and the work will be done. I spray down the bike, brush the Gunk (a paste that turns grease into a brown soapy substance) into the chain, derailleurs, freewheel, and chainwheel teeth, and anywhere else that needs it, then blast it away with a strong stream of water. Next I wipe the whole bike down with a rag, spin the chain to help it dry out, and relubricate it with one of the special bicycle or motorcycle products made for the purpose. I like the type that sprays on and penetrates before thickening into a grease; I then wipe the excess off the outer links so the chain won't pick up more grit quickly. The job is finished by putting touches of a penetrating lubricant, such as LPS or WD-40, on the pivot points of the derailleurs, on the brake springs, and where any cable goes in or out of a housing. These substances will drive out water and prevent rust as they lay down a light film of lubrication.

Now, I realize that water and machinery generally don't mix. I know that the last thing some riders would do is purposely put water on their bikes. But I've used my method for several years as a regular Monday procedure and I've yet to encounter one problem that can be blamed on it. In fact, after a weekend of racing my bike is often covered by things like Coke and iced tea, and there is no way to get that sticky stuff off except with a good washing. I've even been known to wheel my bike into a car wash and give it a dose of high pressure. Of course, every time I use a hose I make sure not to direct the water in such a way that it will enter the internal bearings. This means special care around the hubs, headset and, of most importance, the bottom bracket. To make sure no water will enter the holes where the crank axle passes through the bike, wrap small strips of cloth or pipe cleaners around each side.

Those who don't believe that water can do a bike any good will use a damp sponge or soft cloth to wipe down the frame. They like to keep the paint job protected with a good automobile cleaner/wax, which helps remove foreign substances that are picked up from the road or spilled on the bike. (For those of us into Gunk, it is futile to spend time waxing the frame, because the chemical will strip if off. I've found that a quick application of spray-on furniture polish works great to keep the finish gleaming. I like to use Pledge, which cuts grease as well as a cleaner/wax and leaves the bike smelling so sweet that bees follow me around.)

After the frame is clean and dry, individual components can be wiped off and relubricated. If the power train is really dirty you may want to get out a small stiff-bristled brush and a pan of your cleaning solution (I recommend kerosene or diesel fuel; don't use gasoline, which is explosive and very harsh). With the chain removed and the wheels out of the frame so tires can't be damaged by any spills, hold the pan under each derailleur and the chainwheels as you scrub out the grime. Then wipe everything clean and put touches of your penetrating lubricant on the pivot points of each derailleur and the places where cables enter and leave their housings. Clean and lubri-

After cleaning the derailleurs, spray a small amount of lubricant into their pivot points. Locate them all by working the gear levers back and forth, then give the cables a squirt wherever they enter and leave housings. Use a rag to wipe off excess lubrication and catch overspray.

cate the brake system, too, but do the cleaning by wiping with a rag, not by using kerosene—brake pads will be ruined by solvents.

Chain Maintenance

To remove the chain on any bike with derailleurs you must use a rivet extractor. There is no master link as on a 1- or 3-speed bike (it would be too thick to fit through the gear system), so place the tool on any link you wish. With the pin lined up directly against a rivet, turn the handle slowly and watch to see that the rivet begins to move out the other side of the chain. If it doesn't, back up and try again or you'll surely break the pin. When the rivet protrudes a ways, take the tool off and see if you can snap the chain apart. No? Then drive the rivet out another turn or two and try again. The idea is to avoid pushing the rivet all the way out, because if you do, it is next to impossible to put it back in again. Also, with the rivet still in the side of

When using a rivet extractor, push the rivet through to the outside only as far as necessary to snap the chain apart. If you do it right, the rivet will still protrude to the inside enough to hold the chain together when you rejoin it, thus ensuring correct alignment.

the link, the chain will snap back together with everything in alignment, making installation much easier.

There are two basic ways to clean and lubricate a chain, and no matter which you choose the important thing is to do it often. In fact, chain maintenance can make a great difference in how smoothly your derailleur system operates and how long the teeth on your chainwheels and freewheel last. If you allow your chain to become too dry or gummed up, the loss in efficiency is remarkable. If you ride when it has picked up dirt or sand (probably the worst enemy of the power train), wear is increased on every part it touches. The same holds true if you continue to use a chain after it has worn to a point where it no longer fits as designed into the teeth of the wheels it engages.

I think it's perfectly okay to clean the chain right on the bike with Gunk and water. I do it this way by slowly turning the crank and scrubbing out the links on the chainwheel teeth. But other cyclists prefer to remove the chain and soak it in a solvent to dissolve out the dirt and old lubrication. After the crud has been loosened, a toothbrush can be used, if needed, to clean each link. The chain is then hung over the cleaning pan, wiped down, and allowed to dry.

At this point one of two things can be done. The chain can be immersed in a can of light machine oil or motor oil, hung up until the excess has dripped off, and then thoroughly wiped down (you want the lubrication inside the links, not on the outside where it will do nothing but attract dirt). Or you can install it on the bike and then apply one of the special chain lubricants, again making sure to wipe off any excess. Some of these products are actually dry to the touch right out of the aerosol can. I've experimented with a number of different types and found that they'll all work well as long as they are cleaned off and reapplied regularly. Just make sure that whatever you pick is labeled as a chain lube—some products, such as WD-40, are great for cable and derailleur lubrication but don't have the properties a hardworking chain needs.

Of course, before installing the fresh chain you should clean all the parts it touches. After the chainwheels and derailleurs have been attended to as described above, degrease and lubricate the freewheel. This can be done without removing it from the wheel. I just Gunk it,

a

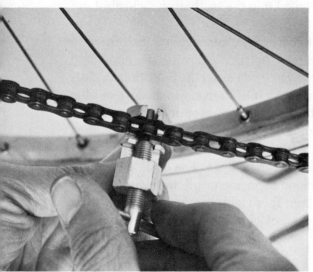

Here is how to remove and install the chain on a bicycle with a derailleur gear system. Since there is no master link, go to any rivet you wish and align the extractor tool's pin with it precisely (*a*). Drive the rivet through (*b*) only as far as needed until you can pop the chain apart with a sideways twist (*c*).

b

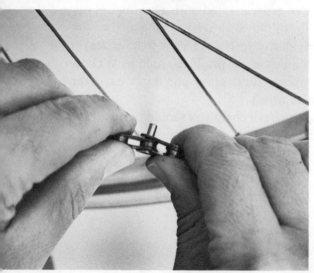

c

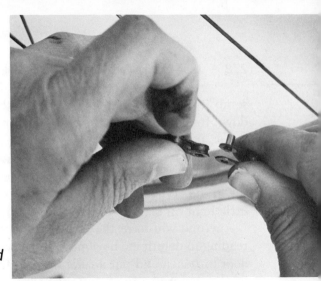

d

When installing, let the protruding rivet (*d*) hold the chain in alignment as you use the tool to push the rivet back through (*e*). Once there is an equal amount of the rivet showing on each side of the link, set the tool aside, grasp the chain as shown (*f*), and flex it side to side. Without this last step the link may be stiff and cause skipping when the bike is pedaled.

e

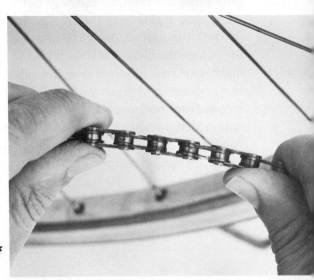

f

scrub it, and hose it, but there is another method just as easy. Sit down Indian-style with the rear wheel flat in your lap between your knees, freewheel up. Take a clean rag and fold it once, slip it between any two cogs, and pretend you're shining shoes. The side-to-side motion will keep the freewheel turning and let you wipe out all the grime. When the whole freewheel is clean, finish by squirting a little light oil or WD-40 into its bearings.

Anytime you have the chain off for maintenance you can take a reading to determine how much it has worn. Stretch it out flat on the floor or bench and put a ruler on it so that the measurement begins on the center of a rivet, any rivet. Then go down the ruler to the 12-inch line. On a new chain this will fall directly on the center of a rivet. If a chain has been ridden even 50 miles it will have stretched to about 12 1/16. With proper maintenance (and if it is a quality chain) that's where it will stay for many more miles. But if it has stretched to 12 1/8 or more, replace it or the wear it causes will misshape the teeth on the freewheel and chainwheels. When that happens it's too late—a new chain will not run smoothly and your only alternative will be to replace the parts. That's a mighty expensive proposition compared to a chain's $7–$10 price tag. With good chain care, a freewheel should last several years, and chainwheels can be good for 10,000 miles.

After pushing the rivet through to install a chain, bend the link to see if it has full movement. Often it doesn't, so take hold of the chain on each side of the tight link and flex it easily back and forth (opposite the way the chain normally bends) until it is free. If you accidentally push the rivet all the way out when removing a chain, don't waste time trying to put it back in. Just go to the next link and drive its rivet the correct distance, then extract and throw away the bad link. Since the chain has some 112–116 links, the loss of one shouldn't make any real difference to the bike's operation, except to make things quite tight when you combine the large chainwheel with the largest freewheel cog (but as discussed in Chapter 4, that's a combination that should never be used anyway). Proceed cautiously and you'll soon get the hang of how far a rivet needs to be pushed until the chain can be popped apart.

Front Derailleurs

Once each year, usually when the onset of winter means the main cycling season is over, it is a good idea to disassemble the bike completely so that all the components can be inspected and cleaned really well, and the frame's nicks and scratches can be touched up. During this annual overhaul, or anytime you remove and reinstall the derailleurs for maintenance or repair, you must know how to put them back into proper adjustment. The methods are basically the same for all brands.

In setting up the front derailleur, position it on the seat tube so that the cage's outside edge is parallel to the large chainwheel and about ¼ inch above the teeth. Almost all front derailleurs have two adjustment screws and an open body. Work the left-hand gear lever back and forth and watch how the derailleur arms move; you can easily see which screw sets the outward limit of travel and which determines how far the cage can return toward the seat tube. With the chain on the small chainwheel and the largest freewheel cog (first or low gear), and the cable loosened at the derailleur, spin the crank and check to see that the chain passes through the cage without rubbing. If it touches the inside edge, turn the low-gear adjustment screw to create the needed clearance. Now put the gear lever into the full forward position and use your needlenose pliers to pull the cable snugly through the derailleur's fixing bolt. Clamp the cable in place, being careful (as always when working on a bike) not to use a lot of force; the small bolts and alloy parts can easily be damaged.

With the chain now on the smallest freewheel cog, try to shift onto the large chainwheel by pulling the left-hand gear lever firmly and fully back. If the chain won't get up there, use the high-gear adjustment screw to let the cage move farther to the outside of the bike. Turn it a little and keep shifting until the chain is climbing up without delay. Once on the large chainwheel, the chain should pass through the cage without any rubbing. The crank arm will come very close to the cage as it passes by, but it shouldn't make contact. If it does, or if the chain shifts right over and off the top of the big

a

To adjust a front derailleur, begin by positioning it so that the cage is parallel to the large chainwheel and no more than ¼ inch above its teeth (*a*). With the cable loosened at the fixing bolt, turn the low-gear adjustment screw (*b*) until the chain will just miss rubbing the inside edge of the cage when it runs through from the largest freewheel cog. Then use a needlenose pliers to draw the slack from the cable as you tighten the fixing bolt (*c*).

b

c

d

Now shift onto the large chainwheel and use the high-gear adjustment screw to eliminate rubbing against the cage when the chain runs through from the smallest freewheel cog (*d*). Proper alignment and clearance is shown in the photograph (*e*). If everything seems in adjustment and yet the chain balks at climbing cleanly from the small to the large chainwheel, shifting may be improved by toeing in the inside front lip of the cage (*f*).

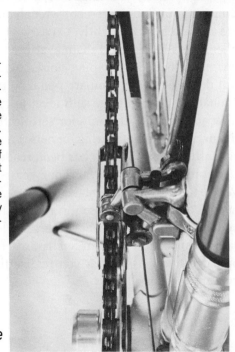

e

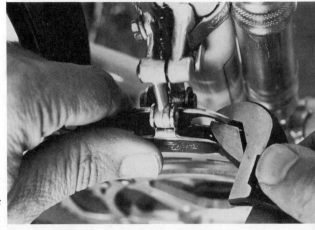

f

chainwheel, turn down the high-gear screw. If the chain drops down around the bottom bracket when you shift back to the small chainwheel, the cage is returning too far to the inside and you need to limit that travel slightly with the low-gear screw.

In summary, there should be no chain rubbing against the cage when in first gear and top gear. If there isn't and the bike is shifting smoothly, you've got it. If everything seems right but you're still having trouble making a smooth and quiet shift from the small to large chainwheel, you might be able to help matters by carefully clamping your 6-inch crescent wrench on the front inside edge of the cage and toeing it in slightly. Go easy—too much might make the derailleur start kicking the chain over the top of the big wheel. Finally, remember that any scraping noises made by the chain against the front derailleur when you are pedaling in intermediate gears can be eliminated by moving the shift lever just a bit to center the cage. The screw adjustments are only for setting the range of motion of a derailleur and have no bearing on noises resulting from the chain's new angle after a gear change has been made.

(A note to those with SunTour gear systems: For some reason— I've yet to hear one that makes much sense—this fine Japanese component company has chosen to reverse the spring action of its front derailleurs. Therefore, when the shift lever is moved forward the chain is shifted onto the large chainwheel—the opposite of all other popular brands. As long as you realize this, the principles of adjustment are the same.)

Rear Derailleurs

Rear derailleur adjustment begins by making sure the mechanism is mounted in line with the frame. The easiest way to check this is to shift the chain onto one of the middle freewheel cogs, then step a couple of feet behind the bike, get down to where the derailleur is at eye level, and take a good look. The line of the chain around the cog and down through the derailleur should be straight; the derailleur should not cause the chain to angle off toward the inside or outside of the bike. If it does, something is out of kilter and the result will be poor shifting, lots of drag, and excess wear. Unless you know that the derailleur has somehow been damaged, it's fairly safe to assume that the cause of the misalignment is a bent dropout or hanger. If this is what you suspect, don't try to straighten it yourself. Take the frame to a shop mechanic who has the alignment tools and know-how to set things in order. Before you do you might as well make some other checks for frame straightness, which are discussed later in this chapter.

Assuming the derailleur is in line, adjusting it is a simple procedure. Begin by making sure the rear wheel is centered in the frame (use your index fingers to feel if the rim is equidistant from the chainstays behind the bottom bracket). Shift the chain onto the large chainwheel, put the right-hand shift lever fully forward, and loosen the cable where it is attached to the derailleur. Now sight from behind the bike. What you want to see is the chain making a straight drop from the cog to the derailleur. If it doesn't, locate the high-gear adjustment screw and turn it until proper alignment is reached. Like most front derailleurs, rear units have two screws. On many models you can simply look into the mechanism and see which one determines the limit of outward (high-gear) travel and which stops inward (low-gear) travel. On derailleurs with enclosed bodies, the screws will be marked with something like "H" or "Hi" and "L" or "Lo."

Now pull the cable through the fixing bolt with enough firmness to take the slack out but not so much that you might cause the derailleur to move out of position. Tighten the bolt, spin the cranks, and shift up and back down several times to make sure the chain drops onto the small cog without hesitation and then runs quietly. If it doesn't, back off the high-gear screw by quarter turns until the sluggishness is gone. This setting is now correct and you can proceed to the low-gear adjustment.

Turn the crank and shift onto the small chainwheel, then pull the right-hand shift lever all the way back so the chain will move to the largest freewheel cog (low gear). Do this very gingerly, because if the derailleur is out of adjustment it could throw itself and the chain into the spokes—and other than breaking a frame this is one of the most expensive disasters in cycling if it happens while you are actually riding. That's why so many inexpensive bikes have metal or plastic "pie plates" between the freewheel and spokes. Good bikes

a

To adjust a rear derailleur, shift the chain onto the large chainwheel and the smallest freewheel cog, then loosen the bolt that fixes the cable to the derailleur. Using the high-gear adjustment screw (the one whose end is in contact, or on enclosed models, the one marked "H"), turn it in or out (a) until the chain makes a straight line around the cog and down through the derailleur when you sight from in back of the bike. Then gently pull the slack out of the cable and tighten the bolt (b). Now shift onto the small chainwheel and the largest freewheel cog, using the low-gear adjustment screw to attain a straight chain line from the cog down through the derailleur (c).

b

c

with good gear systems don't need them; even though the derailleur will be alarmingly close to the spokes when you are in low gear, it will never touch them as long as it is in adjustment.

Use the low-gear screw and check from in back of the bike until the chain line is straight, then try several firm shifts to make sure the chain pops into the big cog cleanly but without any tendency to climb over the top. If you're the nervous type you can then turn in the screw a little bit just to give another millimeter or two of clearance between the derailleur cage and spokes. As long as the shift into low gear is still crisp you're welcome to play it safe. This is also the step to take if you ever hear a soft, rhythmic brushing sound from the rear of the bike when you are riding in low gear. That's the sound of the spokes nipping at your derailleur, and you'd be wise to stay out of the big cog until you can make the adjustment.

Anytime the chain is on one of the middle cogs and you hear a clatter from the back of the bike, get rid of it by slightly repositioning the derailleur with the right-hand shift lever. The noise happens because the derailleur isn't left directly under the cog after a gear change; the chain may be brushing against the next larger cog or it may be angling off toward the next smaller one. Either situation will

Whenever you hear a clatter from the rear end of the bike after shifting, it is because you have not left the derailleur directly under the cog you are riding in. Make a slight movement with the gear lever until the chain no longer rubs against the adjacent cog.

increase wear and decrease efficiency. Be aware of this and soon you'll be able to tell which direction to move the derailleur by the slightly different sound the misalignments create.

Once the derailleurs are adjusted they need only periodic cleaning and lubrication to keep working well; on quality gear systems the adjustment screws should hold their settings indefinitely. However, cables may need occasional tightening, especially when they are new and prone to stretching. To check for this, have both shift levers in the full forward position and look for slack in the cables along the downtube. If there is some, open the fixing bolt at the derailleur and gently pull the cable through.

Should either derailleur ever fail to hold the position you leave it in, the problem is insufficient tension in its shift lever. Turn the little loop or wing nut at the base of the lever to snug it up. Finally, ensure that all your work in adjusting the gear system will last by never laying the bike down on the derailleur side. A rear derailleur pushed out of position in this way could very well wind up in the spokes the first time you shift into low gear. I've seen this happen, and it can result in extensive damage—bent spokes, bent rim, and ruined tire when the wheel suddenly jams; bent chain and bent dropout when the derailleur is eaten alive.

Stretched gear cables can result in slow and imprecise response by the derailleurs. Check for slack along the down tube after shifting so that both levers are fully forward. If needed, open the fixing bolt at the derailleur end and pull the cables snug again.

If you find that the chain won't remain in position after you shift, you need to increase the tension in the gear lever. Most models come with a wing-nut–like tightener so an adjustment can be made easily, even while riding.

Brake System

Brake-system maintenance revolves around keeping the cables lubricated and adjusted. If the long lengths of housing are improperly serviced it can result in sticking cables and the use of an inordinate amount of hand strength. This is very critical when riding in hilly terrain, especially on tour with a loaded bike. Even with a brake system in tip-top shape, hands and arms can become quite fatigued from squeezing the levers on long descents. In this or any type of riding, safety is on the line when it comes to being able to easily and accurately control the speed of the bike.

For reasons discussed in the chapter on equipment, I recommend sidepull brakes over centerpulls. But no matter which system you have, the adjustment procedures are nearly identical. Of course, the ability of any brake system to work well depends in large part on the condition of the rims that the pads contact. If rims are out of true, out of round, or dinged up or have a foreign substance on them, you'll have to remedy the problem before you can expect to have good braking. We'll take a look at wheel maintenance later in this chapter.

Begin a brake-system overhaul by removing the housings and cables. Set them aside for now. Take the wheels out of the frame to give yourself easy access and use a clean cloth to wipe all the grime out of the brakes themselves; you can do this while they are mounted on the frame just as easily as if you removed them. Except under extreme conditions there is no need to use a solvent to clean the brakes (if you do, remove the shoes and pads first). Now put a pencil tip of grease or drop of oil on the spot where the spring contacts the caliper arms—two places on each brake. Inspect the brake pads for anything that has become imbedded in the rubber.

Wipe down the cables with a clean rag and coat each one with a thin film of grease. This will reduce friction and help protect them against corrosion. I like to play it doubly safe by also squirting a lubricant into the cable housing, using the thin tube that most spray lubes come with. Check the ends of both housings to make sure there are no burrs that could snag the cable. Sometimes the housing is crimped where it enters the top of the brake lever (it'll always happen if you turn your bike upside down to work on it—a definite no-no), and you should get rid of this bad ¼ inch with your needlenose cable cutter. Be careful not to create a burr when you do it.

Before installing the cables, spend a minute with the brake levers. Now is the time to tighten or even reposition them if you need to. To do this, pull the lever handle down to the bar so you can get at the clamp screw or bolt that you see inside. When finished, squirt a little lubricant where the handle pivots in the lever body. Then insert the cables and slide on the housings, making sure they seat fully into the top of the levers or rubber hoods. Put the wheels back into the frame—be certain they are centered—and now you're ready to adjust the brakes.

The procedure is the same for the front and rear. First, squeeze the calipers with your hand to see that the brake pads make proper contact with the rim. The pads should be in the same plane as the rim and neither above nor below. If one end of the brake shoe is open, make sure that end faces the rear of the bike or the rotating wheel will pull the pad out. Now let your third-hand tool hold the pads against the rim as you channel the cable into the fixing bolt. If your brake system has a quick-release cable mechanism it should be in the closed position, and the cable-adjusting barrel should be screwed down for a fresh start. (Unlike riders with centerpulls, sidepull owners don't necessarily need a third-hand tool, though using one does make the job a little easier. The handy $2 gadget holds the pads to the rim so both hands are free to work with the cable.)

A third-hand tool makes brake adjustments much easier. It holds the brake pads to the rim, freeing your hands to work with the cable and its fixing bolt.

After the cable is attached and the third-hand tool removed, you may find that the pads stay in contact with the rim. If so, give the brake lever several hard pulls and let it snap back. This will stretch the cable and get rid of any kinks in the system, as well as double-check that nothing will pop loose the first time you brake hard on the road. Also, I like to leave two or three threads worth of slack in the cable-adjusting barrel so I can let the brake open farther, if needed, without having to undo and reset the cable.

Perhaps the problem you'll encounter most often with the brake system is pads that don't contact the rim simultaneously. Or worse, a pad that stays against the rim when the lever is released. This is easy to correct on centerpulls because the caliper arms are attached to a stationary plate which is in turn bolted to the frame. Simply take the brake in your hands and pivot it until the pads are equidistant from the rim, then snap the lever a couple of times to make sure they are going to stay that way. You may need to loosen the large center bolt before you can move the brake, but you shouldn't have to. In fact, it's a good idea to keep it just loose enough to move by hand—if a hard blow such as a fall knocks the brake off center you'll be able to set it straight without needing to dig up a wrench.

Sidepull owners don't have it so convenient. Despite all its advantages, a sidepull brake can be a headache to keep centered. However, Campagnolo and some other quality models make the job easier by machining flat sides on the center bolt which allow a thin wrench (in Campy's case a 13mm cone wrench) to be used to position the brake. There is no way centering can be accomplished with simple hand strength, though. Real difficulty comes on older and inexpensive models without the flats, and this is a main reason why sidepulls gained their reputation for being hard to adjust. To center a brake like this you need a screwdriver (or punch) and hammer—it's a crude operation, but it works. Place the screwdriver on top of the spring on the side of the brake that is away from the rim. Tap it down until the pads become equidistant, then firmly tighten the bolt that fixes the

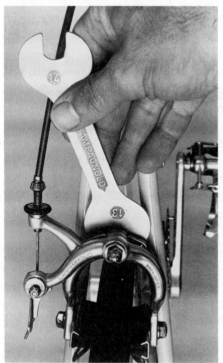

Centering a sidepull brake so that the pads are equidistant from the rim is a snap on models designed with a flat face on the center bolt. The Campagnolo brake accepts the 13mm end of the hub cone wrench.

Inexpensive sidepull brakes have an annoying habit of keeping one pad much closer to the rim than the other. The easiest way to center a brake like this is to tap the spring on the side that is away from the rim until the pads are equidistant. Snap the brake lever to make sure the position holds, then firmly tighten the large nut that holds the brake to the frame.

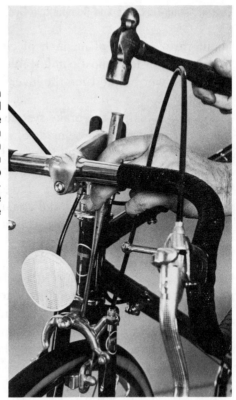

brake through the frame. With luck the brake will remain properly positioned for a reasonable time. Of course, when you are shopping for a new bike or a brakeset, don't consider any sidepulls that aren't engineered with centering flats.

When you pull on the lever handle there should be some play before the pads hit the rim. If there is hardly any, your fingers will remain quite extended and you won't have good leverage. In addition, a brake adjusted too tightly means that a rim which gets the least bit out of true will rub the pads. I like to have about an eighth of an inch of clearance between each pad and the rim, a margin that will let most wobbles pass through cleanly. This is important in racing, especially in criteriums on city streets where there are manhole covers and cracks and patches on the pavement. A rear wheel can get knocked out of true without the rider's realizing it, even though the rim is rubbing a pad and cutting his speed. For this reason, Roger Young and some other top competitors play it really safe and keep about three-eighths of an inch of clearance. I recommend you go with whatever feels most comfortable, just as long as you can get full braking power by the time the lever handle is ¾ inch from the handlebars.

The only parts of the brake system that should need replacement under normal use are those made of rubber—the lever hoods and the pads. Since I must pack and transport my bike so much each racing season, the hoods take quite a beating and I change them a couple of times a season. But if you don't have to put your machine through this kind of wear and tear, and if you use a rubber conditioner such as Armor All, hoods can last until you wear them through. Brake pads, on the other hand, should be replaced at the start of each new season if you ride your bike in all sorts of conditions. Sun, rain, the passage of time, and chemicals picked up from the road all combine to harden the rubber compound and steal its stopping power. Otherwise, if the pads have "feet" they should be replaced whenever these sections have worn down to the main block. I think one of the best improvements you can make to any brake system (with the possible exception of Campagnolo's) is to replace the stock pads with those made by Mathauser.

Squealing brakes? If the noise isn't caused by something to do with the rim—some models have serrated sides that send out a loud buzz as they eat up brake pads—then the problem can probably be solved by changing the angle at which the pads strike the rim. Proceeding very carefully, slip your 6-inch crescent wrench onto the bottom of the caliper arm and bend it just enough so that when the brake is applied the front of the pad will contact the rim first. If after you make this adjustment to all four you still have noise, go to another brand of pads. Again, Mathauser and Campagnolo are superior even in their quietness.

Wheels

Wheel maintenance is critical to efficiency, reliability, and safety in cycling. Hubs that are improperly lubricated or adjusted will steal your energy. Problems with tires and spokes can leave you stranded in the middle of nowhere. Rims which are out of true or somehow damaged will hamper the performance of any brake system, no matter how well it has been adjusted. Still, if you have wheels of good quality to begin with, there is no reason you shouldn't be able to keep them in excellent shape in your own workshop. Only when a wheel has to be rebuilt for some reason do I recommend taking the job to a professional.

Obviously you can keep the need for wheel maintenance to a minimum by the way you ride. Though the wheel components are by themselves light in weight and quite fragile, when properly assembled they have remarkable strength and durability. If you complement this with sensible riding techniques, a bike's original wheels can easily last for years. Playing the biggest part in this is how you deal with road hazards like potholes, railroad tracks, and curbs. There's no big secret to it—avoid hitting them if you can, and if you can't, then slow down and lighten up. That is, sort of sit like a jockey with your crank arms parallel to the ground so you can get your weight up in the air as the wheels pass over the hazard. It's sort of a floating, see-saw motion as first the front wheel and then the rear makes contact. Once you're good at it you'll even be able to lift the front wheel right over a low obstacle and set it down gently as the rear gives it a light bump. Of course, this technique won't protect your rims very well if your tires aren't up to proper pressure—that's always a must before you go riding.

But no matter how carefully you ride or how good your wheels are, it is inevitable that they will get out of true from time to time. A twitchy feeling when riding on smooth roads, jerky braking action, or simple observation will tip you off to a wheel that has developed a side-to-side or up-and-down wobble. The first condition is most often caused by faulty spoke tension and is quite easy to correct in a few minutes' time. But a wheel that has become out of round usually indicates a deformity in the rim caused by an impact, and this can be harder to correct.

In either case, the instrument of salvation or further ruin is called a spoke wrench. These come in various styles and often sell for less than $1 (be sure you get the size that exactly fits the nipples of your spokes). The key to using this tool is to proceed cautiously by making small adjustments. Anytime you seem to be making the problem worse or if nipples are becoming so hard to turn that they strip, round off, or cause a spoke to break, stop right there and seek help. But it needn't come to that if you understand the principles behind wheel construction and the trueing process.

Wheel Trueing

Looking at a front wheel with 36 spokes (the normal number for 10-speed bikes), you will see that 18 spokes go to the rim from the left flange of the hub and 18 go from the right flange. They alternate all the way around the rim, making the construction of a front wheel basically a matter of lacing the spokes in the chosen pattern and then tightening them uniformly. Ideally this would result in a rim that is exactly centered between the hub flanges and that spins in a perfect circle. In actuality, perfection is impossible due to the "man" in manufacture of the parts, but we can come close by making adjustments to individual spokes. We can pull a certain small area of the rim to the left by tightening the spoke that travels to it from the left flange. Conversely, if we take tension off that same spoke by loosening it, this part of the rim will move slightly to the right. Or we can pull it to the right by tightening either of the two neighboring spokes, because each of them goes to the hub's right flange. Turning a nipple counterclockwise with the tool tightens the spoke; clockwise rotation loosens it.

To remove a wheel's side-to-side wobble you must first determine exactly where it is located. Professional mechanics use trueing stands that sometimes cost hundreds of dollars, but there are stands made for home use that sell for as low as $20. It's great to have one of these, because you can get the wheel out of the frame, remove the tire and work on it unhindered. Adjustable arms show exactly where the out-of-true sections are, making it easier to do an accurate job. The traditional alternative has been to true wheels while they are still in the bike, spotting wobbles by watching the rim pass through the brake pads. This can work, but it makes it a bit tough for someone who is trying to learn. Once you know what you're doing, though, it's easy to touch up a wheel right on the bike.

Small wobbles should always be taken out by making spokes tighter rather than looser. This is because, in general, a tightly tensioned wheel is stronger than a loose one. Begin by going around the wheel with your hands and squeezing pairs of spokes. This lets you check their relative tightness, and you might just find one or two that have vibrated loose. If so, tighten them until they are as taut as their neighbors, and that may be all it takes to bring the wheel into true.

If there are no loose spokes and the rim has, for example, a small movement to the right, go to the spoke nearest the middle of the wobble that connects to the left flange of the hub and tighten its nipple half a turn. Then spin the wheel to check the results. If that wasn't enough, another half-turn will probably do it. If the wobble to the right is larger, locate its center and tighten that left-flange spoke a half turn, then go to the left-flange spokes immediately before and after and tighten them a quarter turn. Spin the wheel and proceed as needed. It's always better to undercompensate and have to come back around a second, third, or even fourth time rather than over-tighten and create additional problems.

Should it become hard to turn the spoke nipples enough to draw the rim into true, this is the time to also loosen (clockwise) those that go to the opposite flange. Proceed cautiously by quarter and half turns and continually check progress. Especially during work on large wobbles it is best to true by loosening and tightening alternate spokes.

If while attempting to straighten a badly out-of-true wheel you get to a point where some spokes are too tight to turn any farther and their opposite-flange counterparts are almost flaccid, what you've got is a bent rim. There is nothing to do but replace it, and at the same time you should have a new set of spokes installed. It's a job that a good bike shop mechanic can handle easily, and so can quite a few cycling enthusiasts. Although a description of wheel building is beyond the scope of this chapter, I don't want you to think that it is necessarily beyond your ability as a mechanic. If you are interested in learning how to construct wheels, consult Jobst Brandt's excellent new book on the subject, *The Bicycle Wheel.*

A wheel that shows no side-to-side wobble might still need true-ing. You'll know it when you are riding down a smooth road and there is a rhythmic bouncing sensation. Watch the rim spin past the brake pads and you can see the reason—a section that rises above (or perhaps dips below) the steady circle that the rest of the rim makes. If it's a hop, you need to pull that section down. Determine the length of the too-high area and which spokes go to it. Let's say that six spokes seem to be involved. Tighten the two in the center of the hop half a turn each and the two on either side of them a quarter turn. Check progress by spinning the wheel and apply more inward pull, if needed, by proceeding in the same manner. Because you are giving fairly equal tightness to spokes going to each flange, the rim will tend to be pulled down but not much to the left or right, leaving the wheel in good side-to-side true. If the rim has a dip instead of a hop, reverse the procedure and loosen the spokes involved. Go easily and see how the rim responds. If the whole thing starts off shaped like an egg (or begins to look like one), you may be in for more than a rookie wheel truer can handle. But by using this general procedure you should be able to help most up-and-down problems so that the bike will roll more smoothly and brake better.

The trueing technique for a rear wheel is the same as just described, even though its construction differs from the front in one major way. Because of the width of the freewheel, the rim is not centered between the hub flanges but rather between the outermost axle nuts. For this to happen the rim must be pulled to the right (freewheel side) by one of two ways: Either the 18 right-flange spokes are tightened several turns more than the left ones, or the right-flange spokes are shorter than the left and all 36 are tensioned about equally. The effect is called "dishing" and you can easily see that the freewheel-side spokes make a flatter angle to the rim than those from the left flange. This produces a wheel that is inherently weaker than a front wheel in which all spokes are of equal length, angle, and tension, and until recently there has been no way around it. But Shimano, always the innovator, has just introduced new hub models which are designed to greatly reduce rear-wheel dishing.

Spokes

You should rarely experience broken spokes if your wheels are built with well-matched components of good quality. But if the spokes are cheap or they have become fatigued with use, breakage can be a constant problem. (Because of the fatigue factor it's always a wise move to install new spokes whenever a wheel is rebuilt, even if they have not been breaking. Lacing on a new rim with used spokes might save you some money today, but there will almost surely be problems down the road.) Spoke breakage can also be the fault of the hub or the match between it and the spokes. For example, if there remains a small gap after the spokes fit through the holes in the flange, the movement that results as the wheel rolls along the road can cause the heads to snap off unendingly. The solution here is to go to thicker gauge spokes which fit tightly through the flange. It's sad to say, but some new bikes have been known to come with this ready-made problem. You might be able to spot it and avoid buying one by looking closely.

When a spoke does snap you'll probably hear it or feel it, and that's your notice to stop immediately and get it out of the wheel. A broken spoke can do no good and it could lead to major damage, especially if it is behind the freewheel (spokes almost always break at their bend through the flange and more often than not on the free-wheel side of the rear wheel, because of the extra tension required for dishing). I once saw a perfect example of the disaster that can re-sult when a rider ignores a pop in the rear wheel and later shifts into a low gear. In this case the protruding spoke snagged the derailleur cage and the next thing the rider knew he was sprawled in the road, looking at a pretzeled wheel and destroyed derailleur that had frac-tured the dropout as it was ripped backward. So for the sake of safety and your pocketbook, dismount whenever you hear a telltale snap, find the culprit, bend it double, and unscrew it from the nipple. Check to see how badly the wheel is out of true and open the brake's quick release if necessary to prevent the rim from hitting the pads. Ride cautiously until you get back home, because the wheel is in a weakened state.

When replacing a spoke you should remove the tire, tube, and rim strip if you have clinchers; those with tubular wheels can get by with peeling away the tire just in the area around the work. If it's a front wheel, insert a spoke of identical length and thickness through the hole in the hub flange (try to use the same spoke brand if possible; take your wheel or the broken spoke down to the bike shop for a match). Pay strict attention that you follow the wheel's over/under crossing pattern as you channel the spoke to the rim. You will have to snake it around a bit, but try not to give it a severe bend. Then screw on the new nipple and tighten the spoke until it feels as taut as those around it. Finish by going through the regular trueing procedure and the wheel will be back in tip-top shape. Clincher owners must make sure that the end of the new spoke (or any spoke) doesn't extend through the nipples so that it could puncture the tube. File it down if it protrudes.

Rear-wheel spoke replacement follows the same routine, but you must also remove the freewheel. Even when the broken spoke is on the left side of the wheel you'll have an easier time if you get the cogs out of the way (see procedure below). As with the front wheel, make sure the new spoke is identical to those it is joining. Remember that there may be a different length on each side of the wheel. After the spoke has been installed and the wheel trued, put the freewheel and tire back on and fasten the wheel into the frame. (Always remove and install the rear wheel with the chain positioned on the smallest cog; this keeps the derailleur as far out of the way as possible.) Finish the job by running through the gears to make sure everything is in adjustment.

Freewheel Removal

To take the freewheel off the hub, remove the wheel from the frame and keep the tire inflated. Remove the quick-release skewer from the axle. Insert the freewheel-removing tool fully into the unit's notches or splines and run the skewer back through the axle (handle on the left side), leaving out the two little conical springs. Screw the

Tools for removing freewheels from hubs come in many different designs, and few are interchangeable. For this reason it is a good idea to buy the same brand of freewheel should you need another for racing or touring.

When removing a freewheel, use the quick-release skewer, minus the two conical springs, to hold the removal tool tightly in place. Standing over the wheel with the freewheel on the right side, exert downward force with the wrench until the free-wheel breaks loose. Then loosen the quick release before proceding further or you may damage it.

nut onto the end of the skewer until it contacts the freewheel re-mover. If all looks properly engaged and aligned, tighten the skewer very firmly to prevent the remover from slipping and damaging the freewheel. This is very important when there are just two small cogs interlocking the remover and the freewheel.

If you have a bench vise, clamp it on the remover tool so that the wheel is held in a horizontal position. Take hold of the wheel at three and nine o'clock and turn it counterclockwise as you press down. As soon as the freewheel gives, stop and loosen the quick-release skewer or you will damage it. You can usually finish unscrewing the free-wheel by turning the tool with your hand. If you don't have a vise, a large crescent wrench will work. Hold the wheel vertically in front of you with the freewheel on the right side and apply downward (counterclockwise) force with the wrench. Again, as soon as the free-wheel breaks loose remove the skewer. If your wheel isn't equipped with a quick-release hub, use the axle nut to hold the remover in place. But no matter how you do it, if it seems that the tool is moving

a

To remove the freewheel, first unscrew the quick-release system and take out the small conical springs (*a*). Insert the removal tool fully and precisely into the freewheel (*b*), and secure it with the quick-release skewer (*c*). (Note: the multi-splined tool shown offers the most foolproof operation; whenever you replace a freewheel, look for a new one that will accept such a tool.)

b

c

d

With the wheel in position (*d*), apply downward (counterclockwise) force with the wrench until the freewheel breaks free, then loosen or remove the quick-release skewer before you continue unscrewing the freewheel (*e*).

e

against the freewheel instead of making the freewheel unscrew from the hub, stop immediately, realign the tool, and make it tighter. Otherwise the notches will be damaged and it may be impossible to get the freewheel off without tearing it apart and using a pipe wrench on the body. There is almost no chance that it will come to this if the freewheel is designed to accept a multi-splined tool, which is something to keep in mind whenever you're shopping for a new one.

You can help ensure that the freewheel will come off without difficulty if you apply a little grease or an anti-seize product to the threads before putting it back on the hub. No tools are needed for installation—just screw on the freewheel hand-tight and the pull of the chain will do the rest. Be very careful not to cross its steel threads with the softer alloy of the hub—if the freewheel doesn't spin on easily, then back up and start again. Should you change freewheels, be sure that the new one matches the hub's threads or else serious damage to the alloy could result. If in doubt, check with your dealer or the authoritative source for such information, *Sutherland's Handbook for Bicycle Mechanics*.

Hubs

The wheel hubs should be opened, cleaned, greased, and adjusted at least once a year, more often if you ride much in wet weather or in places where there is a lot of dust or sand. This is the only internal-bearing maintenance I'll be detailing, mainly because it is the easiest to perform and it requires the least outlay for special tools. I think everyone should be able to handle hub maintenance, and if you enjoy this kind of work then there is no reason not to branch out and have a go at overhauling the crank, headset, and pedals, all of which are similar to the hubs in mechanical concept. These parts should also receive a thorough cleaning and repacking once every year or, as I'll describe later, whenever inspection discovers the need for immediate attention.

Anytime you have occasion to pull a wheel out of the frame, use the opportunity to check the axle adjustment. Remove the quick-release skewer and turn the axle with your fingers. It should have a smooth rotation. If you try to move the axle up and down or side to side, there should be no play or only the tiniest bit (some mechanics prefer slight movement, for reasons we'll soon see). Now hold the wheel by the ends of the axle and give it a spin. Tune in to what you are experiencing—there should be no roughness, no catches in the rotation, no grinding. If any of this shows up and you have recently repacked the hub, you need to adjust the axle cones. If it has been months since the hub was last maintained, you should open it up to check for anything that might have gotten into the works. In either case, to work with the hubs you will need two pairs of cone wrenches (two having ends of 13mm and 14mm, two with 15mm and 16mm). These are thin tools that fit the flats on the conical axle nuts which contact the bearings in each side of the hub. At times you'll need to apply a good deal of force with them, so you should spend enough to get a set which will hold up. Campagnolo cone wrenches are virtually indestructible, but Sugino and Bicycle Research make strong models which sell for half of Campy's price of about $7 each.

Hub work is the same for front and rear wheels, the only difference being the need to remove the freewheel in order to clean and repack the rear (the axle can be adjusted with the freewheel in place, but it is much easier when it's out of the way). When removing the rear axle, always work from the left side so that the right-side parts can remain on the axle and in their same relationship to it. When the axle is reinstalled there will then be no chance that the spacing under the freewheel has been altered. You can work from either side of the front hub; for my instructions, though, I'll assume we're operating from the left side of each hub.

Before disassembling a hub, look right into the end of the axle and rotate it from the opposite side. Any oscillation means that the axle is bent, a much more common occurrence with rear axles than fronts. The reason is obvious once you get the freewheel off and see how much of the axle's right side is unsupported after it leaves the hub. Don't be too shook up if you see an out-of-round rotation—I daresay there aren't many 10-speed bikes with perfectly straight rear axles, and a slight bend doesn't seem to hurt a thing. However, if yours looks quite bent, and if you find signs of uneven wear on the cones or in the races where the bearings roll, you should take the axle to a bike shop and buy a replacement. It is best to get new cones, lock washers, and nuts with the axle so there won't be the danger of old threads and new not fitting together snugly.

To remove the axle, take off the nut, lock washer, and cone from its left side only and pull it out of the hub. Do this over a rag so that if any bearings fall out they won't roll away. Now use a rag to wipe clean all axle parts and set them aside. (There is no reason to use a cleaning solvent for any aspect of hub maintenance; it's simply not needed, and if you should fail to remove all traces of it the result will be contamination of the new lubrication.) With the wheel flat in your lap, use a small screwdriver to coax the bearings down through the hollow hub and into your waiting hand; then flip the wheel over and do the other side. Put the bearings where they won't get away and now you're ready to clean the hub itself.

Most hubs have pressed-in dust caps that cover part of the opening on each side. These caps can be pried out to make cleaning and re-greasing easier, but you can certainly do the job well enough with them in place. I don't like to remove them, because they tend to bend easily, and sometimes they won't hold tight anymore after they've been out and back in several times. Either way, use a clean rag to wipe out all traces of the old grease.

At this point the entire hub has been disassembled and cleaned and you can now inspect the parts for signs of uneven or excessive wear. If there is pitting or other damage, you should consult with your bike shop about the possibility of replacing the worn parts. It is usually an easy matter to buy new axle assemblies, and sometimes new bearing races can be pressed into the hubs. As for the bearings themselves, replace all of them anytime some begin to lose their bright silver finish. If you do your hub repacking on a yearly basis, go ahead and replace them at that time whether they appear to need it or not. Bearings cost just pennies apiece and it's worth it for peace of mind. Count out how many you need of each size—all hubs do not use the same size or number—and take along one from the front and rear to ensure an exact match.

Reassembly begins by coating the hub bearing races with a moder-ate amount of quality grease. Oil should not be used because it is too light to stay in place; on the other hand, lubricants such as automotive wheel bearing grease are much too heavy. There are several greases made specifically for bicycle hubs, and you're welcome to read the labels and price tags and choose what suits you best. Many mechanics like Campagnolo Special Grease, figuring that if this is what Campy uses to lubricate its hubs, cranks, headsets, and pedals then it must be perfect. It does work very well, but at about $4 for 100 grams it is more expensive than any other brand. Still, this amount will see you through many hub repackings and it has all the qualities needed to hold up through a year's worth of riding.

Once the grease is in place, gently tap in the dust caps (if they were removed) and lay in the bearings. The same number goes in each side; if you're confused about how many, just fill up the race until a small space remains—a space too small for another bearing. The grease will hold the balls in place if you've applied enough. Now apply a light layer of grease to the face of the cone that is still on the axle and put the axle through the hub. Thread on the opposite cone, also greased, until it contacts the bearings. Slip on the lock washer, screw on the nut finger-tight, and now you are ready to make the critical adjustments.

The parts on the right end of the axle haven't been disturbed through this whole procedure, but check now to make sure they are tight. Using the cone wrenches, slip the proper size onto the flats and put another on the outside nut. Firmly try to tighten them toward each other (there will be little or no movement). Now rotate and wiggle the axle. Depending on whether there is too much play or it is tight, screw the left-side cone toward the bearings or away from them, respectively. When the axle will spin smoothly with no play, put a wrench on each outside nut and simultaneously turn them toward each other. This will have the effect of tightening the left-side nut against its cone, but it won't cause the cone itself to turn, thanks to the lock washer between them. However, because of the tiny bit of give in the threads the cone will press farther in and probably make the hub feel slightly tight if you spin it now. Regardless, the next step is to lock the three parts on the left side of the axle firmly together, using the same procedure described for the right side at the beginning of this paragraph.

Now spin the wheel in your hands. Too tight? That's usually the

a

Begin hub overhaul by removing the nut (*a*), lock washer, and cone (*b*) from one end of the axle only, always working from the left side on the rear hub. Withdraw the axle and coax out the ball bearings with a screwdriver (*c*). Once the hub has been disassembled and all parts have been wiped clean (*d*), coat each side of it with a moderate amount of quality grease (too much grease will increase resistance and may ooze out, attracting dirt) and lay in the bearings and axle (*e*). The dust cap of the hub has been removed (*f*) to give a better look, but it is not necessary to remove when doing routine maintenance. Finish by threading on the axle parts and using the cone wrenches (*g*) to perform the adjustment procedure described in the text.

b

c

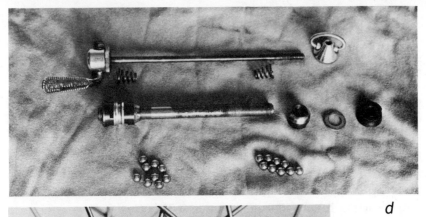

d

e

f

g

case at this point, but if you've done a good job so far it'll be close to correct. Make the final adjustment by putting a wrench on each cone and trying to screw them away from each other—that is, pull your right hand toward your body as you push the left hand away. Apply a steadily increasing force until you feel the give, then check how the wheel spins. Still a tad tight? Okay, try the wrenches again, but before resorting to any inordinate force it is better to loosen the axle nut on the left side and start the adjustment afresh. There's a lot of give-and-take to hub adjustment, and even the best mechanics usually need a few minutes to get it just right.

Once you think you've got it just right, you might be chagrined to find that you've adjusted the tightness out just a hair too much and now there is a hint of looseness when you wiggle the axle. Hold on, because this isn't necessarily bad. There's a theory that goes like this: A hub that is perfectly adjusted out of the bike will be tight as soon as it is installed. I believe it. The reason is the considerable inward pressure on each cone assembly when the wheel is fastened into the frame. Therefore, I like my hubs to have a small amount of play, play that allows for this squeezing effect. This gives me assurance that I'm not rolling around on tight hubs, which will cause both them and me to wear out faster. Of course, hubs that are too loose will also result in excessive wear, so you should check for this by holding the installed wheel at the rim and working it side to side. If you feel lateral movement, you must go back to the axle and adjust out all but minimal play.

The same adjustment procedures should be followed anytime routine inspection turns up a hub that is too tight or loose. But if you are as precise as possible when assembling your hubs after repacking them, and if they are made by one of the quality companies, there will be little need for further attention as the miles go by.

Tires

Since the tires provide your one tenuous contact with the earth when you are on the bike, and since they are the only thing between whatever you ride over and your rather fragile rims, they deserve serious attention. This begins with keeping them inflated to proper pressure—the first rule of tire maintenance. On most clincher tires the recommended pressure is imprinted right on the sidewall and normally falls between 65 and 100 pounds per square inch. This helpful information usually isn't found on tubulars, but most of the general-purpose models take 85–100 psi. Air pressure should be increased when the weight on the bike (rider and/or load) is above normal, and decreased slightly when the roads are wet or very hot. Under normal conditions it's customary to keep the rear tire inflated 5–10 psi more than the front, but the important thing is that there be only the slightest flattening of the tire where it contacts the road. It's best to use a gauge so you'll know exactly how much pressure is in each tire, but many riders go by a thumb pressed into the tread or the sound when it is thumped. The tendency when using these two methods is to overinflate.

Because correct inflation is so important to safety, efficiency, and tire life, I recommend that you have a floor pump with a pressure gauge at home, and a frame-mount pump for emergencies on the road. I think the reason many people ride around on underinflated tires is that they rely on getting air at gas stations whenever they happen to think about it instead of having a pump handy before each ride. Their penalty is excessive tread wear, risk of rim and tire damage with every pothole or set of railroad tracks that loom up, and a bike that pedals and handles sluggishly. Then when they take air from a gas station's high-volume compressor, they run the risk of blowing a tire right off the rim. It happens hundreds of times a day.

After proper inflation, the chief concern is avoiding punctures. It is possible to ride for thousands of miles without having one, and I've seen riders have two within minutes. Luck plays a big part, of course, but so do road conditions and riding habits. Steer around likely-looking dangers (broken glass, patches of gravel, damaged pavement, etc.), avoid roads that pass through debris-strewn industrial areas, and don't ride your bike across lawns or fields where there can be trouble in the form of sand spurs, thorns, and so on. Finally, use tire savers or make it a habit to brush off each tire every few minutes. Reach out and put a gloved palm or couple of fingers on top of the front tire, then do the same with the rear (this part can be unnerving at first but it really isn't dangerous; just slide the back of your hand down the back side of the seat tube and then go to the tire—don't let your hand lodge between the wheel and frame). A couple of seconds on each tire will knock off anything that has been picked up and is on the way to causing a puncture. And don't worry—neither spinning tires nor slivers of glass have ever injured my fingers.

When the inevitable does happen, you will have a tube and/or tire to repair. The procedure for tubulars is somewhat more involved than for clinchers, but the basic patching process is the same. I'll detail clincher repair first, then go into the specifics which tubular owners must also deal with.

Clincher Repair

With the wheel out of the frame, inspect the tire carefully for signs of what it was that caused the flat. If you find it stuck in the tire, leave it there for now so it can help you locate the hole in the tube.

Begin tire removal by first depressing the valve to release any air that may remain, then go to the opposite side of the wheel. Carefully insert a tire lever under the bead, pry the edge of the tire over the rim, and hook the lever's notched end on a spoke. Move over about four spokes and use the other lever in the same fashion, but instead of hooking it, run it along the edge of the rim until the entire side of the tire has been lifted over. Put the levers aside and use your fingers to pull out the entire tube except the valve stem. If you found something sticking in the tread you can now lay the tube on the tire to locate the hole. Should it not be apparent, pump some air into the tube and put your ear near the area. Once you've found the hole, make an X across it with a ball-point pen. Then remove the tube entirely and pull the tire up and off the rim. Now remove the object from the tire and thoroughly feel all the way around the inside to make sure there is nothing else sticking through. If there is, you may have more than one hole to patch.

Should nothing be in the tread to indicate the location of the puncture, remove the tube entirely and give it some air. Run it slowly by your ear and you will probably hear the hiss. If not, immerse sections of the partially inflated tube in water until you see the telltale bubbles. Mark the hole and wipe down the tube—it'll have to be completely dry before you can patch it. (A leak that causes a tube to deflate slowly over a period of hours or even days can be hard to find. If your tubes have Schrader valves, the first thing to do is make sure the air isn't escaping through a loose valve core. Check for this by pumping the tire to pressure and putting a seal of saliva across the valve opening. If a bubble forms, that's it. Tighten the valve core by using the little two-pronged gizmo that comes as part of some pencil-type air gauges, or pedal over to your nearest friendly bike shop or gas station and borrow theirs. Check the other valve while you're at it.)

Patching a tube is an easy job. Everything you'll need for several repairs, including instructions, is in the compact $2 kit you can buy at any bike shop. I recommend a European brand, such as Rema, because the patches are usually thin and tapered at the edge; there is no advantage to a thick patch and it can make a noticeable lump under a lightweight tire. The basic procedure is to (1) roughen the area around the hole with the scraper provided; (2) apply glue to an area slightly larger than the patch; (3) apply the patch when the glue has become tacky (always use the smallest patch possible); (4) press the patch down firmly, especially at the edges; (5) sprinkle the area with talcum powder so that the patch won't stick to the inside of the tire and be pulled off the next time you remove the tube.

A small hole in the tire does not need to be patched, of course, because it has nothing to do with holding air. But if something has really gouged through the tread and it's a tire worth trying to save, you can apply a patch to its inside in the same manner just described. Keep an eye on it during subsequent rides, because the pressure could make it split open further or allow the tube to bubble up. If a tire has suffered sidewall damage or has begun to split above the wire bead that runs around its inside circumference, junk it. These problems are likely to allow the tube to protrude and blow out.

Before reinstalling the tire and tube, take a moment to inspect the inside of the rim. Make sure that no spoke ends are extending through the nipples. File off any that are, or this could be the cause of your next flat. Also check the seam where the rim is welded together and file away any sharp edges. Arrange the protective rim strip so that it covers all the nipples.

Begin the remounting procedure by pumping just enough air into the tube to give it some body. Two or three strokes should do it. Place the tube into the tire, making sure there are no creases or twists. Put the valve stem through the hole in the rim (don't pull it down firmly yet) and, using your hands, work one side of the tire onto the rim all the way around. Now begin to do the same with the other side, proceeding in both directions from the valve stem. When you get to the last few inches, depress the valve to let out all the air. Finish mounting the tire by forcing it up and over the rim with your thumbs. Do not use the tire levers unless there is just no other way; it's very easy to pinch the tube between the lever and the rim at this point. Once the tire is on, work around the circumference with your hands to be certain it is down into the rim and the tube is not protruding anywhere. Then push the valve stem up into the tire and pull it out firmly, making sure it is perpendicular to the rim. This "locks on" the tire by putting the thickness at the base of the valve on top of the bead.

Now start adding air and watch to see that the tire is seating properly all the way around the rim, on both sides. You'll notice a line, called the bead line, molded into the rubber along the lower edge on each side of the tire. This should appear just above the rim on a properly mounted tire, but sometimes it'll dip below for a few inches and then reappear. If this is the case when you have inflated the tire to recommended pressure, you should add a few more pounds until the bead line pops up. If it still won't seat as it should, let the air out and work the tire with your hands, then try again. If it's really stubborn you can apply something slippery along the side of the tire. Saddle soap works well; don't use anything with a petroleum base which could harm the tire or impair braking if it gets on the rim.

Beyond keeping them properly inflated, there is little routine maintenance needed for clincher tires. If the spirit moves you, go ahead and give your rims and tires a good cleaning once in a while with a brush and a bucket of soapy water. Armor All can be used on the sidewalls to keep the rubber preserved, something to consider if you live in a dry climate.

Tubular Repair

The procedure for patching the tube is the same as for clinchers, but almost everything else is different when it comes to repairing a tubular tire. For starters, locating the hole in the tube can be quite difficult unless whatever caused it is still lodged in the tire or has made an obvious hole. You can still pump in some air and listen closely, and you can put it under water, but the fact of the matter is that the leaking air will follow the path of least resistance, which usually means out through the hole at the base of the valve. You may have to pump the tire quite hard before enough air is forced through the puncture to locate it.

The repair can't be done without the proper materials, so purchase a kit made specifically for tubular tires. The Velox kit is widely available and for about $2 has everything needed (needle, thread, thimble, sandpaper, patches, and glue) except a razor blade, rubber cement, and some talc. Have these items at the ready and there should be no problem making a good repair. The procedure will take longer than when working with a clincher, but it isn't difficult.

Once you've peeled the tire off the rim and located and marked the puncture, go to the inside circumference and carefully pull away the base tape in the work area (about 2 inches on each side of the hole). You may need to use the blade of a small screwdriver or the like to do this; always proceed cautiously through these steps, taking care not to rip anything or cause further damage to the fragile tube. Now use the razor blade to nip through the stitching which allows the tire to encase the tube (and which gives tubulars their other name, "sew-ups"). Cut the whole 4 inches exposed under the base tape, remove and throw away all the pieces of thread, lift aside the strip of chafing tape, and pull out the section of tube.

When you've found the hole put a little X on it with a ball-point pen, then look at the opposite side of the tube to see if whatever punctured it went all the way through. If so you'll have to put on two patches. Also inspect the tire itself, both inside and outside, and remove whatever it was that caused the flat. As with a clincher, it is possible to patch the inside of the tire in the event of a tear or gouge; some patch kits come with a piece of canvas or similar material for doing this, or you can use a piece of the casing from a junked tubular. Holes in the tread can be filled with a general-purpose black rubber cement sold at hardware stores. After the inside patching is done, dust on some talcum powder to dry up excess cement.

Before sewing things back up, give the tube some air to make sure there are no other leaks. Then deflate it and tuck it back into the tire, being careful to avoid twists and folds. Lay in the chafing tape so that it will protect the tube from being abraded by the stitching. Now you're ready for the needle and thread, which should be used double—insert the thread through the needle's eye and bring it back down about a foot, cut it off there, and tie the ends together. Using a simple overhand stitch, begin about ½ inch into the existing thread and proceed ½ inch past the 4-inch opening you've made. Use the same holes made by the original stitching and be careful not to pull the thread too tight or it could slice through the casing. When finished, cut away any loose ends and apply a light layer of rubber cement to the thread and to the inside of the base tape. As soon as it gets tacky, carefully lay the tape over the stitching. Then pump in a few pounds of air and give the repair enough time to dry thoroughly.

What happens to the tire next is for you to decide. Some riders (usually rich ones) don't use patched tubulars for anything but spares, keeping one strapped under the saddle for the next time a puncture strikes. Others don't have any qualms about using repaired tires for general riding and training, but they would never consider competing on one. But I have raced on patched tires a number of times and I don't think there is any risk if the damage was a simple puncture and it was repaired correctly. However, if a tubular has had sidewall damage, that's when I draw the line. Sidewalls are made of fabric with a light rubber coating, and they are quite thin to save weight and provide flexibility. Therefore, they are easily damaged when scuffed against something or if tires are ridden when underinflated. If a sidewall blowout occurs it may be possible to repair it with an internal "boot" fashioned from a section of old tire, but it is best used for a spare from then on.

Gluing on a Tubular Tire

Whether the repaired tire or a new one is going to be mounted on the rim, the procedure is the same, and it's critical to your safety on the bike. Unlike clinchers, which sit deep within the rim and are held on by nonexpandable wire beads and air pressure, the primary thing that keeps tubulars in place is glue. Not ordinary glue, but special compounds designed or adapted specifically for cycling use. I've used several European brands, including the popular Clement red, but all of them seem to loosen up at road temperatures above 90°F. This makes them not quite right for a lot of the U.S. cycling season, even though they work fine on the Continent. In fact, after some U.S. races my valve stems have ended up at quite an angle to the rim, indicating how much the glue has let the tire slip around—and how close I was to flat tires caused by stems tearing loose from the tubes. Lately I've turned to the new glue made by the French company Wolber, and I've been using an auto trim adhesive from the 3M Company, No. 8031. Both keep their grip in the heat and they also

Why did this rider crash? The rear wheel tells the tale. He was going through a corner at high speed and the tubular tire was not glued on well. It rolled partly off the rim, the wheel buckled, and he learned a hard lesson about the importance of proper tire maintenance.

set up quicker than other brands. While most of the traditional glues require a 24-hour drying period before the wheel can be ridden safely, No. 8031 will let you charge around sharp corners within the hour.

Gluing on a tire can be a messy job, but it usually becomes less so with experience. For my description I'll assume we are working with a new rim and new tire, which will let me cover all phases of the process. Not all these steps are necessary if the components have had glue on them before.

First, mount the new tire on the wheel without any glue involved. This is done to stretch the tire if necessary; you don't want to have to fight with a tight one after the glue has been laid down. To mount the tire, stand over the wheel facing either side and with the valve hole at twelve o'clock. Put the valve stem through the hole. Now firmly stretch the tire onto the rim, working each hand around its circumference in opposite directions from the valve. When you get near the bottom, flip the wheel over (valve is now at the bottom) and move your hands closer and closer together as you work the last section of tire onto the rim. Fight like the dickens to make it get on there. Then inflate it hard and let it sit for a couple of hours; when you're ready to mount it for real it won't be nearly so difficult. If, however, you just can't make the tire fit, set the wheel aside and get some isometric exercise: Stand with your foot through the tire and give it a firm, steady upward pull, rotating it after a few seconds until you've stretched it from several directions. This will do the job, but it should be the last resort—you'll know why when you hear those ripping sounds coming from that nice new $20 tire.

After finishing the stretching process, prepare the tire for final mounting by applying a thin coat of rim glue all the way around the base tape. (If the glue is in a tube, knead it for several minutes to make sure it is mixed; if in a can, stir it well.) Spread the glue evenly with your finger or a brush, then set the tire aside. Now prepare the rim surface by first filing off any sharp edges on the ferrules or spoke holes (if nonferruled). Wipe the surface with a clean rag so there is nothing that will interfere with the glue's holding power; acetone can be used, if needed, but don't clean a rim with any petroleum product, such as kerosene, which will leave a film. At this point some mechanics suggest using a corner of the file to mark a series of X's or grooves all the way around the rim surface. They feel that this gives the glue something more to adhere to, but I'm not so sure it makes any difference. If you do it, just be sure not to gouge too deeply.

Now apply a thin bead of glue between each ferrule (don't put any into the holes) and spread it out evenly. Set the wheel aside until the glue is hard, which may take minutes or hours, depending on the brand. Then put on a second coat just as thinly, and when it has become tacky you can mount the tire in the manner just described. Be as careful as you can or you'll have a sticky mess on your hands, not to mention all over the rim and tire. When you get around to that last section of unmounted tire, try to pull it up and over so you can set it onto the rim; if you slide it over the edge you'll smear the glue. Now add a few pounds of air and spin the wheel so you can see if the tire is straight. Center it as best you can by moving it around with your hands, making sure the valve remains perpendicular to the rim. Then inflate the tire to pressure and let it sit until the glue sets. If glue has oozed out from under the tire you have used a bit too much. Either wipe it off now or wait until it has dried and you can peel it away. Remove any that has gotten on the rim with acetone or a car-care product made for taking off road tar. Be careful not to get these chemicals on the tire's sidewall.

If you are working with a used tire and rim, you don't have to go through all the above steps. There is no need to put any more glue on the tire's base tape, and one fresh coat on the rim should do it. Again, spread the glue thinly and give it a chance to become tacky before mounting the tire. Some riders prefer to do the gluing after the tire is on the rim, lifting up the tire section by section and spreading glue under it—you may find that this method is less messy. After a rim has received glue about six times you should clean it down to bare metal before making another application. Scrape off the old glue with a dull screwdriver or dissolve it with acetone, tar remover, or a solvent made for the purpose and sold in bike shops.

Finally, a word of caution should you come across something known as double-sided tacky tape and think to yourself, "Aha, a way to avoid the mess of using glue." Forget it. The stuff dries out quickly and simply doesn't do the job. I used it before I knew better and it was the cause of my first crash—I rolled a tire on the opening lap of a criterium and came up with a broken finger. It upset me greatly.

Care of Tubulars

Tubular tires are expensive, so it is wise to take measures which will help lengthen their life span. One helpful procedure is to occasionally give the sidewalls a cleaning with a soft brush and soapy water, then apply liquid latex (available at bike shops). This milky solution protects the sidewall fabric from moisture, dirt, road chemicals, etc. New tires come with a coating, but it quickly begins to disappear once they are ridden. Latex will also help recondition the "gumwalls" of clincher tires.

Over in Europe, a top racing cyclist may have dozens of tubulars down in his basement, stored away like a good wine until the passage of time brings them to maturity—"I will ride no tire before its time," Orson Welles might say. The reason is that the rubber of a newly manufactured tire is definitely softer and more prone to punctures and wear than aged rubber. Two to three years is considered ideal, which means that smart riders buy their good tubulars many months in advance of when they intend to use them. Until then the tires are stored in cool darkness, lightly inflated on old rims or hung loosely over wooden rods. Once aged, the tread rubber will show no mark when pressed with a thumbnail, nor will it act like an eraser and give up little particles when it is rubbed. "Green" tires will do both, and they will puncture more easily because they tend to pick up and hold road debris, letting it work through the tread.

Certainly all quality nonvulcanized cotton tubulars and all racing tubulars constructed on a silk casing should be aged. Such tires can cost upwards of $50 each, and to ride them green is like throwing money away. I remember an instance a few seasons ago when a team of riders from Florida competed for a month in the Northeast. Among the equipment their sponsor provided was a batch of top-quality silk racing tires with the cocksure model name "Invulnerable." They were anything but. Having just arrived from the European factory, the tires sounded like popcorn in races that took the riders over any road strewn with gravel. Tires that could have withstood all sorts of road hazards were soon junk simply because the rubber had not been given time to harden.

Many tubulars in the moderate-to-low price range—those meant primarily for training and touring—probably don't need to be aged. For one thing, it is becoming more and more common for these to be made of nylon, which does not harden with time. On the other hand, low-cost rubber tubulars are machine-made and the tread is vulcanized onto the casing. The heat used in this process also serves to harden the rubber, making the tires about as puncture-resistant the day after they are made as they would be after hanging for two years. It won't hurt to age them, however, and if you are able to get a deal by buying in quantity you should go ahead and treat them like expensive silks. If they came in a bundle, break it apart so there is no danger the tires will become stuck together as the months go by. Keep each one inflated lightly to prevent the tube from crimping, and always store tires away from heat and sunlight.

As a final tip on tubulars, it is a good idea to reduce air pressure after each ride when you are using lightweight cottons or silks, the tires you'll most likely be on if you become involved in competition. Letting out half of the racing pressure (110–120 psi) will help keep them from stretching and losing strength. This needn't be done with lower-cost training-type tires, though if yours have latex tubes, which are quite porous, you might as well go ahead—you'll have to add air before the next day's ride anyway. On the other hand, training tires with tubes made of Butyl (a synthetic rubber) are convenient because they usually hold their pressure for a week.

Headsets

We've now looked into a number of maintenance, adjustment, and repair techniques which should be within the capabilities of all serious riders. Three components remain, but working with them can be tricky business and some special tools are required. For this reason, you may wish to leave the overhaul of this equipment—the headset, crankset, and pedals—to your local pro mechanic. As time goes by and you become proficient in the maintenance procedures already outlined, there is no reason you can't learn how to work on the internal parts of these components. Meanwhile, there are things you can do to keep the need for maintenance to a minimum and discover problems before they require expensive repair.

The headset is critical, because it is composed of the parts that connect the steering assembly to the frame. The cups at the top and bottom of the head tube are filled with small ball bearings. When everything is in adjustment, the front wheel will turn freely and fully to each side without there being a hint of looseness. Let's take a look at how to check out the system.

First, stand beside the bike with your hand holding the forward end of the top tube. Raise the front wheel a couple of inches off the ground, then nudge the handlebars so that the wheel swings fully one way, and then back the other. If the pivot in each direction is smooth and complete, fine—the headset is not binding. If, however, the wheel stops short in either or both directions, something is wrong. The headset might simply be adjusted too tightly; the bearing grease may have become thickened by dirt or age; or something could be amiss with the headset installation or even the frame, resulting in misalignment between bearing races. In any case, continued riding could cause damaging wear to the headset.

Next check for headset looseness. You may be tipped off to this by shudders and knocking in the front end when riding on bumpy roads. Find out for sure by picking up the front end of the bike as above and letting it drop. It'll sound loose if it is. Another check is to stand over the bike, squeeze the front brake hard, and rock the bike back and forth. The play in a loose headset will be readily apparent. If the bike is ridden in this condition the headset will be damaged as road shocks cause the ball bearings to dent their races in the cups, resulting in rough rotation.

Even if a headset is kept properly lubricated and adjusted, the day will come when the bike develops what might be called an automatic pilot. That is, a "notch" will form in the dead-center position, the place where the front wheel is pointed (and where bumps are hit) during so much of the riding time. Except in advanced cases this will not affect handling, but it's a sure sign that the headset is on the way out. The extent of the problem can easily be determined by lifting the front of the bike and letting the wheel swing slowly through the straight forward position. Once a headset has become quite worn, the wheel will lock into dead center and resist turning out of it.

In this latter case, or anytime that dents in the races (a condition known as "brinelling") cause the bearings to roll roughly even though the headset is properly adjusted, there are a couple of ways to help things work almost like new. They require special headset tools and the ability to use them, so you will have to see a shop mechanic if you aren't ready for this kind of maintenance. The first procedure is to knock the headset cups out of the frame, rotate each one a different amount, and press them back in. This alters the position of the bearing indentations so they no longer match. Next, rebuild the headset, using loose ball bearings instead of retainers. Many headsets, Campagnolo included, put bearings in round metal holders called retainers to facilitate the installation process—slipping in a couple of retainers is about ten times faster than putting in each small bearing individually. But it also means that each race holds fewer bearings than it can if a retainer isn't used. Therefore, if a worn headset is rebuilt with loose bearings they can't sit in the same indentations. The rotation may still not be perfectly smooth, but you'll be able to get hundreds of more miles out of the headset and perhaps even double its life.

Preventive maintenance for headsets consists mainly of keeping grit and water out of the works. Of primary concern is the lubrication at the bottom of the head tube, which is subject to everything thrown up by the front wheel. One way to help keep out contaminants is to tie a strip of nylon stocking or pantyhose around the bottom assembly (don't use cloth, which will absorb and hold water). Another way is to install a short alloy or plastic mudguard which attaches to the brake bolt and extends about six inches fore and aft of the headset. Both of these methods will delay the inevitable, but perhaps the best choice if you ride often in wet or dusty conditions is to invest in a sealed-bearing headset (see discussion in Chapter 14). They are expensive, but so are frequent maintenance and replacement parts.

Cranksets

Crankset inspection should be a routine part of every maintenance session. There are quite a few nuts and bolts down there, and they can occasionally vibrate loose. In addition, the axle/cup assembly in the bike's bottom bracket can get out of adjustment. If it's tight it will steal your energy and damage the races; if loose, the excess movement will result in uneven wear to the internal parts. Also, the chainwheels will tend to move side to side with each pedal stroke, causing the front derailleur to shift poorly and the chain to rub against its cage.

The first thing to check is the attachment of the crank arms to the axle. If you have a cottered crank, give each pin a couple of light raps with a hammer and tighten the nuts. Go easy—cotter pins are soft, so don't strip the threads. If your crank is an alloy cotterless model (the usual type on today's lightweight bikes), unscrew each dust cap to expose the bolt or nut that fixes the crank arm to the axle. On some brands a thin-wall socket can fit into the opening, but usually you will need a special wrench made for the purpose (available at bike shops for about $5). After you've checked the tightness of each side, don't be tempted to leave off the dust caps so your bike will look like a racing machine. Dust caps are important for two reasons: They keep dirt out of the alloy threads, and they prevent the fixing nuts or bolts from working their way out if they should vibrate loose. Put a little grease on the dust-cap threads, and don't overtighten them or it might be a real problem to get them out next time.

Now check each of the small bolts that hold the chainwheels to the crank arm or to each other. Use moderate force or you're liable to snap one. If you find that one or two of the bolts always seem to be loose, hardware stores sell products which can be applied to the threads to stop the problem. Should one of these bolts ever turn up missing or broken, it's best not to ride the bike or you might bend a chainwheel. Remove one of the good bolts and take it to the shop so you can get an exact replacement. Buy an extra one for a spare.

To check bottom-bracket adjustment, take the chain off the teeth and let it hang out of the way around the bottom bracket (or do this inspection during times when the chain has been removed for cleaning). Grasp a crank arm with each hand and wiggle them back and forth across the bottom bracket, trying it with the arms in various positions. Just a hint of play is okay, but anything more should put you on the road to your local shop for a quick adjustment. (Don't hold the pedals when you do this check; pedals have a little play of their own and this will fool you.) If you can feel no looseness, the bottom bracket might be right or it could be tight, something which is often hard to determine with the pedals and crank arms installed. With the chain still out of the way, give a crank arm a nudge and watch the reaction. If the rotation comes to any sort of sudden stop without a tendency to reverse direction, the bottom bracket is probably tight and you should take the bike in for adjustment before doing any further riding.

Of course, the best way to discover tightness is to take off both crank arms and turn the axle by hand. However, it's never a good idea to remove and reinstall the arms except when absolutely necessary—the soft pins of cottered cranks can be easily damaged, and the arms of cotterless models will begin to draw up too far on the tapered steel axle because of the relative softness of the alloy. With this in mind, I like to adjust the bottom bracket as I do hubs—that is, so I can feel just a hint of play when I make my routine check by wiggling the crank arms. This isn't enough to cause abnormal wear, but it lets me always be sure that the movement hasn't tightened up.

It is fairly easy for dirt and moisture to enter the bottom bracket and contaminate the grease. One reason is that this is the lowest part of the frame, the place where anything inside the tubes eventually settles. Externally, the crank area catches dust, mud, and water thrown up by the wheels. This stuff will accumulate around the crank axle and can get inside through the hole in each cup. (This is why I urge caution when washing the bike—you don't want to accidentally rinse anything into the bottom bracket). Beyond keeping everything wiped clean, some riders like to tie a strip of nylon stocking or wrap a pipe cleaner around the short section of axle between the cups and crank arms. This covers the opening, and it's a measure I recommend if you ride in dusty or sandy areas. (Note to folks with Campagnolo cranksets: never pedal backward. Campy has engineered screw-type threads into each cup's opening, the purpose being to wind foreign matter away from the internal parts as the axle turns. By pedaling backward—something that serves no useful purpose anyway—you run the risk of actually helping contaminants get into the works. This design innovation, plus the protective plastic sleeve that covers the Campagnolo bottom-bracket movement from cup to cup, helps the grease remain clean between yearly overhauls. Still, the bottom bracket, along with the bottom headset assembly, is where a sealed-bearing unit can pay off if you ride in unusually dusty, sandy or wet conditions.)

And if you've ever wondered why some frames have holes, slots, or some kind of design cut out under the bottom bracket, part of the reason is that this allows water to escape, not sit in there and cause corrosion. Holes also help prevent condensation in the tubes, because they let inside air temperature fluctuate with the outside. And a cutout gives the builder a chance to take off a little weight while adding a distinctive design touch. Some people worry that the missing metal might make the bottom bracket weak, but most of the world's best frame builders obviously don't agree.

Pedals

Quality pedals don't need much maintenance. I know riders who simply ignore them season after season, finally going to a new pair when the alloy cage, not the internal movement, becomes too worn. But repacking pedal bearings is not difficult, and once you get the hang of working on hubs you can probably handle the job easily. The axle/cone/bearing designs are similar and all you really need for pedal work is a thin-jawed wrench for taking them off the crank arm (the left pedal has a backward thread), a tool to unscrew the dust caps (often a crescent wrench or channel-lock pliers will work), and a metric wrench that fits the axle nuts.

Check the need for pedal adjustment by spinning it and working it side to side while it is on the crank arm. Rotation should be smooth but with no more than a hint of lateral play. However, pedals can pass these tests and still need a little attention, because they are frequently the source of creaks and ticks from the crank area. These irregular noises have annoyed and exasperated many a rider who has unsuccessfully tried to get rid of them by overhauling the bottom bracket and pedals. Before going into the internal parts, try these simple remedies: First, remove each pedal, grease the threads, and screw them back on. Often ticks are the result of a minute movement between the steel and alloy threads, and the grease tightens the seal. Second, put a little light lubricant such as WD-40 on the places where the pedal cage joins the body. This will get rid of any creaking sounds caused by movement between these parts.

Random Tips

There are many tricks of the bike-maintenance trade, as you'll find when you become more experienced with your own machine and have the opportunity to observe or work with good mechanics. Even experts frequently pick up new techniques and must make an ongoing effort to keep up with the ever-advancing component industry. Periodicals such as *Bicycling* magazine and *Velo-news*, the bike-racing newspaper, frequently carry technical articles by top mechanics. Reading them is a good way to learn procedures which can be applied during your own maintenance sessions.

Here are a few more tips for the care of your bike.

Use mudguards in early season. I've mentioned the many benefits of keeping your bike clean, but in the late winter and spring, when it's hard to resist getting back on the road after the confinement of winter, weather conditions can often have you looking as if you've been competing in a cyclocross. One of the smartest things you can do for these sloppy weeks is install a pair of full-length mudguards. It's just amazing how well they protect a bike and rider from the dirty, salty snowmelt and puddles left by spring rains. In fact, mudguards are a good permanent addition for a second bike that is used for training or commuting. Tourists and fitness riders will find them of constant benefit, too, and the old complaint about air resistance has been lessened with the introduction of narrow styles for bikes with tubular and lightweight clincher wheels. I recommend the resilient plastic models like those of Bluemels and Esge, which sell for about $15 a pair. They are easily installed on any frame that has eyelets on the front and rear dropouts; there are adapters for frames that don't.

Keep saddles clean and dry.   Bad weather and perspiration will soil all-leather saddles and nylon models with leather tops, so an occasional cleaning with saddle soap is a good idea. For about $2 you can buy an Ideale seat cover, which is made of waterproof clear plastic that will stretch to fit over any racing-type saddle. You can pack one of these in a jersey pocket on days when rain is threatening, and it makes good protection whenever you wash the bike or carry it on the outside of the car. If a leather saddle ever becomes soaked, let it dry at normal room temperature rather than near a heat source, which could make it shrink and crack.

Prevent the stem and seat post from sticking.   A couple of times a year you should pull the seat post and handlebar stem out of the frame. This is done to prevent them from becoming bonded to the tubes, something which happens all too frequently. Perspiration is the main culprit as it seeps down and causes a corrosive reaction. If you periodically remove the post and stem and coat them with grease, you should be safe. (Before doing so, use a piece of tape to mark each part's depth so you won't lose your riding position.) Should one or the other become stuck tight, get on down to a bike shop for some expert help. Too many frame tubes have been bent or crimped by strong-arm efforts to free frozen parts. A good mechanic will know several relatively safe remedies, but the best cure, by far, is prevention.

Lubricate away the creaks.   Sometimes when you are climbing and putting a lot of muscle to the handlebars you will hear creaks. If your stem is already greased as it should be, the noise is probably coming from the bar/stem junction. Loosen the stem's binder bolt so you can slide the bars over to one side, give the center section a good greasing, and wipe off the excess when you've got everything back in place. Saddle noises can occur where the metal undercarriage joins the nylon or leather, or where it contacts the seat post. Make sure all bolts are tight and give each spot a light shot of WD-40.

How to Check for Frame Damage

Finally, the workshop procedure I hope you'll never have to do—checking your crashed bike for frame damage.

It's almost as sure as death and taxes that you will take a fall sometime, but unless it's an end-over-end tumble or you actually run into something (or something runs into you), frame damage is usually confined to scratches and maybe a minor dent. However, a frame that has been knocked out of alignment even slightly can cause problems with everything from riding in a straight line to shifting gears. Sometimes an expert can straighten or "cold-set" the tubes, but if they have been crimped by an impact the frame may be a total loss. Bent forks can be replaced at some cost, though if they have been heavily impacted it means there could well be more expensive trouble in the frame's head tube area.

Of course, if a frame has been badly damaged it won't take an expert to tell. But even if it seems to have come through the crash okay, it's good for peace of mind to be able to check it out with a few simple tests. First, look closely at the paint around the fork crown and the lugs adjoining the head tube. If there is any sign of cracking or bulging, the frame has been bent. It might still seem ridable, but handling and safety will be marginal because the front wheel has been pushed back under the bike. The result is unstable steering and the possibility that your foot will hit the wheel during turns.

If the frame has been twisted by the impact, you may be able to see this by taking out the wheels and standing a few feet directly behind. The seat tube and head tube should line up precisely. If they make any angle to each other, the frame is bent. This means the bike will no longer track straight—the wheels won't be in alignment, which will increase rolling resistance and cause excessive tire wear. The bike will also tend to veer to the side.

Another alignment check can be made with a length of string and a ruler. Attach one end of the string to the left rear dropout, stretch it around the head tube, and then back to the corresponding place on the right dropout. Now measure the distance from the seat tube to the string on each side. If there is a difference, the rear end of the frame has been pushed over, and this can result in chain misalignment and poor shifting, among other problems.

Inspect for a bent fork by kneeling at the side of the bike and looking at the line the head tube makes with the upper section of the fork. It should be straight down to the point where the blades naturally curve forward. Check further by slipping in a wheel to see if it is equidistant from each blade where it passes through the top of the fork. If not, turn the wheel around. If it is off to the same side, one of the blades is bent, or at least bent more than the other. A bike with a damaged fork should never be ridden, because there is always the risk that a bump could cause it to break completely.

If any of these inspections turns up signs of frame damage, the next step is to take the bike to a mechanic or frame builder who has the tools and experience to make the needed repairs. You can help him (and save some labor charges) by first removing every component that you can. If you are fortunate, he will be able to muscle the frame back into alignment and you can ride it again safely. If not, it's better to have the choice of paying for a new fork or replacement tube, or even a whole new frame, than risk a more severe accident on a dangerously weakened, ill-handling bike.

CLOTHING

16

One of the things I like best about cycling is how good riders look when they're wearing the proper attire. The clothing of the sport is colorful, practical, and above all functional. It is designed to be form-fitting, giving cyclists a sleek and lean appearance both on and off the bike. As you move into long-distance riding or racing, wearing the proper clothing becomes all the more important for comfort and performance. There are just a few differences between what works well for touring and for competition, and I'll point these out as we now look into what makes the well-dressed cyclist.

Feet First

While well-designed jerseys, shorts, headgear, and gloves are all important, there is one item that is absolutely essential: cleated shoes. I consider shoes the most important component you will ever buy, next to the frame itself. They must transfer every bit of energy you are putting into the pedals, so the top brands are biomechanically designed to help position the feet at an angle which aids efficiency and power. Also very important is the protection they provide against uncomfortable pressure from the pedals.

Just as runners must pay from $30 to $60 for training and racing shoes, you must be prepared to spend $50 or more for quality cycling shoes. That's a lot of money, but with proper care a pair will last several seasons. Virtually all cycling shoes are manufactured overseas, primarily in Italy and West Germany, and good bike shops usually carry several brands. It is rare for a regular shoe store to stock them, but some athletic stores are beginning to.

Cycling shoes come in European sizes, and widths are mainly a function of the country of manufacture. Most Italian companies, for instance, seem to produce narrow shoes. Try on several models and

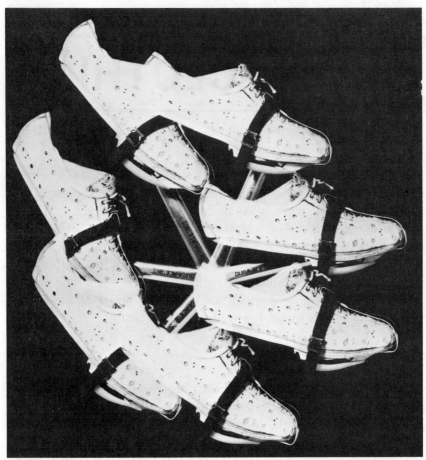

(*Photograph courtesy of American Shimano Corporation*)

make sure the pair you buy fits snugly but doesn't restrict the toes—if the shoes seem comfortable enough for walking they are probably one size too big. Shoes will always stretch, especially after they've been soaked on rainy rides or by perspiration. If they are not relatively tight when new you will soon feel movement during fast or forceful pedaling—very disconcerting.

One feature often overlooked in shoe selection is the arch. It should help provide support along the entire length of the shoe, keeping foot movement to a minimum and preventing the ankle from rolling inward. This is important for good pedaling technique and reducing foot fatigue on long rides. Arch inserts, available at athletic stores, can be added to shoes that don't provide enough support.

Even expensive shoes sometimes have nothing but a paper-thin piece of leather covering the inside sole. This lack of padding is the main cause of what is known among racers and long-distance riders as "hot foot." It results when the bottom of the foot is kept pressed against the shoe long enough to restrict circulation in the capillaries. The pressure is compounded because feet tend to swell during long rides, and the result is a very uncomfortable sensation of heat. Unknowing riders will try to put out the fire by squirting their feet with a water bottle, but what they really need is resilient foam insoles, such as those made by Spenco. These will allow enough relief from pressure to prevent the circulation problem or at least keep it to a minimum. As an added benefit, the addition of insoles can help older, stretched-out shoes fit snugly again.

The leather uppers should be supple, be stitched with heavy thread, and have a plentiful number of ventilation holes. Some interesting design touches have shown up in recent models by Adidas and Sidi, including the use of nylon-mesh sections for lighter weight and even better ventilation.

The Italian-made Duegi cycling shoe is among the most popular. Each pair comes with a tool for the adjustable cleats.

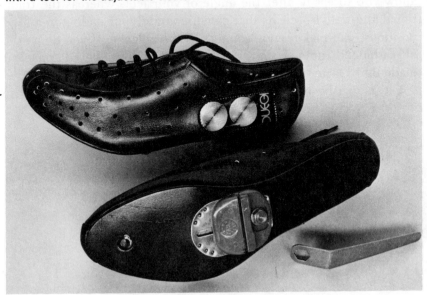

There are three types of soles, with leather the most common, followed by wood and plastic. Often leather shoes will have an internal metal shank to give them additional stiffness. This is important because if the sole flexes or allows the pedal to be felt by the foot, it will be working against comfort and efficiency. Generally, you should get the stiffest sole possible, but realize that the stiffer it is the more road vibration you will feel (this is another reason to use foam insoles). Soles should have holes like the uppers, not just for ventilation but for letting water escape on rainy rides.

The cleats are your primary connection to the bicycle, and their position on the bottom of the shoes must be precise. Maladjusted cleats are probably the greatest cause of knee problems in cycling. When they are properly positioned, the balls of the feet will be directly over the pedal axles. I like each foot to be aligned parallel to an imaginary centerline running through the length of the bike, but some riders use a slightly pigeon-toed position and a few angle each foot differently. Such individual preferences, and the fact that knee problems caused by cleat position may take a number of miles to show up, are why I recommend buying only those shoes which have adjustable cleats already attached. Most do nowadays. This will allow you to easily alter the angle of your feet, whereas the traditional alternative—cleats that come separately for nailing in a fixed position—can make repositioning a real headache. If you do go the old-fashioned route, I suggest you use the adjustable add-on cleat made by Pavarin, just to be on the safe side.

Cleats can be metal, plastic with metal slots, or all-plastic. The

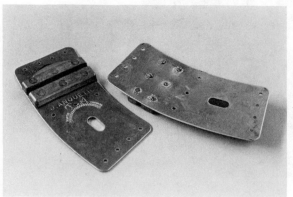

The long T.A. road cleat is a good choice for soles that can use some added stiffness.

main feature to look for is a deep slot so there is little chance of feet accidentally pulling out of the pedals. I recommend all-plastic cleats because they will not wear down the alloy cages of the expensive pedals many good bikes are equipped with. Worn pedals can cause improper foot alignment and subsequent injury. Most shoes with factory-attached cleats have plastic ones, primarily because they are less expensive and lighter than metal.

I've worn most of the top shoes—Adidas, Puma, Sidi, Detto Pietro, Duegi, and others—and have found Vittoria's Super Prestige model to be the best. It has all the required ingredients, plus an extra touch or two. The anatomically designed sole is made of wood for lightness, strength, and stiffness, and it has a thin layer of cork to cushion the ball of the foot. This unique feature improves comfort without introducing any serious amount of flex. The cork also absorbs moisture to prevent slipping. The factory-mounted nylon cleats have a fairly deep slot and can be adjusted over a wide range of positions. They are fixed directly into the wood with two bolts instead of one, which makes them very secure. At about $60 the Vittoria SP isn't the most expensive cycling shoe, but I don't think there is a better model on the market.

Riders on tour who make numerous stops during a day's pedaling may be tempted to forgo cleated shoes and wear the models by Avocet, Detto Pietro, and others which are designed for both cycling and walking. The soles of these shoes have grooves which act as cleats, and they contain stiffeners to cut down on pedal pressure. They are certainly better than riding in running shoes or sneakers, and they

Although many cycling shoes now come with adjustable cleats already attached, Pavarin makes an alloy model you can put on yourself. This helps get around a common problem—nailing on cleats and then finding they are slightly out of line and need to be moved.

cost less than quality cleated shoes, but that's where the advantages end. I think a serious tourist who will be covering 80–100 miles a day for several days should emphasize riding performance, not walking. It may take a few seconds to change out of cleated shoes and into a pair of sandals or sneakers, but the time spent pedaling between stops is what really counts.

Shoe Care

The first rule in caring for cleated cycling shoes is never to walk in them. Of course that's impossible, but do try to keep it to a bare minimum. Walking will damage the cleats and heels, though lightweight nylon taps can be tacked on to protect the latter. Of more serious concern is the softening that will occur to the heel counter. The rear of the shoe must withstand quite a bit of force as you pull through the back of the pedal stroke, and a weakened heel will allow foot movement. This could result in friction and raw spots, and will almost surely prevent you from pedaling at your best.

Protect the leather uppers by frequent cleanings with saddle soap and polishing. This will help you look snazzy while keeping the shoe leather supple, comfortable, and water-resistant. You should also apply shoe polish to the bottom of the soles so the leather won't soak up water on a rainy day. (Water repellency is an advantage of plastic and treated wooden soles.) If your shoes do get soaked, help them dry out and retain their shape by stuffing them with wadded-up newspaper after removing the laces. Don't put them too near heat, as rapid drying can harden and crack the leather. Afterward, give them a cleaning and polishing.

Socks

Important to foot comfort is using the right type of sock. Although some riders like to go without, I think socks are necessary for several reasons. Cotton or wool (or a fabric blend that is primarily one of the two) will pull perspiration away from the feet and let it evaporate. Socks will also absorb sweat and any other wetness that comes down the legs—your feet won't slip in the shoes and your skin won't be subjected to any dyes and chemicals released by the leather. Socks also provide protection against shoe seams and laces, which can really wear on your feet as the miles go by. Another advantage is that they help prevent small pieces of road debris from getting into the shoes. Finally, they may save some skin if you should take a fall. Most riders prefer socks that are just over ankle-high. You don't need anything more than that, especially not knee socks—the extra length is of no benefit (except for warmth in winter), and if you are caught in a rain they will become very heavy.

Cold-Weather Foot Protection

Since cycling shoes are designed to keep the feet well ventilated, this presents a problem when riding during cold-weather months. As the temperature drops, the body automatically reduces circulation to the extremities in its attempt to keep the torso warm. This makes hands and feet quite susceptible to the chill air. Hands are easily protected, as we'll soon see, but foot comfort is a big problem for many riders.

There are a number of possible solutions, some of which are inexpensive and easily tried. You can wear two pairs of wool socks (best if used with old shoes which have already been stretched too large for summer riding). If that's not enough, wear a plastic sandwich bag between the pairs. Your feet might get damp from condensation, but the cold wind won't get to them. To nullify the ventilation holes you can use tape or pull on a heavy sock over each shoe, cutting out a place for the cleats to come through. All of these methods will help in moderately cold weather.

Another solution is to purchase a pair of winter cycling shoes. These are made without ventilation holes, and some models have high tops, sort of like old-fashioned football shoes. Their advantage is that they are fully lined with thick fleece, which insulates against the cold as it lets the feet breathe a bit. If they are soaked by the rain, however, it may take several days for these shoes to completely dry out. Another drawback is that they are hard to find and quite expensive. In fact, I really don't think they are worth buying for the minimal benefits they offer.

For cold-weather cycling, foot protection is a must. There are various makeshift ways to try to keep cold wind out and body heat in, or you can opt for foot covers, like Duegi's, which have openings to expose the cleat.

Perhaps the best answer, and certainly the one gaining the most popularity, is booties that go over regular summer shoes and extend up the ankle. These futuristic-looking coverings are water-resistant, insulated, and designed to let the cleats do their job, and they are thin enough so that you probably won't need to alter the position or size of your toe clips. At this writing the most available model is the one supplied by the Italian company Duegi. The price is modest, about $20, and I've found they do the job quite well. Even when wet they keep heat trapped in and your feet will stay reasonably warm.

Fabrics for Cyclists

In recent years there have been some major changes in the materials used to make cycling clothing. For decades there was but one choice for serious tourists and racers—wool. The reasons for its popularity then are the same that keep it a favorite today. Wool, being a natural fiber, has properties which make it the best material for virtually every temperature and weather condition. It helps riders retain body heat in the cold, yet in the heat it produces a cooling effect as it wicks perspiration away from the skin to let it evaporate. In the rain, wool helps insulate against chill and doesn't have the cold, clammy feeling of other wet fabrics.

But 100 percent wool garments are expensive and they are not easily cared for. They have to be hand-washed and dried carefully lest they wind up shrinking or losing their shape. Cyclists have always been willing to grin and bear these drawbacks, but today we no longer have to. New manufacturing techniques are producing all-wool materials and wool/synthetic blends that don't need special handling. In fact, many are machine-washable and can be put through the cycle many times without danger to fabric or construction.

The second most popular material is cotton. This is the best choice for anyone who has an adverse skin reaction to wool, and I advise wearing a cotton jersey anytime the temperature is above 70 degrees. Cotton seems to feel cooler than wool in warm weather, but it is not as warm in the cold. In modern jerseys, cotton, like wool, is often blended with one or more synthetics—fine as long as the natural fiber makes up at least 50 percent of the material.

I recommend blends because the clothing will generally be less expensive than if made of 100 percent wool or cotton, it won't shrink as much (if at all), and it tends to be more durable. It's also not as heavy and it ventilates better. When I first began cycling everyone told me to wear 100 percent wool everything because it is the traditional material in Europe. Now that I've raced there I understand why. In Europe it rarely gets over 75 degrees most of the season, and in that type of climate wool works best. But in the United States most of our racing is done at temperatures above 75 degrees, and this makes the lighter and cooler blends an advantage.

Jerseys

A cycling jersey serves four functions. First, it has rear pockets for carrying food, water, and other items. Second, it protects the body against the elements. Next, it will save skin in the event of a fall, more so if an undershirt is also worn. Finally, a jersey can be decorated with the name of your bike club or racing sponsor, and it can be very colorful and attractive to the eye. The latter is important for safety in traffic and also for comfort—light colors tend to be cooler in summer, while dark ones will absorb the sun to help keep you warmer in winter.

During a long tour or race anything can contribute to fatigue after a while. That's why it's important to look for good construction in a jersey. Seams should be unobtrusive. The sleeves should not be too tight or too short. The overall fit should be snug so that there is no excess material to bunch up or hang loose to catch the wind. A well-made jersey has a definite form-fitting taper. You'll find some variations in collar design, and I recommend the style that comes up fairly high on the neck when it is zipped shut. This helps keep out the chill in cool weather.

A very important consideration when choosing a jersey is the construction of the rear pockets. They should be large, deep, and strongly stitched so they won't tear loose. Three pockets are much better than two because you will be able to balance what you are carrying, especially important if it is somewhat heavy. For example, with two pockets a bottle of water will be always be tugging around to the side, and this can be quite bothersome; with three it can sit squarely in the middle and hardly be noticed. When you are riding, the pockets should be low enough on your back for easy access yet should not droop over the saddle—pocket position is actually the factor which determines the correct overall length of a jersey. The tops of pockets are sometimes fitted with elastic or buttons to help hold them closed when empty so they won't catch the wind. But if the jersey is well designed this shouldn't happen anyway.

Some jerseys are made with a pair of pockets in the center of the chest. While a tourist might find these handy, I don't recommend them for a racer. They act like a couple of air scoops, and anything you put in them will cause the jersey to hang down in front of you. It's easy for something to fall out when you are riding in a stream-lined position, and besides, you'll find that it's actually easier to reach into a rear pocket.

There are a number of widely available jersey brands. For years a favorite has been Sergal of Milan, Italy, which produces clothing for all types of riding. Though fairly expensive (a wool road jersey falls in the $30–$40 range), Sergal's quality in design and construction makes it hard to beat. You'll see other European brands as well as clothing made in the United States, Mexico, and the Orient when you visit a well-stocked bike shop. Using the guidelines I've just given, you should be able to look over any item and decide if it has the right material and design to meet your needs. It's also smart to check with other riders to see which brands sold in your locale have given them good service.

What you wear under a jersey depends on the temperature and the kind of riding you're doing. When it gets into the 70s or higher I don't wear an undershirt unless I'm in a race, such as a criterium, where there is going to be a lot of bike handling. If I go down, the jersey will slide against the undershirt and leave me without most of the skinning that would otherwise occur. For reasons stated above, I think wool is the best material for an undershirt, followed by cotton, and a blend with a synthetic is fine. If your local bike shop doesn't carry wool undergarments you might try a camping or mountaineering store.

Jerseys should be washed frequently, certainly after every ride in the warm-weather months. It does the material no good to dry out after being saturated with body salts, and you might experience skin irritation if a jersey is worn more than once between cleanings. Just follow the manufacturer's label instructions; if in doubt, hand-wash in cool water, using a mild liquid detergent. Rinse thoroughly and get out the excess water by squeezing, not wringing, and then roll the jersey tightly in a towel. Otherwise the heaviness might make it stretch out of shape when it is hung up to dry. Avoid drying any of your natural-fiber cycling apparel in hot sunlight or it may shrink.

Skin Suits

While the same style of jersey is ideal for both touring and road racing, if you plan to do much time trialing I strongly suggest the purchase of a one-piece "skin suit," such as those made by Descente and Pearl Izumi. They are much sleeker than even a pocketless track jersey tucked into shorts—you can really feel how much easier the wind goes around you. The fabrics for one-pieces are always shiny, lightweight synthetics. There is chamois sewn into the seat and

For racing, a skintight one-piece suit is a definite advantage. You can actually feel the air go around a lot easier when wearing one. They are practical only for time trials, criteriums, and track events, however, since there are no pockets for carrying the food and water you need in road races.

usually some extra padding to make up for the thinness of the material. Prices range from around $50 to $100, but with proper care one of these outfits will give you several seasons of use—and a real advantage every time you go off the line in a time trial. Look for a fit that leaves no baggy areas when you're in your racing position, and be careful not to buy a suit that is so tight it could restrict circulation. I once wore one that was a size too small and it practically cut me in half.

Shorts

As with jerseys, the traditional materials for shorts are wool and cotton, but a mixture of either with a synthetic fiber is probably the best choice in terms of durability. The breathability and absorbency will still be there, but the shorts will retain their shape better and be easier to care for. A good wool blend is hard to beat.

Along with the new one-piece-suit technology have come shorts made entirely of synthetics, such as Lycra, which are very light and yet wear well. You can tell them by their shiny, almost wet appearance. The fit is snug and they keep their shape even in the rain because the material won't absorb water. The price is in the same $30–$45 range that you'll pay for quality wool shorts, and I suggest you consider having a pair or two if you will be racing. But for touring they aren't as comfortable or practical as shorts made with natural fibers.

The cut of a good pair of cycling shorts will make them look pretty ridiculous for casual wear. The rear should be high to keep the small of the back covered when you are bent over the bars, and the front should be low so there is no extra material to bunch up. The legs should extend to at least midthigh, and the inside of the legs should be longer than the outside to help keep the shorts from riding up between thighs and saddle. The waist will have either an elastic band or a drawstring—I recommend the latter, because elastic tends to stretch when it gets wet. Actually, many riders, myself included, always wear suspenders to prevent shorts from sagging when soaked by sweat or rain. Choose suspenders which have plastic or plated metal clasps (this keeps rust to a minimum) and straps that are about an inch wide. White suspenders are best, because some colored ones will bleed their dye into your jersey, undershirt, and skin.

The most important part of cycling shorts is the leather chamois. Its purpose is to provide a soft, smooth, and absorbent surface in the area of greatest pressure and friction between the rider and the bike. This is so critical to comfort and the prevention of saddle sores that it is well worth the extra few dollars it takes to buy the best shorts you can. As in jerseys, Sergal is the preference of many. You will see in these shorts the things that go into quality design: a thick, smooth, perfectly contoured chamois with no protruding seams or edges, covering all areas where friction can occur.

Riders differ on whether to put anything on the chamois before a ride. I prefer to just rub it soft and put the shorts on, but others apply everything from baby oil to baby powder. Anything that has a petroleum base, such as Vaseline, will make the chamois harder to clean, so some riders prefer a water-base product such as Noxzema. The main objective in using any of these substances is to further reduce friction, and the chamois can also hold medication if broken skin or sores do develop. A pharmacist will be able to recommend a suitable product should you be in need.

However, if you keep your shorts and yourself clean, skin problems

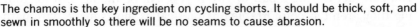

The chamois is the key ingredient on cycling shorts. It should be thick, soft, and sewn in smoothly so there will be no seams to cause abrasion.

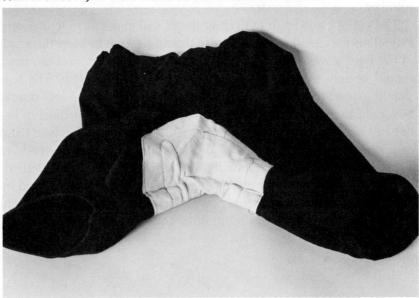

should be minimal at most. This takes some effort when on tour, but personal hygiene is really the same for any rider anywhere. Use a disinfectant, such as rubbing alcohol, to swab the crotch area before and after every ride. Clean the shorts after each use to prevent the buildup of bacteria—if you have any minor crotch irritations and you ride in dirty shorts you are simply courting disaster. Wash them by hand, using a mild detergent, and let them air-dry. Some riders feel that hanging the shorts in sunlight will kill bacteria, but I think all it does is cause the chamois to harden and crack. Either way, it often takes a day or longer for the leather to dry completely. This makes it necessary to own at least two pairs of shorts so you will always have a clean pair to wear.

While jerseys are available in every hue of the rainbow, when it comes to shorts Henry Ford said it best: You can have any color you want as long as it's black. The reason is simple. Black won't show those unsightly brown stains that are picked up from most saddles, and black shorts give you a place to wipe the grease from your hands after you've stopped to change a flat or make a mechanical adjustment. Any other color just won't do.

Headgear

Cycling caps are an inexpensive (less than $5) but valuable part of a rider's attire. They help keep long hair off the face and they aid in sweat absorption and evaporation. The caps I'm speaking of are the ones that usually carry some company's logo. They are made of cotton with a small bill in front and an elastic band sewn into the back. One size is supposed to fit all, though you'll find plenty of variation. Look for a cap that fits snugly enough not to blow off in the wind but isn't so tight it'll give you a headache. As with jerseys, a light color is what you want for summer use because it will reflect the sun's rays.

A cap can really help your comfort in hot weather if you soak it frequently with a water bottle, but on a cool or rainy day it helps hold in body heat. In fact, some models are made of nylon or have a special coating to make them water-resistant, and there may be a little insulation on the inside. In dusty conditions a cap keeps grit out of your hair.

The small bill can be used in several ways. You can have it forward and folded up to allow full vision, or you can flip it down as a sun visor or to protect your eyes from falling rain or the spray coming up from another rider's wheel. On a hot day when the sun is overhead or behind you, turn the cap around and let the bill shade the back of your neck.

Of course, a cap won't be needed if you are using any cycling helmet other than the leather strap model (a cap can be worn either under it or over it and used as just described). Although I always wear my "hairnet" when I race—the rules require a helmet—I confess to being a member of the old school that rarely uses head protection at any other time. But I don't suggest that you follow my example. In fact, I probably would wear a helmet while training if I wasn't able to ride such lightly trafficked roads. I advise wearing a quality plastic helmet designed specifically for cycling if it adds to your confidence or if you must ride on busy roads. If you are relatively new to cycling and are still developing your bike-handling skills, wearing a helmet is all the more important. Sometimes a beginning rider is his own worst enemy when it comes to reasons for falling. Hardshell helmets will protect against all types of blows, and,

There are many choices in helmet design. Pick the style you like and that fits you comfortably, then wear it every time you ride.

as statistics show, head injuries are the leading cause of death due to cycling accidents. The leather strap model is light and airy but it offers minimum protection at best.

Recent advances in hardshell-helmet design have done away with most of the complaints riders have had in the past. The major brands now on the U.S. market—Bailen, Bell, Brancale, MSR, Pro-tec, and Skid-Lid—generally weigh less than a pound, are adequately ventilated, easily fastened and removed, filled with padding materials that can absorb skull-cracking forces, and are reasonably priced at about $40 or less. These helmets offer a wide range of styles, and all meet the requirements for use in sanctioned racing. Many tourists and more and more competitors are showing up in hardshells each year. One of them, Tom Broznowski, became the first plastic-helmeted rider ever to win the U.S. Senior men's road championship when he took the title in 1981. Even in tradition-bound Europe the hardshell is being seen more often, particularly in track racing.

In cold weather the head needs to be protected against heat loss— estimates of how much body heat escapes through the head and neck range to 40 percent. To keep this to a minimum I recommend sock hats or wool caps which can be pulled down low enough to cover the ears and the back of the neck. If you wear a plastic helmet you can tape up the ventilation holes and wear a skier's wool headband across your ears. When shopping for cold-weather headgear it's a good idea to visit a store that carries clothing for hunters. There will be a wide selection of hats in bright red and orange, which makes you much more visible to motorists when you're squeezing in a ride just before dusk on a cloudy winter's day.

Gloves

Gloves are an important safety item. There are a number of brands, and most are similar, having padded leather palms, half fingers, a mesh or perforated leather back, and an adjustable wrist strap. I prefer a Velcro closure to a metal snap, which is not as easy to use and can rust. Gloves provide a number of benefits to make their price of $10 to $20 a bargain. First, they cushion hands against road vibration and help prevent blisters and raw spots on a long ride. They improve the grip on the handlebars, particularly in wet conditions. They catch moisture coming down the arms and are handy for wiping away sweat that gets into the eyes. Should your tires pick up debris from the road, you can reach down with a gloved palm and brush it off. Finally, gloves can save the skin on your hands should you crash—it's an automatic reaction to break a fall by putting your hands out, and the damage to bare hands can be painful and quite slow to heal.

When shopping for a pair of gloves you'll find that because of variations in the cut some brands fit better than others. The ends of the half fingers should be snug but shouldn't restrict circulation. In fact, this tightness often presents a problem when taking the gloves off. Instead of tugging at each finger and trying to work it up, it's best to peel the glove from the wrist so that it comes off inside out. Look for good stitching throughout the construction, especially at the ends of the fingers. Maintenance consists of washing the gloves when they become dirty or sweat-soaked; I just toss mine in with a regular wash load.

For cool weather I recommend full gloves made of wool, leather, or an insulated material. When it's quite cold, mittens may be more comfortable, since they pool the heat of the fingers (you'll find you

Cycling gloves protect hands from numbing pressure and also from damage in case of a fall. Look for a model that offers a padded palm, Velcro closures, and a mesh back for ventilation.

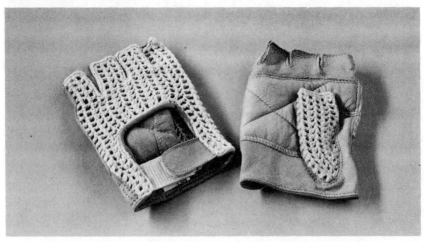

can still work the gear and brake levers without difficulty). An important feature to look for in any cold-weather glove is a high and tight wristband; you can lose a surprising amount of heat and comfort if there is exposed skin between the top of a glove and the end of a sleeve. Shop for full gloves and mittens in sporting-goods stores— there is no need to pay the high price for fancy imported models sold in bike shops. As with winter hats, you might consider the extra safety in wearing bright-orange gloves made for hunters.

Foul-Weather Gear

Riding in the rain needn't be a soggy, cold, uncomfortable experience, thanks to the new man-made fabrics now being used in rainwear. The best of these is Gore-Tex, which has the uncanny ability to let moist air out while preventing water from coming in. Thus it solves the age-old dilemma with wet-weather clothing: If the material effectively stops rain, how can it keep a rider from becoming just as wet from heat buildup and condensation? The Gore-Tex synthetic fabric does it with a weave that permits the passage of water vapor but not water molecules. Many in the new generation of running suits are made with Gore-Tex, and more and more manufacturers are using the material for cycling apparel as well. The suits have a separate jacket and pants, and they work well for all cycling activity except racing, where their bagginess is bad news. The important features to look for include Velcro closures (especially at the wrists and cuffs), enough tightness in the legs to keep material out of the bike's power train, a hood that doesn't block vision and can be used either over or under a helmet, enough length in the jacket and pants to keep all parts of the body covered in every riding position, and a color that will stand out in murky weather. Yellow is best.

The drawback to Gore-Tex suits is the price: $100 or more. This may understandably make you wonder if you really need one. The investment might be justified for extended touring, especially when riding in areas of the country where wet weather is prevalent, such as the Pacific Northwest. Otherwise, cycling through an occasional summer shower really isn't so unpleasant that you need to go to great expense for protection. In fact, I've found that the main concern in rainy riding is to stay warm, not dry. Simply wearing wool clothing will help a lot in this regard.

Check into a lightweight nylon cycling jacket such as racers use in wet weather. It won't stop the water for long but it does a good job of cutting the wind. It traps in body heat well, making wetness of little concern, and nylon dries quickly once the rain stops. The best models have mesh ventilation panels or zippered openings down each side, which help air circulate without allowing in the wind. They are designed to hug the torso and arms closely so they won't work against efficiency by catching the air. Look for a model cut long in the back so it will hang over the seat and keep out rear-wheel spray.

If you are caught by rain in the middle of a ride and you don't have any protection with you, it is important to keep the wind off your chest once you are wet. The best way is to stuff a newspaper, aluminum foil, plastic bag, or something similar up the front of your jersey.

As for the legs, you're probably better off leaving them bare in all but the coolest wet weather. Bare of clothing, that is, but a liberal application of baby oil or petroleum jelly will increase comfort markedly. (This is one of several reasons why serious cyclists keep their legs shaved.) These substances will coat your pores to help you retain body heat as they make rain and wind flow right by. There is so much water hitting the legs from front-wheel spray that any material (with the exception of Gore-Tex or something rubberized) will soon become wet, heavy, and quite a hindrance to your pedaling. Besides, the torso and head are what need protection against heat loss, not a pair of working legs.

Cold-Weather Clothing

When the weather is chilly but dry, keep your legs protected with a pair of tights, which are just like regular cycling shorts but with long legs. Some models have zippers at each ankle, and there may or may not be chamois in the seat. I prefer mine without. They are less expensive this way, and chamois isn't needed if you wear shorts underneath. It is a lot easier to wash out a pair of chamois shorts than a pair of full-length tights, which can be used a number of times between cleanings as long as they are not worn next to the crotch. Also, the double layer of cloth around the lower torso helps keep the cold wind out and adds to sit-down comfort, especially early in the season when you may be doing more miles than the posterior is ready for.

A traditional alternative to tights is leg warmers, which are basically tubes of cloth with elastic at both ends. You wear them with regular shorts, and they cover your bare skin from there to the socks. I've used these and do not recommend them. They shrink up with washing, they slip down and expose bare skin, and the thigh band often rubs uncomfortably against the saddle. Tights are much better. Arm warmers, on the other hand, work well and are especially good on days that start off cool and then warm up. Since your arms stay relatively quiet on the bike, arm warmers aren't prone to slipping down, and they can easily be removed and stored in jersey pockets once the temperature rises.

Only on the coldest days will riders in competition wear tights. The reason is that the material, even though it hugs the skin, catches quite a bit of air. Instead, racers will keep legs warm by using the same technique recommended for wet weather—liberal applications of baby oil or petroleum jelly.

Upper-body requirements in cold weather start with the head, foot, and hand protection discussed above. The next area of major concern is the neck—sore throats and breathing problems can result from wind hitting this part of the body. My favorite solution is to wear a big cotton bandana. I tie it at the back just as if I were going out to rob a stagecoach, but instead of wearing it over my face I put it under my chin and tuck the excess cloth into the jersey collar. This does a fine job of stopping the wind and holding in warmth. A turtleneck undershirt also works well. By wearing one that has a high percentage of wool you'll also have the best foundation for torso protection.

The key to dressing right in cold weather is to wear several layers of light clothing rather than one or two thick items. The layers insulate better because they trap more air, and if you start getting too warm you can peel one off. It's always the case that the first miles feel the coldest, so overdressing is a common mistake. On winter rides I usually wear a long-sleeved wool undershirt, then a short- or long-sleeved jersey (depending on the conditions), followed by a warm-up suit top. In competition I'll forsake the last item and stuff a section of a newspaper up my jersey. The hard work keeps me plenty warm, and the paper blocks the wind from my chest.

Despite all this cold-weather attire there's still going to be one patch of skin in need of protection—the face. I've used a ski mask in frigid weather and it worked well. It certainly kept drafts out of my neck, and even though ice formed around the nose and mouth, this didn't present any difficulty. I recommend the style that has the mouth cut out; without this, icing could be more of a problem. On less severe days I sometimes apply petroleum jelly or a liberal

When the weather turns cool, wear long tights and several layers of jerseys to trap body heat. When the temperature drops even further, cover the head to overcome the main avenue of heat loss, and add full gloves and extra foot protection; you should be able to ride comfortably even as the mercury goes below freezing.

amount of my wife's skin lotion. This helps against both the coldness of the air and its drying effect.

By dressing in the manner and clothing I've described, I have been able to ride at zero degrees. Though an hour is about the limit in that kind of cold—zero is equivalent to 32 below when pedaling at 15 mph—I've found that it's possible to ride as long as desired on days when it's in the 20s.

GLOSSARY

AEROBIC—describing an intensity of exercise below the level which produces lactic acid faster than the body can dispose of it. Thus, oxygen needs are continuously met and the exercise can be continued for long periods.

AERODYNAMIC—describing a design of cycling equipment or a riding position that reduces wind resistance.

ATTACK—an aggressive, high-speed jump away from other riders.

ANAEROBIC—describing an intensity of exercise past the point where the body can cope with its production of lactic acid and need for oxygen. Thus, the exercise level cannot be sustained for long.

BEARING RACE—the area of contact for ball bearings in components such as the headset, pedals, hubs, and crankset.

BLOCKING—legally impeding the progress of riders in the pack to allow teammates in the break a better chance of success.

BONK—a state of severe exhaustion caused mainly by the depletion of glycogen in the muscles. Once it occurs, there is no means of quick recovery.

BOTTOM BRACKET—the part of the frame where the crank is installed.

BRAZING—a process in which the tubes of a bicycle frame are joined together with melted bronze or, less commonly and more expensively, silver.

BREAK, BREAKAWAY—a rider or group of riders who have escaped the pack.

BRIDGE, BRIDGE A GAP—to catch a rider or group that has opened a lead.

BUNCH—the main cluster of riders in a race. Also called the group, pack, field, and peloton.

BUTTED TUBE—a type of tubing found in expensive bike frames, the metal being very thin throughout except at each end, where it thickens to provide the needed strength at tube intersections.

CADENCE—the rate of pedaling, measured in revolutions per minute of one foot.

CALIPERS—bicycle brakes actuated by hand levers.

CARBOHYDRATES—simple sugars and starches which provide a quick source of muscle energy. They are plentiful in fruits, grains, potatoes, breads, pasta, etc. and are stored in the liver in the form of glycogen.

353

CARDIOVASCULAR—pertaining to the heart and blood vessels.

CATEGORIES—the division of USCF classes into smaller groups, based on ability and/or experience.

CENTURY—a 100-mile ride.

CHASERS—those who are trying to catch a group or a lead rider.

CIRCUIT—a road course which is ridden two or more times to compose the race.

CLASS—a division of USCF racers based on sex and age. Also, something a talented pedaler is said to have.

CLEAT—a metal or plastic fitting on the sole of a cycling shoe with a groove to engage the rear of the pedal cage.

CLINCHERS—conventional tires with a separate inner tube.

COTTONS—moderately expensive tubular tires for training and racing, constructed with cotton thread in the casing.

CRITERIUM—a mass-start race covering numerous laps of a course that is normally about one mile or less in length.

DROPPED—describing a rider who has failed to keep pace with the group he was riding in.

ECHELON—a pace-line formation in which each rider is behind and to the side of the person immediately ahead, the purpose being to nullify the effect of a crosswind. For example, if the wind is coming from the left, the line of riders will angle off to the right side of the person in front.

FIELD SPRINT—the dash to the finish line by the largest group of riders remaining in a race.

JUMP—a quick, hard acceleration.

LACTIC ACID—a by-product of hard exercise that accumulates in the muscles and causes pain and fatigue.

LAW—League of American Wheelmen, a national organization for touring cyclists that also actively works for cyclists' rights in the legislative arena. Office address is Box 988, Baltimore, MD 21203.

LEAD OUT—a race tactic in which a rider accelerates to his maximum speed for the benefit of a teammate in tow. The second rider then leaves the draft and sprints past him at even greater speed near the finish line.

LSD—long, steady distance. A training technique which calls for continuous rides of at least two hours, done entirely at a firm aerobic pace.

LUGS—metal fittings at the intersections of tubes in a bicycle frame.

MASS START—events such as road races and criteriums in which all contestants line up together and leave the starting line at the same time.

MAXIMAL OXYGEN CONSUMPTION (max VO_2)—the maximum amount of oxygen that a person can consume in one minute. It is basically determined by heredity and is an indicator of potential performance in endurance sports.

MINUTEMAN—in a time trial, the rider who is one place in front of you in the starting order. So called because in most TTs riders start at one-minute intervals.

MITERING—a frame-building process in which the ends of tubes are shaped to fit flush against the tubes they intersect, thus making a more secure joint.

MIXTE—a bicycle frame design which has two straight tubes going from the head tube to the rear stay ends, both being attached to the seat tube where they pass by. This produces a frame with riding characteristics similar to those of a "man's frame" even though the top tube is eliminated.

MOTORPACE—riding behind a motorcycle or other vehicle that breaks the wind.

OFF THE BACK—describing one or more riders who have failed to keep pace with the main group in a race.

OFF THE FRONT—describing one or more riders who have broken away from the main group in a race.

OVERTRAINING—deep-seated fatigue, both physical and mental, caused by training at a volume higher than that to which the body can adapt.

PACE LINE—a single-file group formation in which each rider takes a turn breaking the wind at the front before pulling off, dropping back to the rear position, and riding in the other's draft until at the front once again.

PANNIERS—large bags for touring that come in pairs and are mounted on a rack that positions them along each side of the rear and, sometimes, the front wheel.

POWER TRAIN—those components directly involved with making the rear wheel turn, i.e., the chain, chainwheels, and freewheel.

PRIME—a special award given to the leader on selected laps during a criterium, or the first rider to reach a certain landmark in a road race. It is used to heighten the action. Pronounced "preem."

PSI—pounds per square inch.

PULL, PULL THROUGH—take a turn at the front.

PULL OFF—move to the side after riding in the lead so that another rider can come to the front.

QUADRICEPS—the large muscle in front of the thigh, the strength of which helps determine a cyclist's ability to pedal with power.

REPETITION—each hard effort in an interval workout.

ROAD RACE—a mass-start race that goes from point to point, covers one large loop, or is held on a circuit longer than those used for criteriums.

ROAD RASH—any skin abrasion resulting from a fall.

ROLLERS—an indoor training device that works like a treadmill for bikes.

SADDLE—bicycle seat.

SADDLE SORES—skin problems in the crotch which develop from chafing caused by the action of pedaling. They can range from tender raw spots to boil-like lesions if infection takes place.

SADDLE TIME—time spent cycling, the purpose of which is to condition the body to handle the demands of longer rides.

SAG WAGON—a motor vehicle which follows a group of riders, carrying equipment and lending assistance in the event of difficulty.

SET—in interval or weight training, a specific number of repetitions.

SILKS—expensive, very light racing tires constructed with silk threads in the casing.

SIT ON A WHEEL—to ride directly behind someone and receive full benefit of the slipstream.

SLINGSHOT—to sprint around a rider at high speed after taking advantage of the slipstream.

SLIPSTREAM—the area of low air resistance behind a moving cyclist.

SNAP—the ability to accelerate quickly.

SOFT-PEDAL—to rotate the pedals without actually applying power.

SPEED WORK—fast training using techniques like intervals and motorpacing.

SPIN—pedal at high cadence.

SPRINT—a short acceleration to maximum speed.

STAGE RACE—a multi-day event consisting of point-to-point and circuit road races, time trials, and, sometimes, criteriums. The winner is the rider with the lowest elapsed time for all stages.

TEAM TIME TRIAL (TTT)—a race against the clock with two or more riders working together.

TEMPO—hard riding at a fast cadence.

THROW THE BIKE—a racing technique in which a rider will push the bike as far ahead of his body as he can at the finish line, hoping to edge out another sprinting rider.

TIME TRIAL (TT)—a race against the clock in which individual riders start at set intervals and cannot give aid or receive it from others on the course.

TOPS—the part of the handlebars between the stem and the brake levers.

TRAINING EFFECT—the result of exercise done at an intensity and duration sufficient to bring about positive physiological changes. These include increased lung capacity, increased number and size of blood vessels, increased maximal oxygen consumption, reduction of body fat, improved muscle tone, increased blood volume, lowered resting pulse, etc.

TUBULAR OR SEW-UP—a lightweight racing or training tire which has the tube permanently sewed inside the casing. The tire is glued onto the rim.

TURNAROUND—the point where the riders reverse direction on an out-and-back time trial course.

UP ON THE FIELD—describing the amount of time or distance a lead rider or group is ahead of the main race pack.

USCF—United States Cycling Foundation, the organization in charge of amateur bicycle racing in America. It makes the rules, sanctions the events, and licenses the competitors. Address 1750 E. Boulder St., Colorado Springs, CO 80909.

VELODROME—a banked track for bicycle racing.

WIND-UP—steady acceleration to an all-out effort.

BIBLIOGRAPHY

RACING

All About Bicycle Racing. Mountain View, CA: World Publications, 1975.

Complete Bicycle Time Trialing Book. Mountain View, CA: World Publications, 1977.

Cycling. Rome, Italy: Central Sports School (CONI), 1972.

Matheny, Fred. *Beginning Bicycle Racing.* Brattleboro, VT: Velo-news, 1981.

McCullagh, James, ed. *American Bicycle Racing.* Emmaus, PA: Rodale Press, 1976.

Simes, Jack. *Winning Bicycle Racing.* Chicago: Contemporary Books, Inc., 1976.

Ward, Peter. *King of Sports—Cycle Road Racing.* Yorkshire, England: Kennedy Brothers, Ltd.

TOURING

Bicycle Touring Tips Brochures. Missoula, MT: Bikecentennial. (Six pamphlets on various aspects of touring.)

Bridge, Raymond, *The Bicycle Camping Book.* Harrisburg, PA: Stackpole Books, 1974.

————. *Bike Touring.* San Francisco: Sierra Club Books, 1979.

Cuthbertson, Tom. *Bike Tripping.* Berkeley, CA: Ten Speed Press, 1972.

Hawthorn, M., E. Hawthorn, and J. Mafchir. *The American Youth Hostels' Bike Hike Book.* Harrisburg, PA: Stackpole Books, 1976.

The Cyclists' Yellow Pages. Missoula, MT: Bikecentennial, 1979.

Heilman, Gail. *The Complete Outfitting and Source Book for Bicycle Touring.* Marshall, CA: The Great Outdoors Trading Company, 1980.

Tobey, P., and T. Tucker, eds. *Two Wheel Travel—Bicycle Camping and Traveling by Bike.* Mountain View, CA: World Publications, 1974.

Wilhelm, Tim and Glenda. *The Bicycle Touring Book.* Emmaus, PA: Rodale Press, 1980.

GENERAL INTEREST

Anderson, Robert. *Stretching.* Box 1002, Englewood, CO 80110, 1975.

Ballantine, Richard. *Richard's Bicycle Book.* New York: Ballantine Books, 1978.

Beinhorn, George. *Food for Fitness.* Mountain View, CA: World Publications, 1975.

Books About Bikes. William Allan, bookseller, Box 315, Englewood, CO 80151.

Brandt, Jobst. *The Bicycle Wheel.* Menlo Park, CA: Avocet, Inc., 1981.

Campground and Trailer Park Guide. National and regional editions. Chicago: Rand McNally Co.

Coles, Clarence W., and Harold T. Glenn. *Glenn's Complete Bicycle Manual.* New York: Crown Publishers, 1973.

Cooper, Kenneth. *Aerobics.* New York: Bantam, 1972.

Cuthbertson, Tom. *Anybody's Bike Book.* Berkeley, CA: Ten Speed Press, 1971.

DeLong, Fred. *DeLong's Guide to Bicycles and Bicycling.* Radnor, PA: Chilton Book Co., 1978.

Greenhood, David. *Mapping.* Chicago: University of Chicago Press, 1964.

Inside the Cyclist—Physiology for the Two-Wheeled Athlete. Brattleboro, VT: Velo-news, 1979.

Kolin, M., and D. de la Rosa. *The Custom Bicycle.* Emmaus, PA: Rodale Press, 1979.

————. *Understanding, Maintaining and Riding the Ten-Speed Bicycle.* Emmaus, PA: Rodale Press, 1979.

Mirkin, G., and M. Hoffman. *The SportsMedicine Book.* Boston: Little, Brown, 1978.

National Atlas of the United States. Washington, DC: U.S. Dept. of Interior, Geological Survey, 1950.

Powers, E., and J. Witt. *Traveling Weatherwise in the U.S.A.* New York: Dodd, Mead & Co., 1972.

Reynolds, Bill. *Complete Weight Training Book.* Mountain View, CA: World Publications, 1976.

Sloane, Eugene A. *The New Complete Book of Bicycling.* New York: Simon and Schuster, 1974.

Sutherland, Howard. *Sutherland's Handbook for Bicycle Mechanics, Third Edition.* Berkeley, CA: Sutherland Publications, 1981.

Woodall's Campground Directory. Editions for Eastern U.S., Western U.S., North America, and Canada. Highland Park, IL: Woodall Publishing Co.

Woodland, Les. *Cycle Racing and Touring*. Levittown, NY: Transatlantic Arts, Inc., 1977.

PERIODICALS

American Wheelmen. Box 988, Baltimore, MD 21203. Official publication of the League of American Wheelmen. Sent to LAW members; not available by subscription. Twelve issues per year.

Bicycling. 33 E. Minor St., Emmaus, PA 18049. Covers all aspects of bicycle usage and has detailed test reports on equipment. Nine issues per year.

BikeReport. Box 8308, Missoula, MT 59807. Published by Bikecentennial and sent to all members. Six issues per year.

Cycling USA. c/o U.S. Cycling Federation, 1750 E. Boulder St., Colorado Springs, CO 80909. Official USCF publication sent to all licensed riders; also available by subscription. Twelve issues per year.

Velo-news. Box 1257, Brattleboro, VT 05301. Photos, news articles, and features about national and international racing, including extensive calendar of events and result listings. Eighteen issues per year.

INDEX

INDEX

ABOUT THE AUTHORS

Like most Americans, Tom Doughty was an enthusiastic bike rider as a kid. And, like most Americans, he traded those two wheels for four just as soon as he could get a driver's license. But now he has come full circle, preferring to use a bike whenever and wherever he can. In fact, his rediscovery of cycling has enhanced his life so much that he says without reservation, "I am one of the luckiest people in the world. I have found something that I really like to do. I'm good at it and I have the financial and organizational support to be able to spend a lot of my time doing it. I'm talking about riding a bicycle."

For Doughty, riding means training and racing more than 10,000 miles a year. He appreciates how nicely a bicycle can be used for other purposes—commuting, long one-day trips, extended tours, and, of course, simply pedaling for the sheer joy of it—and he has experienced them all. But it is in the hard, fast world of competition where his talent is strongest, and his achievements have elevated him to the U.S. Olympic Cycling Team.

Born on July 24, 1952, Doughty grew up on an Indiana farm and remembers using his bike as a way to get to the nearest town, six miles away. Not until his student years at Ball State University, however, did he become aware of what cycling really had to offer. His introduction came in the form of the Ball State Bikeathon, a campus race very much like the Indiana University Little 500 featured in the climax of the hit movie *Breaking Away*. Doughty, a strapping athlete who had entered Ball State on a basketball scholarship, was recruited to ride for one of the teams. He excelled and, one thing leading to another, was asked to come in for testing in the lab of Dr. David Costill, Ball State's renowned exercise physiologist. The results showed that Doughty was physically on a level with the finest European professional cyclists.

Thanks to this encouragement, as well as the discouragement of being soundly thrashed in his first off-campus race against good amateurs, Doughty decided to get serious about cycling. He pushed ahead his Master of Business Administration program so he would finish in the winter term of 1976, then he headed to Florida for the first intensive training of his life. By the following June he made the Olympic Cycling Team as an alternate; from then on it has been a steady progression. He has been selected to the National Road Team each year through 1981 and raced overseas in major

379

international events and the world championships. He won a gold medal in the 1979 Pan-American Games, then was one of the first riders chosen to race for the United States in the 1980 Olympics. Although the boycott canceled the trip to Moscow, Doughty excelled that summer by winning two national championships and setting a new American record of 52:25.9 in the 25-mile individual time trial.

Now a management consultant with Borg Warner in Chicago, Doughty maintains his great enthusiasm for cycling but is at the age where he must step aside for younger riders at the national level. In fact, his only regret in the sport is that he did not begin riding seriously until the ripe old age (by the standards of elite athletes) of twenty-three. "I wasted quite a few valuable years in the wrong sports," he says, "and when I did enter cycling I had almost no one to help me along. Good advice can make a great deal of difference to any developing cyclist, and today's riders are fortunate to have the chance for much better guidance than I did.

"That's one of the reasons I'm writing this book. I want to help other people discover the enjoyment of cycling, of doing it well, without having to go through all the mistakes and experimenting that I did. Cycling is a skill. If you know how to do it well it's a lot more rewarding."

Coauthor Barbara George is the founder/owner of *Velo-news*, the oldest and most respected journal of bicycle racing in North America. Since beginning business in 1972 she has published more than 150 issues of the paper and several cycling books, and written three for other publishers (in addition to this one). Her husband Bob is widely known in cycling as one of the premier race photographers.

Coauthor Ed Pavelka has a degree in journalism from the University of Florida and worked for five years as a bicycle shop manager and mechanic. In 1977 he was named editor of *Velo-news,* and he remains closely allied with the publication, though also freelancing from his home in southern Vermont. A member of the U.S. Cycling Federation's Veteran class, he has raced and ridden for fitness since 1971.